PETER
LLOYD
CAVANAUGH

CONSEQUENCE

Tenth Anniversary Issue
Spring 2018

Volume 10

EDITOR   George Kovach

SENIOR ASSOCIATE EDITOR   Catherine Parnell

ASSOCIATE EDITORS   Olivia Kate Cerrone
                                John M. Lewis
                                Mitch Manning

ASSISTANT EDITORS   John R. Coats
                                Jose F. Diaz
                                Jonathan Papas

ART FEATURE EDITOR   Anne Kovach

GRAPHIC DESIGNERS   Stephanie Odeh
                                John Polizzi

WEB DESIGNERS   Josh McCall
                                Betsy Walker

CONTRIBUTING EDITORS
        Kevin Bowen   Askold Melnyczuk
        Martha Collins   George Scialabba
        Fred Marchant   Roy Scranton
                                Afaa Michael Weaver

ADVISORY BOARD
        Susan Cheever   Pamela Painter
        Hester Kaplan   Bob Shacochis
        Alexandra Marshall   Tom Sleigh
        Jill McDonough   Brian Turner
        Askold Melnyczuk   Jane Unrue

Consequence Magazine
P.O. Box 323
Cohasset, MA 02025-0323
consequence.magazine@gmail.com

CONSEQUENCE *is an international literary magazine published annually, focusing on the culture of war. Subscriptions ($10/yr.) are available online and by mail to the address above. International addresses add $10/yr. Submissions are welcome between March 1 and September 30. We accept only online submissions sent to us through our website's Submissions page. Visit our website www.Consequencemagazine.org for guidelines. We are an independent, non-profit magazine, and a 501(c)(3) charitable organization. Your donations are tax-deductible.*

Editor's Note

The photographs taken by Virginia Dwan and featured in this issue were selected from her book, *Flowers* (Radius Books 2016). Straightforward and clear, they appear at first as traditional statements in black and white about the consequences of war. But look again at these repeated images of military cemeteries that initially seem so alike and so familiar. One after another rank and file of identical markers extend from a particular moment in time and point of view to a vanishing point that is both past and future. If you were to walk toward the horizon in any one of Dwan's photographs into that white, unnatural symmetry, you would find just beyond the trees vast stretches of land held in reserve for new graves. Now step back and notice how the peripheral space stretches in all directions, not attempting to contain what is alive and what is not. This is a patient, capacious response that never shies away from the obscene banality of war. Rather, it intentionally compounds and accumulates images to embody overwhelming loss. Still, despite the visceral sensation of wanting to turn away, we cannot escape the contradiction that a manicured, military arrangement of the dead is not, as Dwan shows us, without a disturbing kind of beauty. Do the frequent ceremonies at Arlington or any national cemetery make war honorable and easier to accept?

Virginia Dwan named her book of photographs *Flowers*, referring to Pete Seeger's Vietnam-era song of resistance, but now, four generations of "permanent war" later, that title echoes with a renewed sense of irony. Like the woven refrains in a ballad or a hymn, each image in *Flowers* connects the one before it to the one after. To make the continuation of war tangible, *Flowers* comprises a series of images printed on one long, heavy sheet that folds together like the fabric of a bellows—as though the country's national cemeteries stretched without interruption from Long Island to San Francisco, and then collapsed in on themselves. The necessary effort to view these accordion-like panels of contiguous images subverts the habit of turning a page and moving on. Dwan's tactile layout forces you to handle each successive photograph as distinct, yet like others. It's necessary to pause and think about this process, and perhaps even accept the responsibility of seeing. You have to choose to continue the journey. It's a moral as well as an aesthetic choice.

In Seeger's song, the rhetorical question "where have all the young men gone" equates soldiers to men, so it's fitting that the lyrics include the words "lone time ago." Today, women return from war with the same visible and invisible wounds as men. They write and create art about combat and the many forms of devastation that war causes, but their work does not get the same attention or opportunity for publication as men's. And for far longer than women have soldiered, they have contributed to war narratives as witnesses, survivors, doctors, nurses, journalists, mothers, sisters, partners and spouses. It's obvious that their voices are essential for a full and nuanced understanding of what is at stake when we accept if not support the decisions made on our behalf by an elected elite.

The 10th Anniversary Issue of CONSEQUENCE focuses on the enormous contributions made by those women who write and create art in response to war. Since this magazine's founding we've sought their perspective and insight, their wisdom and mastery. It's very satisfying to look back, mark the names, compare the numbers and find that since 2008, more than half of our authors have been women. Numbers, of course, don't indicate what you will realize when you read their work. We need the strength and empathy of women for all of us to be strong.

—George Kovach

Fiction

Nonfiction

Play

Book Reviews

2017 Consequence Prize in Fiction
Selected by Siobahn Fallon

2017 Consequence Prize in Poetry
Selected by Danielle Legros Georges

Fiction

KATEY SCHULTZ

Taking Flight

This is what it would taste like: candied moisture, a wet slice of sunlight in the mouth. It's market day; the dingy streets of Imar beckon. There might be nuts, fresh bread. There might be produce—an apricot—and there it is again, a craving for fruit seeping from Aaseya's mind to her mouth, her taste buds sprung to life. It's hardly enough, and what is a life, if not lived fully? She wants the fruit. She wants her freedom. She wants to do everything she shouldn't. She shoves back her purple headscarf and walks to the open window of her small, second-story apartment. She sticks her torso out and leans, hanging her head upside down. Her hair dangles like a black flag in the breeze. Positioned like this, she won't have to look up the street at the remains of her family compound. She won't have to wish she'd died in there three years ago, too.

Quickly, she hoists herself upright and her vision shifts between sun splotches. A molten feeling fills her skull as blood drains downward and rights itself throughout her body. She leans against the windowsill and looks toward the sky. The taste is still there. An apricot. Sweet and earthy. Warm. Amazing, how a single thought can bloom like a saffron crocus, infusing the body, her body. Seventeen years old and no one would have guessed this life. Not her father, not her mother or her siblings, all of them gone, leaving only an obstinate Afghan girl in a rushed marriage to Rahim, a desire for fruit, and a village the size of a flea.

"Silly woman!" a child's voice taunts from below.

"Taking Flight" is the first chapter of *Still Come Home*, a novel in progress.

A different child giggles. "She's the dishonorable one. The one who's shameful."

Ba haya. Shameful. Aaseya rights her headscarf and studies the two boys standing across the narrow street, their brown eyes as wide as grapes. Behind them, a smaller boy with a dense crop of hair crouches against the corner of a building, examining the dirt. The sun throws light across their bodies in a wash of pale yellow, illuminating their black-topped heads into little, golden orbs. Somewhat like desert flowers, but no, there's nothing lovely about these boys.

"Go home to your mothers!" Aaseya shouts and waves them off. "You're useless to me!" The two bigger boys run and cackle, quickly out of sight. The small boy remains, engrossed in digging. "If you think you've got something to say to me, you might as well get out of here, too," Aaseya shouts. "I won't hear any of it."

The boy stands, his face soft and thin. A desert flower, after all. His eyelids blink slowly open and closed. He looks about six years old and sickly, covered in dirt. For a moment, she remembers the communal bathhouse where her mother scooped water over her head and sang: *Aaseya comes from the village of sun / my dearest, my jewel / my shining smart one.* But here, she faces a barrage of insults. No cushioned embrace. No clean, white steam and sweet melodies or even the basic company of another woman who believes in her. She barely believes in herself anymore, what with her naive hope for an education. Her petty, circular obsessions about the past. More— her private, pitiful habit of pinching her own arms until they bruise purple. Everything in life feels like a bargain between impossible choices. Just as soon as desire surfaces, forces larger than the desert rise against her. It makes her impatient, quick to judge. From there, it's easy to think everything is insufficient. But some good always remains. It has to. Even outside her window. Even in the middle of a war. Even in a village that insists on the wrongness of her life.

The boy looks at the ground, hair flopping in front of his face, then quickly snatches something from the hole and walks across the street to stand beneath Aaseya's window.

"Well," she says, "which is it—are you starving or homeless? Or both?" She thinks of her younger brother Alamzeb, perhaps the

9

same age as this boy before he died. But Alamzeb never looked so sheepish or frail, so starved.

"Muuuuh," the boy says. He holds a small object toward her. It's indecipherable at first, but as the boy twirls it in his fingertips, metal catches the light and sends a beam outward like a flare.

"Put that away!" Aaseya scolds. It's a brass shell casing and by the look of the boy's pockets, there are more. War scraps are a common sight, but these casings are shiny. Recent.

The boy closes his fist around the brass and frowns, yet there's still a query in his gesture, some need to know.

"You can't sell it, if that's what you're wondering. It's worthless. It's toxic. Boys used to get in serious trouble for playing with things like that. You want something to play with? Hold on."

She turns from the window and dashes toward her chest of belongings inside. An old carved cup. A swatch of fabric. A stick of incense. As she rummages through her thin collection, it strikes her that there's nothing here a boy would want. She unfolds and refolds a sweater. The smell of wood smoke and old sunlight rise from the soft fabric. There's not a single item here worth saving. The chest has been coveted and tucked away, but is effectively empty. She returns to the window, but the boy has disappeared. There's only her ruined former home up the street, the one she thought she'd live in forever. There's only the sun, stretching across the sky in its slow climb. Her father Janan used to tease her about that—asking whether the sun chased the moon or the moon chased the sun. Though the war has continued since his death, Imar is the same. Loyalties still shift from block to block, day to day. Family feuds and Pashtun decrees still trickle down; it's inconceivable to imagine a world where destiny doesn't reign. Whether commanded by the sun or the moon or the heavy hand of Allah, life is endured.

Thinking of her father, Aaseya feels a sudden bolt in her chest, as though a bird is tugging her by the heart, beckoning outward, toward the street. She dresses quickly in her burqa, before caution can object. On her way out, she grabs the empty water pail and curls a fistful of *afghanis* into her pocket. The bazaar awaits. Maybe some chai, some chickpeas. Some raisins for a sweet delight later this week. Maybe, even, an apricot.

SCHULTZ

◊

Outside, the heat clings to Aaseya in an instant. The air feels soupy, three-dimensional. It envelops everything around her—gray buildings, crumbled walkways, tangled rebar—and fills the vacant lots with thick, pulsing space. She shifts the fabric of her burqa to create a cave between her eyes and the cloth, where the breeze from her movement can eddy. She vaguely remembers when women didn't have to wear burqas in Imar, though most still chose to. Fabric tangles at her calves as she walks briskly, hoping she'll go unnoticed. A useless water tap stand sits at the edge of the street, where the alley meets the pathway. The American military installed it years ago, trying to befriend her parched community—three hundred people, largely cut off from outside contact. Within a few months, that tap stand was as dry as the well her mother's aunt had thrown herself down in despair.

A scent of spoiled rubbish wafts from one of the crumpled homes. Aaseya steps onto the street, passing a block of clay shacks with crooked roofs and sparse window curtains. It's the walking, more than anything, that pleases her, the suggestion that she could just keep going. Growing up, her father Janan spoke of large cities like Kabul or other countries where women ran businesses and earned degrees. He even had a crank radio for a time, and the family would gather to listen to broadcasts from the BBC. Aaseya's playmates said it was all farfetched, on par with fables the elders liked to tell. But within the walls of her family compound, Aaseya felt as free as a skylark. Today, the bazaar will have to be enough.

A few blocks along, she approaches Rahim's sister Shanaz's house, where she'll leave the water pail outside the compound gate. Shanaz's sons fill it for Aaseya each day, walking an impossible distance over the ridge and back—a half day's journey and a heavy load. It's no small kindness, and Aaseya tried to thank her in-laws once, but was only met with stony condemnation. "Don't bother me with your overtures," Shanaz had said. "If you really want to do good, you'll give my brother a child." But there was more to it than that; Aaseya's unaccompanied forays to the bazaar were like a continual slap across their faces. *Ba haya.* It's not as though she doesn't understand what's expected of her. Around her elders, she acts one way. A few years ago, to avoid notice from the Taliban, she acted another. As far as the Americans, if she sees them, she takes what she can get and turns her back on the rest. But even these maxims didn't save her family and now, they're hardly enough to make her stay inside. Remain obedient. Never dare to want for anything and most especially to leave home without a man to protect her honor. Aaseya isn't persuaded by any of it. What's honorable about entrapment?

She sets the pail outside Shanaz's gate and picks up her pace. One blessing of her burqa is the narrow window it provides at this juncture, in particular, where she can spare herself the view of her old family home across the street simply by steadying her gaze straight ahead. Everyone knows about her early wartime tragedy, the hurried marriage to her father's cousin Rahim at the age of fourteen, sparing her from orphanhood. That she can't bear children is another story making her worthy, perhaps, of execution had she any elders left to humiliate. Now, Aaseya behaves dishonorably, an embarrassment. Most neighbors avoid her like a contagion.

A playful cry breaks loose from within Shanaz's courtyard, followed by a gaggle of children laughing. Through the melee, Shanaz barks instructions. Brief silence, and then the *wind-whisp-thwap* of a switch across skin. Feet scuffle and a child cries softly, then whatever game was interrupted seems to pick up again. Aaseya hears it all— young boys and girls roving within their family courtyard, a few older women directing children this way and that, and of course, Shanaz, her voice loud and thunderous, hovering over them all.

"Aaseya!" Shanaz shouts.

Aaseya turns around to see the woman's hooked nose pressed through the grate of the courtyard gate. She feels immediately sandwiched, condemnation on one side of the street and a horrible stain of loss on the other. Could the ground simply open up right here? Swallow her? She'd likely let it take her, but then there's Shanaz. Such righteousness. Aaseya won't stand for it.

"You get back here!" Shanaz shouts again.

"I don't have time," Aaseya says. There might be bread left if she hurries. Maybe some ghee. Then again, she might only find maggot-riddled cucumbers. She hates the uncertainty, hates the apricot, her foolish optimism. It would be easier to dispel hope entirely.

"If you're going to the bazaar, my brother should be with you."

Aaseya blushes and retreats to Shanaz's gate. The woman stands squat and square, fists punched into her soft hips. Folds of skin gather around her jowls, contrasting with her tightly-set headscarf. Several grown daughters have joined her inside the gate, carrying with them the scent of cumin and fresh mint. Their hands look greasy and charcoaled, marked by effort.

"Rahim's working the creek beds. You know as much," Aaseya says. She folds her arms across her chest and waits for what may come.

"Just look at you," Shanaz says, "letting the heat of the day spoil your womb! Walking around, unattended! What next?"

Her voice descends like a slap but Aaseya holds herself steady. Admonition or otherwise, attention of any kind provides an odd balm. If it weren't for Shanaz, Aaseya might feel invisible most days. When no further insults come, Aaseya nods bitterly at the remains across the street. There it sits, a historic stain marking her as a Western sympathizer. Piles of rocks avalanche onto the sidewalk, the only reminder of her childhood home. Seeing it always feels like another explosion. So much had been lost, though Aaseya remembers finding part of the radio afterwards, sifting through the rubble. Sometimes, she imagines that if she could get it to work again, she could tune in and hear the voices of her family, their laughter.

It's not as if she could bring them back. As if she could piece her parents together out of pebbles and mud. Here, her father with his wide palms. There, her mother's soft face. Alamzeb's dusty knees. Her cousins, aunts, uncles, reconstructed from chalky remains. She'll never know why she was spared, but certainly not just to be subjected to Shanaz stomping her foot, or the ridiculing stares of her daughters aimed like arrows at Aaseya's throat. Certainly not to spend the rest of her life in Imar, a place weighing on her like so many stones over a grave.

"Well," Aaseya says, growing brave. "Look at it!"

13

"I look at it every day," Shanaz says. She takes in a sharp breath. "But you should know, Aaseya; there are worse things than losing your family."

Aaseya studies Shanaz's face—how suddenly slack it appears. Something's shifted. The old woman's cheeks burn with color. Everyone understands that the only thing worse than death is shame. But what would Shanaz know about any of that? Aaseya's felt her share of shame. Someone had tipped off the Taliban, certain Janan was colluding with the Americans. True, her brother Alamzeb had angered a squad one afternoon, but he was so young. True, Janan had welcomed soldiers into his family compound, but only for cultural conversation. Could kindness get you killed? An Afghan prided himself on hospitality and good impressions. Janan modeled that, perhaps too much. Many nights, Aaseya lies awake trying to guess who might have spread the rumor. Sometimes, she even imagines it was Shanaz, whose meddling authority extends from block to block surrounding their homes. There's a subjective logic to it, the way one family can bring down another, though there was never anything afoul between Janan and his neighbors. Trying to pinpoint blame in a village that's at the mercy of history and culture seems about as effective as praying for rain. Aaseya hustles away from the gate and already, Shanaz has turned her back, a dark cloud in retreat.

◊

When she's a few blocks from the crossroads, she knows she should turn around. Permission to go further isn't granted. Leaving the water pail with Shanaz is a necessary exception; even Rahim grants her that much. It wasn't so long ago she could walk with her father in public, wearing only a headscarf. But now, to remain outside the home unattended—Aaseya should shrink at the thought. She's one of only a few women who still pushes this boundary in Imar because it's not in her nature to hold anything back. Not hope. Not fear. Perhaps most of all, not ambition.

She turns down the main thoroughfare. A few rusted cars are parked haphazardly, half on the pedestrian pathway, half in the road. A blue scooter lies in a ditch, its kickstand mangled. She crosses

14

the street to avoid its path; no one has dared go near it for years, the prevailing rumor being that it was planted with a bomb. Imar had only seen two such ambushes in Aaseya's lifetime, both manned by a suicidal mujahideen on a scooter who aimed for the Americans who patrolled the village frequently during those early years of fighting. Seeing the scooter sets Aaseya's suspicions reeling again. She's heard about fellow villagers swapping allegiances throughout the war. Her father was resourceful enough to outwit such dishonesty, though in the end, what did his skill matter? The abandoned scooter—in a village with no gas stations, no electricity—only confirms that betrayal and indignation share the same bed in Imar.

The neighborhood itself remains quiet today. Hardly a hint of human occupancy other than the occasional tails of smoke rising from courtyards. Like little prayers. So many women tend those fires amidst various daily tasks. Most of them never knew Ms. Darrow, the visiting English teacher who came about the time the tap stands were installed. Most of them weren't born to such a worldly father. Most don't look at the horizon and see a line to follow, either. Aaseya longs to have classmates again, or at least another girl to share her dreams of progress. She can't afford to let go of hope, its private comfort like the lead thread in an embroiderer's hand. Lose that and the entire pattern gets disrupted, so much gone to waste.

A few blocks ahead, Aaseya hears the cry of animals for slaughter, sons bargaining on behalf of their mothers. It's a spectacle of activity: the smell of dung, the dry taste of the desert, people coming and going—enlivening the mud-cooked pathways in flashes of teal, maroon, sun-gold, deep purple. Men loiter, scuffing their dirt-coated sandals against the ground. At the edge of the bazaar, beggars wait.

"Food?" a girl pleads. Her bone-thin back presses against the corner post of a bazaar tent. The girl stares at Aaseya and whimpers her incantation: "Allah. Allah. Allah."

Behind the girl, narrow rows of tents and tables form a humble economy. Aaseya remembers studying her father as he bargained kindly but firmly, Aaseya often the only young girl in sight. Walking arm-in-arm with Janan through the bazaar, she thought then she might marry a man like him. Someone who was respected and lived openly, escaping ridicule. Someday, she might even command as much independence herself.

"Please," the begging girl speaks again. "Sister, *please*."

Aaseya brushes past, unnerved. The girl's voice rings like a threat in her ears. Where are those English teachers now? Where are any teachers, for that matter? No one cares to educate girls in Imar anymore. Finding water. Raising boys. Hatching rumors. Exacting revenge. These things matter. An orphan girl is just another kicked-up rock along the road.

Aaseya tries conjuring the bird in her chest. Its gentle tugging and sweet song. *My shining smart one.* With the bird, she can draw herself out. She can press her heels into the warm skin of the earth, open her lips to the sun, and keep walking—*ba haya* be damned. She can make purchases or trade. She can even wander home the long way just to remind herself that another way is possible. One step at a time. Block by block. Like verbs forming at the tip of her pencil, lead pressed hard into the pages: *ran, run, ran, run, run.*

She's placed her hand over a particularly ripe apricot when she sees them. Both stand nearly six feet tall, lean and limber as the cougars rumored to patrol the nearby slopes. How many years has it been since she's seen Taliban fighters in public? They're even laughing, as though one fighter has just told the other a joke. It's not so much their ammo and weapons as their iron stares and meticulously draped turbans that give them away, black kohl ringing their eyes. Both men have bundled their turbans at the top, swooped them below their chins, then swaddled them across their faces, leaving only a slit for the eyes. She doesn't dare look directly, but that tiny opening of fabric, that suggestion of identity—she feels fused to its possibility. If given the chance to show only one thing about herself, what might she reveal?

The fruit vendor *tsk-tsks* and Aaseya feels a slap across the top of her hand. So few vendors will sell to her—this un-right, supposedly Pashtun woman wandering the streets—and certainly not this vendor, not now that she's lingered too long, coveting the apricot immodestly. She turns from the booth and crosses to the other side of the path. Here is Massoud. Maybe he'll sell to her today. The naan smells so fresh she can almost taste it, and she's drawn to its doughy,

16

charcoaled musk. She reaches out to select one of the toasted loaves. Of all the people she suspects could have started the false rumor about her family, she has never considered Massoud. His daughters also went to Ms. Darrow's language lessons. He even speaks to Aaseya sometimes, if there's no one in line and he can busy himself with tasks as they whisper. But Massoud has spotted the fighters too. As quickly as Aaseya approaches, he turns his back. She angles her body closer to his table display, as if the loaves of bread might stand in for her family, but Massoud offers no indication that he's going to help her.

From the corner of her eye, she sees the fighters make purchases several booths away. The apparent leader moves deftly, his hands bloodied at the knuckles. He selects cucumbers, dates, a satchel of almonds. Only a portion of the exchange is visible through the screen of Aaseya's burqa and she shifts on her feet to bring a different view into focus. Money flashes—crisp, green, US dollar bills—passed like poison seeds from the fighter to the vendor. Two-days' walk from a base, a handful of years since any occupation, and here—an Afghan vendor taking American dollars without pause? She hasn't seen that currency since Ms. Darrow showed the schoolgirls her purse one day, all the womanly items it contained. Such a treasure, then; now, the image sends shrapnel through her chest. The money can mean only one thing—the Americans are coming, and if the Americans are coming, these Taliban will be waiting. Imar will become a mere backdrop to their battle with one inevitable outcome: disaster. Aaseya wouldn't believe she's seen the bills if it weren't for what happens next, the vendor casually making change and, that fast, the little boy from outside her window rounding the corner at top speed and running into the fighters, knocking the currency to the ground.

"Pest!" The leader kicks at the boy tangled in the fabric of his *dishdasha*. Several more bills drift through the air and coins tumble from his pocket.

"You dog!" shouts the other fighter. Both grab for the money.

The boy stands and dusts himself off. In the scuffle, a fresh date has fallen from his pocket and rolled into the dirt. He reaches for it, but not fast enough.

17

"What's this?" the Taliban fighter says, mocking. He swoops down and takes the date. "Looks like we have a thief here."

The boy's eyes widen.

Aaseya leans toward Massoud's booth. "Do you see this? Friend, you have to do something."

"Get," Massoud says, barely a whisper. He won't look at her.

"I'll leave," she says. "Just forget I was here. Go help that boy."

"You get!" Massoud says again. "Get back and away. I refuse to let you endanger me, you dishonorable whore."

The fighters look up, curious, and Aaseya's breath escapes in a wave. She rushes toward the boy. "There you are!" she says, grabbing his bony shoulders. She looks at the ground, addressing the fighter humbly. "I'm sorry. My son was only doing errands for me."

"Muuh-uuuh," the boy blathers. He empties his pockets—shell casings, old springs, a broken pair of sunglasses, a plastic button. The stash tumbles from his hands as he tries offering it to the fighters.

"Over here," Massoud calls. "One free loaf for any servants of Allah, the most merciful, the most powerful."

The fighters look up and with that, Aaseya and the boy are gone, slipped behind the nearest booth, between the side flaps of tents, past the hookah stand and the butcher's table, through a small huddle of goats, ducking under a display of headscarves, pushing through the line for the kebab vendor, and then it's just Aaseya—the anonymity of her burqa, the stifling air, the bird in her chest beating its wings. Where did the boy go? Disappeared again, as elusive as water. She knows he made it through the butcher's station, where they both slowed down to dodge hanging carcasses above the slippery ground. Maybe he hid amidst the scarves and *keffiyehs*.

Aaseya looks for him briefly, then hurries out the far end of the bazaar toward the dead end of town, where the old schoolhouse looms like a bad memory. It hurts to think how many days she spent believing Ms. Darrow would come back. That studying was not only her privilege, but her right. Beyond the schoolhouse, an overflow block for vendors' booths and tents opens up. It's quiet now, more like a park or garden space for nomads who might pass through Imar. At the end of the park, the tight walls of mountains forming either side of the Imar valley meet in a U-shaped trap. Aaseya has heard another village lies not too far beyond that ridgeline, though nobody she knows ever traverses the upper slopes. Imar has always been described as cut off, physical isolation a part of her daily existence for as long as she can remember. But before the upslope begins its steep climb, the loop road arcs along the base of the valley and back around the bazaar, paralleling the edge of town and wrapping round to the entrance of the village. She meets the road and walks steadily, occasionally checking over her shoulder to see if she is being followed.

Before long, the loop road ends and opens toward the wider road leading out of the valley. It's a junction Aaseya knows well, occasionally allowing herself to walk this far from the apartment. From here, the view widens down the length of the valley, and outward to the uninterrupted desert and she can imagine how it will be when they first arrive—tails of dust, the reek of gasoline, the strangeness of their pink skin and different language. Do the Americans know what's waiting for them? How little it takes to disrupt a life? Even if she tried, there'd be no stopping whatever those dollars have set in motion. She studies the view one last time, considering. She's never stepped past this point, but she imagines it would be the beginning of something better. Somewhere in the near distance, Rahim must be digging in the creek beds, his makeshift job of forming bricks only possible in the wake of war's destruction as families slowly rebuild. Somewhere else nearby, there must be Taliban, too. She recoils at the thought, as if something is being pulled from her grasp and sucked into a vacuum of cold. She turns her head from one side to the other, letting the panorama of horizon in through the screened view of her burqa. Some mornings, the sky here fills with pink and orange tendrils that unreel like spools of yarn, stretching from north to south. But now, the sun sits mid-sky, the world hyper-saturated in blues and browns. She folds her arms and pinches the flesh where her forearms crease at the elbows; a slight twinge across her skin. She pinches again and thinks of the apricot, how promising its texture. Hardly a spot of mold. She pinches again, recalling Shanaz's admonitions, the possessive timbre of her voice. Heat blooms across her forearms and she pinches again, so tender. She imagines sinking her teeth into the apricot, holding the pit in her mouth. How she would clean the sweet flesh away with her tongue and find the pit in the center. She can see it clearly—that apricot pit like a missile careening from her mouth, through the screen of her burqa with piercing speed as she yells every curse imaginable in the face of those Taliban. Those imposters. Those loathsome creatures riddled with more lice than the roadside carcass of a dog. She's lucky she survived. That's what Rahim always tells her. That's what Shanaz wants her to believe, and just as surely as she imagines that apricot pit zeroing in on its target, Aaseya feels the skin across her forearms break beneath her fingertips, bleeding into clarity.

There's no denying it; Shanaz was the one who tipped off the Taliban. The Taliban believed her, mistaking Aaseya's family compound for an American hideout. The Taliban reduced her fate to one moment of dust and vibration that stole everything from her but her own heartbeat. They hurt Ms. Darrow, hurt everybody, and although the Americans may be coming soon with their own measure of fate, it's too late. It's not enough. Aaseya has her own explosions to carry out and now she envisions Shanaz with black kohl around her eyes. She wants the Taliban to rape Shanaz, to kill her, but then Aaseya's vision shifts and her enemies turn to face her. Warmth moves across her fingertips—blood, the only proof she's still alive— and as her accusers point their fingers at her, mocking, the apricot pit explodes on target. Body parts pepper the open desert like so many seeds of war.

◊

As Aaseya approaches her apartment, she hears the sound of bare feet not far behind. How bad will it be if the fighters followed her? She sees herself tossed onto the ground, legs spread. Sees them spit on her, burn her hair, her eyes. Maybe it's her due, catching up. She never should have survived the blast. Rahim and Shanaz might even be grateful if she died, released from association with her daily disobediences.

"What is it?" she says, and turns to face her follower.

The boy must have stayed close, after all. Feeling floods her limbs and she looks at her burqa, noticing a few small dots of blood

20

where the fabric sticks to her arms. She almost rushes to him in relief, then remembers he might be timid. Most wartime orphans are.

He points to the tap stand near Aaseya's apartment steps.

"There's not any water," she shrugs.

The boy crosses the street and Aaseya marvels at his little brown calves as flat as kebabs, his twiggy arms hanging from shoulders that jut outward like wings. There's some measure of peacefulness about him, or at least, possibility. Maybe it's his innocence she finds charming, his age alone permitting unawareness of what's headed their way. He moves the pump slowly, tiny frame working hard against the pressure, but nothing comes. He looks at her again, untrimmed hair flopping around his eyes and ears.

"What's your name?" she asks, and when he points with excessive gestures toward his chest, she understands that he must be mute.

"Oh. *Zra?*" she asks, pointing at her heart.

He shakes his head, then points back and forth between his heart and his mouth.

"*Shpeelak,*" she says, meaning whistle.

Wrong again. The boy moves his hands from his lips to the air in front of him, as if pulling something from his mouth.

"*Ghazél!*" she says at last, quieted by the irony—a mute boy named "song."

He nods enthusiastically, then does a little dance in the street, his face opening into a charming grin.

"Wait here." She heads toward her apartment and up the stairs. And so it begins—Aaseya tossing down a stuffed date and Ghazél catching it skillfully, the two connected mid-air by an invisible thread.

Fiction

MALINA DOUGLAS

The Museum of Australian Oddities

If we were in Australia, this wouldn't have happened. People there are bold and bronzed and full of action. *They* wouldn't be sitting in a bombed-out building, hiding from gunfire. They'd be too busy windsurfing and sea kayaking and having barbecues and whatever else they do, far away across the seas.

◊

I am building a museum of Australian oddities. I am building it out of rubble. I collect objects: A rusted knife that could be Crocodile Dundee's, sand that I can pretend is from East Gippsland, a fragment of bone from a rare type of wallaby. Don't tell anyone it's actually chicken, from Thursday's dinner.

Mother had stuffed wads of newspaper into the fire and blown softly until the flames licked our battered old pot. We burn what we can find—chair legs, warped boards, the leftover fragments of houses, ripped apart. She'd sat on a slab of concrete boiling the chicken, sometimes prodding it with a shard of a wooden blind, until the dark smoke set her coughing and the gray dusk made her squint. My sister and I had circled the pot like sharks. I'd barely eaten. My stomach was a ravenous beast, ready to devour everything in sight. When it was finally ready, we had torn off strips of meat and stuffed them into our mouths. We'd pulled the chicken apart until there were only bones left and we'd sucked on the bones and our greasy burnt fingers. I'd pulled one off and slipped it into my pocket.

◊

DOUGLAS

Ever since our flat exploded, we've been camping in the rubble. As night falls over us skeletons of burned out buildings become shadows.

"It's okay," I tell my family. "I'm building the Museum of Australian Oddities. One day, people will come from all over the world to see it."

"That's nice, darling," says Mother. She is squatting, scrubbing the pot with a blackened rag and a bucket of water. She is looking away. I follow her gaze to a darkened doorway in the distance.

When we sleep, we find a spot in the shell of a burned-out building and build a nest of cardboard and old clothes. All three of us snuggle up together, my mother, my sister and I, for safety and warmth.

In the morning, after a bit of bread and an orange between us, I set off hunting for artifacts.

At first, my sister tries to tag along.

"It's a dangerous expedition," I tell her. "It must be done alone."

She scrunches up her face and huffs away, to play with her doll limbs in the dust.

I climb through a blasted-out window and my shoes crunch on broken glass.

I walk beneath severed wires, hanging in tangles. I step over mangled furniture, lift up boards and climb over piles of objects crunched and flattened beyond recognition. I find a long and twisted piece of metal that reminds me of a snake, but it's not realistic enough. I cast it aside.

I pick up jagged bits of stone that look like fossilized crocodile teeth and glass beads like opals. Other stones that could be aboriginal axe-heads. I put each stone into my pocket, until they are heavy and bulging.

◊

Returning with my finds, I must keep a sharp eye on the artifacts. My sister grabs a handful of glass beads. I give her a stuffed giraffe head, to distract her, and pry the beads out of her little clenched fist. I wash them in our cooking pot with a tiny bit of water, and scrape off the grit. I tuck each object carefully into my backpack. "Oh, Mus'ad," exclaims Mother. "You're covered in dirt. Hold still." I try to squirm away but she has my face in an iron grip. She scrubs it with a cold dirty rag. I could come back with an armload of golden crocodiles and if there was one bit of dirt on my face, she would notice it first.

◊

Over the last months, our world has been shrinking. Our school got bombed so we had to stop going. At first, I was happy I didn't have to sit for my math test, but after a while it got boring.

One morning, I went to the market with Mother to buy oranges. We walked past walls lined with archways, most of the accordion covers of shops sealed shut. The high dark vault of the Maskuf market was perforated with bullet holes, and light was streaming in, projecting dozens of circles onto the dusty asphalt. They looked so like coins I had the urge to pick them up.

Outside, we heard a gunshot. Across the street, a man dropped dead. Mother clamped down on my hand and hurried me along.

After that she didn't let me out of the house.

Those were long and dull days. We watched television. Crocodile Dundee and Indiana Jones became my two favorite movies. We invented games to pass the time. I hunted the house for treasure and set snares for imaginary beasts.

The day our flat exploded, we'd been cooped up inside for weeks. The gunfire had finished sometime in the night. When we woke up, everything was unusually quiet. Mother sat by the window, waiting. Her head was wrapped in a white scarf like always, her wide face placid, her almond eyes studying every movement on the street.

My little sister was drawing flowers. I drew a crocodile eating her flowers and she crossed it out with angry red marker.

She drew a house. I drew a big rain cloud pouring down on the house. She drew a sun to dry out the rain. I drew a jet plane blotting out the sun. She scribbled on the jet. I protested.

24

Mother heard us, and said, "Stop bickering."

Farida kept complaining.

Mother took away the markers.

"That's it," she said. "We're going outside."

"Outside?" we both asked.

"It's safe now," she declared. We did not argue. Mother was unpredictable. I grabbed my backpack before she could change her mind. Farida brought her dolls. We burst into the sunshine and started running in different directions, but Mother's hard voice sent us back again.

"Stay close," she commanded. We followed her orders. The few people on the streets walked as quickly as we did.

Between rooftops we caught a glimpse of the mosque. It used to have a shining white dome. Now it was ash-gray and scarred with bullet holes.

We walked around all afternoon, down rubble-piled streets and in and out of shops until we felt our legs were going to drop off.

Coming home we confronted a burning, gaping hole. Something was wrong. Were we on the wrong street? No. It couldn't be . . . But it was. From that night on we were sleeping in the rubble.

◊

It's not easy to build a museum, not when your expeditions are cut short without notice.

"It's time to go," Mother tells me one day. I'm sitting on the ground, sorting out my stone collection, picking out the stones that most closely resemble arrowheads and tossing the unwanted ones into a pile.

"Where are we going?"

"To our new home."

"Will there be snakes and spiders there?"

"I hope not."

"Then I'd rather stay here."

"You can't stay here."

Then she tells me my stone collection is too big.

"You can only take it if you can fit it in your backpack."

I'm forced to abandon many promising artifacts, but some of the precious ones have to be smuggled.

I put a few stones in her bag when she's not looking. Only the important ones.

◊

Our new home is a white tent in a sea of white tents.

"Why do we have to have a white tent," I ask Mother. "Why can't we have a yellow tent or a green tent?"

"There aren't any," says Mother.

"Can we paint it yellow?"

"We don't have any paint," says Mother.

"That's no fun."

◊

I display my findings in the sand outside our tent.

Carefully, I lay out each object: the knife, the jar of sand, the opals, the bone. Beneath each one I put a plaque describing the object and its origin. I have written them out neatly on pieces of cardboard. It's enough to draw a curious crowd of children. Suddenly there are hands all over my findings, touching, lifting, snatching.

"Stop," I cry out. "This is a museum!" They scatter.

I rearrange the objects, dusting off each one and replacing its plaque. I wait for more reasonable people to pass by, who will appreciate the items for what they are.

◊

It's boring, being in the camp. The adults don't do much. They sit around and talk and drink tea, mostly. When there *is* tea.

And there aren't any interesting buildings around to play in. From the edge of the camp, there is only sand. I stand there, looking through barbed wire, out to the vast flat horizon. I imagine I'm looking into the Simpson Desert. My little sister is handing me the reins of my camel and I am riding out into uncharted territory.

26

Australians don't sit around and drink tea all day. They have much more exciting things to do, like surfing waves, fighting off sharks, and catching spiders. Or snaring kangaroos with lassos, jumping on their backs, and riding out into the desert. That's what we'd be doing if we were there.

◊

Light filters into a makeshift shelter, where a man is playing the oud. A second man begins to sing. His mournful voice soars above the rapid strumming. He sings of our homeland across the desert, just out of reach.

Mother is holding me in her lap.

"Can we go to Australia," I ask her. I forgot how many times I asked her this, but her answer is usually the same.

She strokes my hair. "Maybe one day," she says, "when you're old enough."

I hate it when adults say when you're old enough. That could be months or years away, you never know.

"I'm old enough now," I tell her. I start to squirm away, but her arms tighten like a vice. The second man has stopped singing. The oud player glances over. His face is streaming with tears. The oud player lowers his head. He begins a new song.

"We'll find a new home," Mother tells me, looking out through the flap in the tent. "*Insha'Allah*." If God wills it.

◊

A slender boy approaches me. He says he's found something, looks like it could be an ancient pickaxe. Would I like to see it?

I wriggle loose and skip after him down the flat dusty road.

CHRISTINE EVANS

Greetings from Fallujah
a ten-minute solo play in seven blog posts

Cast: ZAYNAB, an Iraqi teenage girl, blogging from Fallujah in 2003-4. She's Sunni, but not particularly religious, from an educated professional family. Smart, playful, full of life.

Time & Place: Fallujah, Iraq, 2003-4.
Zaynab's living room, where she blogs to the world from her home—increasingly a war zone.

The time span of this play is loosely pegged to the following timeline:

March 2003: The United States invades Baghdad, delivering "shock and awe."

April 2003: US troops enter Fallujah.

April 28, 2003: US 82nd Airborne Division fires on a civilian crowd protesting the use of a local high school as military headquarters; seventeen protesters die and seventy are wounded. Two days later, US troops again fire on a protest against the killings, resulting in two more deaths.

March 31, 2004: Iraqi insurgents in Fallujah attack a convoy of four US contractors from the private military company Blackwater (recently renamed Academi). Their corpses are dragged through the streets before being hung over a bridge, causing outrage in the United States and prompting combat operations to reestablish US control over the city.

April 4, 2004: US forces launch a massive assault on Fallujah (Operation Vigilant Resolve / first battle of Fallujah).

Staging: This play could be performed in a bare space, with everything suggested by language and lighting shifts. Or it could be done with sophisticated projection design to suggest the landscapes and world of Fallujah. There are opportunities to create a world of echoes (recorded / live sound) and to mix live and recorded video.

Anachronism: While video blogs (vlogs) weren't around in 2003, the play takes poetic license in making Zaynab a vlogger.

Post #1
> (Crackling noise. We see Zaynab checking her webcam, trying to get online. And then . . . ta da! It works!)

ZAYNAB:

Wow. Finally online. It's been so bad this week. Electricity is off half the time. And we're all jammed in here with a sick baby. At night she turns into a baby demon and howls.

And I'm stuck at home because school's closed because of what happened to the Christian students. A group of men got hold of three girls after school and pushed them round because they dressed like sluts, that's what they said. So now—here I am! Trapped with my family!

Anyway, this will be short because Nasir and Mahmoud are both nagging me for the computer. They are really driving me crazy— Mahmoud always does, he's thirteen but Nasir isn't usually this bad. Aunt Morouj, Cousin Nasir and the baby are here because their house in Baghdad got blown up last week. So the house is crammed, everyone's on edge. Mornings—with one bathroom and nine people— we're all just trying not to scream at each other. My mother does scream sometimes. And the baby never stops.

(*In Arabic*) All right, all right! Give me a minute, I'm coming! (*In English*) So. Don't send us more soldiers. Send us some toothpaste instead. And soap! And candles, but not the ones that smell like food. (*Turning*) All right! I'm coming! (*A parting shot*) And men's deodorant!

(The projected image of Zaynab's face freezes.)

Post #2

ZAYNAB:

Online! Hello Earth. Greetings from Fallujah! —Nasir is really annoying me. Today we've had electricity for four hours and he's been online for three of them. He wants to play war games online, can you believe it. Just go outside if you want to play soldiers, Nasir, I said and he yelled at me and said I didn't know anything about the real world. And then he was mean about my essay prize.

I got an essay prize at school; we had to write about heroes. Everyone else did Ali Baba and Scheherazade but I'm bored with them, so I picked Hercules. Zeus's wife made him go insane and murder his own wife and children. And then he had to fight monsters as punishment, but it wasn't even his fault, the goddess just struck him to get revenge.

(Pause)

Everything's about revenge now, the car bombs and snipers and kidnappings and it's really hard to know who's doing what. The mud is getting wetter, my dad says; that's the only thing that's clear.

Anyway, in my essay Hercules restores the ancient canals of Baghdad, instead of just killing monsters, and the water gardens all bloom again. My dad says that Nasir and I will rebuild the country just like my Hercules; he liked my essay. *After it's smashed to bits*, said Nasir. He's so rude. He always talks about our "past glory," blah blah. He wants to be an engineer but he can't even finish school now so he just boils with rage instead. Dad told him, *Be patient, the Americans hop round like fleas, they'll find a new adventure soon and leave us alone.*

30

Ha ha, just like Hercules, I said. *Oh, so the Americans are your heroes?* Nasir said, then he stormed out. Even though it was nearly curfew. Nasir makes me sick sometimes. And Dad's worried about him too, I can tell.

Nasir was in the protest at the school last month, against the Americans using it as a base. That was very bad. The soldiers hid on a roof and shot at them. Everyone was screaming. Hundreds of people got hurt or killed.

Nasir saw people killed and his friend Khalid got shot in the leg. And then two days later there was another protest and they killed people again. So he's an idiot to go back out there.

Especially after dark.

(The light slowly fades. Zaynab looks around anxiously.)

Post # 3

ZAYNAB:

May 16, 2003. Hello Earth, Greetings from Fallujah. Are you still out there? Anyone?

(Pause)

Tonight is the full moon! We can all see the moon. The same moon, all over the world. That's strange.

Well, you know what we did? We had a moon picnic! We were all in an odd mood, it's been quiet lately and we're not used to it, so my Aunt Morouj suddenly says, let's have a moon picnic! We all looked at her like she was crazy—she is sometimes. We can't get soap or candles but there's a huge market in Prozac—but no, she was laughing and said, let's go up on the roof. And suddenly everyone went crazy!

31

Dad dug out the blankets, I made my date and honey cakes . . . well we didn't have dates or honey but I put sugar in and they still tasted divine, and we went up on the roof. No bombs, no guns—a car backfiring made Mahmoud jump, that's all. Even Nasir was in a good mood, he was home for once. He made my Aunt laugh talking about how he'd rebuild Baghdad with space-age robots and solar power—oh, listening to Nasir is like a roller coaster.

(*To us, confidentially*) He is not sensible like me and Mahmoud.

Tonight everyone was happy. The moon was so beautiful. And everyone, even Nasir said my honey cakes were good. And that made me feel like crying. Because in truth they fell apart, they were just semolina and sugar cooked in an oven that kept shutting off so they weren't even cooked through. Oh, and here goes the electricity. I can see the lights shutting off so I'm probably next.

> (Blackout. The sound of cheerful Arabic pop music, then static.)

Post # 4

ZAYNAB:

Hello Earth. Greetings from Fallujah. The mud is getting wetter every day but Al-Chalabi says the situation is "calm and improving." Huh! We've all been cooped up here and the baby demon cries all the time. The boys still go out, Dad tells them not to, but my cousin Nasir does what he likes now and Mahmoud follows him. And I have to stay here with my crying aunt and her crying baby and my mother who is taking Prozac by the fistful but won't give <u>me</u> any, and nobody can go near the windows since the car bomb last week.

I hate babies. I'll never have a baby, especially in a war.

Anyway, things reached boiling point when the baby screamed and screamed, I was looking after it while Aunt Morouj slept, I shook it just a little bit to see if I could scare it quiet, but Auntie saw me and lost her mind and started shouting and slapped me, and I cried and my mother cried and my Dad said the house was full of howling females, so he yelled at us to shut up.

So I decided to do Mahmoud's job that he has stopped doing and take out the garbage, just to breathe my own lungful of air. I was in a very bad mood and wishing the baby and Nasir and my aunt would vanish back to Baghdad, but they can't because their stupid house was bombed. Anyway, I stomped over to the garbage. It stank and it was overflowing so I wanted to hurry, but then I noticed a big round thing in the bin. It looked like a watermelon but it was reddish-purple, not green. I poked it with a stick to see what it was and it rolled over and I saw.

It was a boy's head . . . I felt completely calm, as if I was made of ice. I noticed the green-blue bruises on his cheek. How young he was, his top lip soft and downy above broken teeth. The curl of brown hair on his forehead. He was like a flower, truly, a little crushed but beautiful. His green eyes were open and they looked straight into me.

And then I realized. It was Khalid, Nasir's friend.

—The furnace of Fallujah rushed back into my lungs and I retched. I ran back inside and couldn't talk, I just locked myself in the bathroom until I could stop being sick.

What kind of world is this? What did Khalid do? He looked right into my eyes. And I saw . . .

I am so, so terrified of what Nasir will do when he finds out.

Aunt Morouj says we mustn't tell him.

But that's one of the things I saw in Khalid's eyes.

Nasir will find out.

And then we will reap the wind.

(Static)

Post # 5

ZAYNAB:

Greetings, Earth . . . Allahu al adheem. I don't know what to do, I don't know what to do. You hear that crying? It's my mother. It's my mother. It's my fault. I was always thinking about Nasir, Nasir, Nasir. I forgot my own little brother. And Mahmoud is only thirteen. Was. —I can't think straight. Our hearts are burning to ash. Why? He just sold DVDs! He didn't have any enemies! Nothing makes sense.

And worse is to come. Yesterday they burned the bodies of the American mercenaries. They dragged them from the truck and hung them up on a bridge. Everyone says the Americans will take terrible revenge. All the men have to leave or they will be killed as fighters. Dad says we have to pack for the village right now. But my mother wants to stay and die in her own house.

If I could find the man who shot Mahmoud, I would tear him to pieces.

Write to me. No, don't write. Say prayers. Tell them people live here.

Post # 6

ZAYNAB:

April 3, 2004. Greetings from Fallujah. This might be my last blog. It's very strange—I feel outside of my own face. Like I'm watching myself on TV.

Is anyone out there? Are you going to watch us die on Fox News and CNN?

You should tune in to Al Jazeera. They get much better pictures of civilians.

Our TV's not working. The water's shut off. It's very quiet. The others are sleeping; I don't know how they can. I haven't slept in three days. But it's a relief that they're quiet. When Aunt Morouj and baby demon are awake they <u>both</u> cry all the time now. Thank God we can still get Prozac.

We shouldn't be here. We should have left. But Nasir has disappeared. My father went to find him.

That was two days ago. We don't know what's happened to them. So now it's just me, my mother and Aunt Morouj and the baby. And it's too late to leave. All the roads are blocked off. The city's crouching. Nothing's moving. There's just this terrible waiting. Like rats in a cage.

I'm watching myself, a girl, in this fishbowl. I have that calm ice feeling again that I had when I found Khalid's head. But this time it's Nasir looking at me—I can feel it.

Nasir has such beautiful eyes.

The moon will rise again. Everything does. *Safra tawila*. I'm so cold.

(We hear footsteps running up the road, and up the stairs to the house.)

—Oh God, someone's coming. I have to put my scarf on.

(She looks in the camera / mirror / out to the audience, worriedly adjusting herself. A loud sound of the door being smashed in. Zaynab turns. A frozen moment. White light. Blackout.)

(After a moment, we hear the sound of static. Zaynab appears again, very calm, in a ghostly light. Her movements are slow. She smiles at us, gently. When she speaks, her voice has an echo, or delay, as if broadcast from very far away.)

Post # 7

ZAYNAB:

Hello Earth. Greetings from Fallujah.

Can you see the moon . . . from where you are? All over the world. People see the same moon.

The moon will rise again. Everything does.

How strange.

Safra tawila. I'm so cold.

Tell them . . . people lived here.

> (Zaynab slowly backs away and disappears. Her ghostly projected image lingers for a few seconds. Then Zaynab's image fades to black, too.)

NOOR HASHEM

Recounting Syria

> *We might think of war as dividing populations into those who are grievable and those who are not. An ungrievable life is one that cannot be mourned because it has never lived, that is, it has never counted as a life at all.*
>
> —Judith Butler, *Frames of War*

There are the lives counted as numbers: four hundred and seventy thousand Syrians dead as of 2016, fifty-five thousand of them children, almost thirteen thousand dead by torture, sixty-three percent of all deaths civilian, the Syrian regime responsible for eighty-eight percent of these civilian casualties. Over 6.3 million internally displaced, shuffling between abandoned and inhabited homes of family and friends; 5.1 million refugees, nearly half of them children. More than one hundred and seventeen thousand Syrians detained or disappeared. Before the revolution, Syria had 21.5 million people— around the population of New York State living within an area roughly the size of Washington State.

There are those not counted in these numbers, like the communities of Syrian exiles who left in the 80s, when Hafez Al-Assad cracked down on dissent and tightened the noose of corrupt, Arab-socialist economic policies, making life unlivable. These exiles made homes and families in the United States, in Germany, in Canada, in the UK, in the Gulf States, and in neighboring Arab countries.

Exiles call family inside the country for on-the-ground accounts told through barely-veiled code: *It's raining every hour here* (raining bombs). *We're drowning.* They turn to the news media and count articles, finding too many on Bashar Al-Assad, statements from France, Britain, Russia, China, reports on Geneva II, III, IV, on Iran and Al-Qaeda affiliated mercenaries. On social media, activists swap videos and photos counting the dead, providing evidence of the lives of emaciated children and the elderly starving behind regime-maintained blockades, exposing regime snipers targeting international aid agencies that have waited to get permission from the government to enter besieged towns. The exiles keep updated about local governing councils in liberated areas, discussing short-term humanitarian aid and long-term development projects, supporting the establishment of institutions that will persist even when individuals cannot. And they cannot any longer in Syria.

Then there are the faces and personalities. Exile-run nonprofits escort Syrian refugees across the US. The refugees speak at events attended largely by Syrian-American crowds, confirming stories the attendees have already heard. Exiles travel to Turkey and Jordan, sneak into Syria, then return to report their own accounts of what they already know from counting numbers: the resilient existence of grievable lives.

Survival Stories—Winter 2014

How do you write a story of grief and survival that is not yours, or even yours to tell? What if you were related to it, only once removed? In the words of trauma theorist Elaine Scarry, the Syrian conflict is the entire making and unmaking of my world. But as a Syrian-American, I am privileged, safe.

"I don't care about the Syrian-American experience," says Razan Ghazzawi, celebrated Syrian activist and blogger. Razan was born in the US and raised for a time in Saudi Arabia before returning to Syria. She is American by birthright. Still, she does not feel American by culture or experience.

It is January in Illinois. We have just left a talk given by Razan and Raed Fares at the University of Chicago. Now we are traveling by car to a community function in a nearby suburb. Raed, sitting in the passenger seat, is the man behind the witty Kafranbel banners that are posted from Syria every Friday on Facebook. The banners reach out to the world to comment on the revolution and world politics, advocating for compassionate and strategic action. A few weeks later in Syria, on his way home from his media office, Raed will survive an assassination attempt by the mercenary group of political radicals who call themselves the "Islamic State of Iraq and Syria."

Kenan Rehmani, a Syrian-American working in DC as Director of Operations for The Syrian-American Council, is driving. I sit in the back between my sister, who at the time also works for SAC, and Razan, who stares out the window. Kenan drives through the Chicago streets with the speed of a New Yorker, disregarding traffic lights like a Bostonian, weaving like an Angelino, assuming the right-of-way over pedestrians and navigating the streets with a gut feeling for direction like he's back in Syria. I have only a few minutes before they drop me off at my hotel, on their way to the next event. I don't have much time to ask them about writing the revolution, about what they think of the work done in the safety of exile. Did they feel we were capitalizing on tragedy? What were their thoughts about the politics of representation and navigating the ethics of art?

I tell Raed and Razan that I write about my experiences with Syrian refugees. In nervous, hobbled Arabic, I try to strike a balance between harmonizing with sociable, witty, energetic Raed while matching Razan's stoic, serious, intellectual bearing.

Their eyes and skin tell me they are both exhausted. They are nearing the end of a one-month speaking tour in the US. Raed has been making posters with Syrian-American youth, sharing them on Facebook while his team in Syria continues to upload their own banners from inside his hometown. Kafranbel, the little agricultural village in the northwest of Syria, part of the Idlib countryside, is a place that was liberated early and gained fame for being one of the centers of the revolution. Most of all, it is known for cheeky banners commenting on the state of Syria and the world.

In the car, after Razan says "I don't care about the Syrian-American experience," a tense silence follows.

"Of course, of course," I repeat. The revolution is not mine. It is not for me. If nothing had changed in Syria, my day-to-day life would remain intact. Even now, I only feel its distant reverberations in my access to loved ones, when their Syrian passports expire, their visas are revoked, and their travel indefinitely banned. Still, the revolution is deeply mine, through my family, through my history, through my sentimental attachments to my memories of Syria, through the feelings of helplessness and the survivor's guilt that lurks at every pleasure and success.

Razan sits next to me but she is elsewhere, sometimes frowning at the scene outside her window, at other times looking straight ahead, her eyes locked with determination, as if moving forward through sheer force of will in the fear that if she stopped, she would shatter. Razan is academic, cynical, studied. Raed, on the other hand, is a charismatic chain-smoking lover of humanity who drinks from a deep well of infectious energy. He is tall, his every feature big, exuding a sturdy certainty in his every move. He makes me feel as if we are old, fast friends, as if I am the center of the world—along with everyone and everything else.

Raed turns 180 degrees to look me in the eye. An optimist and maximalist, he wants to exhaust every possible peaceful means to revolution. "We all need to tell our stories," he says. "It is the details that make the issue come to life. When I met the senator last week, he said he was glad that now he could put a face to the conflict." Raed lives under constant bombing. He is the target of assassination. He leaves behind beloved family and friends—not knowing if they will be there when he returns—in order to tour worlds of comfort and security in the constant hope of moving people to care about tragedy enough that it might make some small change in his reality. Still, he is the one reassuring me. He calls me to responsibility, telling me I count too.

Razan speaks again. Her tone is softer now, but her voice is still monotone, the line of her mouth grim, her words clipped, pragmatic and direct.

"We barely have enough electricity in Syria to keep up with the revolution," she says. "As activists," she explains, "we can barely count on an hour of computer time before the power is cut for hours. As revolutionaries, our priority is first and foremost to keep connected with the revolution, with resistance strategies and comrades on the ground, tracking which friends have been detained, released, killed. Even with electricity, access to information is restricted, and even

40

when we manage to secure access, we are under bombardment."

Razan is quiet again. Raed asks that the world care, but Razan reminds me that caring is costly. Caring about the problems of the world beyond our own is a luxury that depends on precious reserves of time and energy. It draws upon the intangible work of our human capacity to extend ourselves. By all measures, Syrians should not be able to afford to relate to experiences outside Syria. They are busy at the task of sheer survival, gathering just enough material resources to eat, to warm themselves, to avoid being torn apart by man or machine.

And yet, as the years drag, and as the world sighs in pity before going about its day, Syrians reach out to comfort the world through photos expressing sympathy for other tragedies. Two years into the Syrian conflict, in a photo of Raed's group in Kafranbel, men and children hold up a banner as they stand in front of a gutted building. What was once an interior room on the second floor is now the structure's façade, the floor beneath it jagged as torn cardboard. A concrete staircase rests on its side, held up diagonally from the ground by split threads of exposed steel rebar bent like veins. The banner reads:

BOSTON BOMBERS REPRESENT A SORROWFUL
SCENE OF WHAT HAPPENS EVERY DAY IN SYRIA.
DO ACCEPT OUR CONDOLENCES

A year later, in 2014, the group shares another photo. In it, their hands are frozen in peace signs, flags of Syrian independence waving behind them, while the banner declares:

WE STAND IN SOLIDARITY WITH THE OPPRESSED
WHO CANNOT BREATHE
#BLAKLIVESMATTER [sic]

In a photo from 2017, two men stand in uniforms of black khakis and Harrington jackets. They wear white helmets on their heads as members of a volunteer-based group of first responders. I know from other photos that the uniforms, depending on access to resources, consist of simple jackets, polo shirts, voyager vests, knee guards, and black tennis shoes. A select few members have black work gloves, while some only have a t-shirt they wear with jeans. These are the articles of clothes that will have to protect them as they pull children out of the rubble of buildings that have crumbled from crude barrel bombs dropped from regime helicopters that often return for a targeted second attack. Still, in the photo, the two White Helmets hold a sign apologizing for not being available to rescue the victims of the Grenfell Towers fire in London.

◊

In Boston a month later, I meet Ameenah and Hiba Sawwan. These cousins are part of another speaker's circuit, this one billed "The Survivor's Tour." Their lives are defined by their persistence in the face of the Syrian regime's chemical attack on Moadamiya, the besieged town where the government obstructed food and medical supplies in one of their "kneel or starve" operations.

The event Ameenah and Hiba speak at is hosted in a posh loft office on the fifth floor of a building on Newbury Street. The walls feature an exhibit highlighting the various cultural attire from regions in North Africa, the Levant, the Gulf, and the Balkans.

Hiba and Ameenah bring dozens of other witnesses with them: the shuhadaa'. In Arabic, it is not only the living who bear witness—so do the dead. The shuhadaa', or shahīd in the singular, is a person who dies an unjust or untimely death in war or peace, and is promised recompense from God. The word's root form is sh-h-d, to witness. Even if you were running across the street for a few loaves of pita bread when you were gunned down, your death is not for nothing. Your death acts as a complaint about the injustices of the world. You are heroic, remembered.

Hiba and Ameenah's witnesses, all martyrs, are preserved in digital files. They are names and images that are snuck across physical borders until they can be uploaded to global servers in the hopes that they will cross the imaginary boundaries separating hearts from minds. On Facebook, so many Syrians post photos of their dead: images of limb-torn bodies and spilt organs, or faces, some

HASHEM

whitewashed in the fine silt of obliterated cities, others mannequin-frozen, blue ashen, heads wrapped in gauze in the custom of Islamic burial. The only relief in the photos is edited in as stock frames made of roses and hearts. There is little public discussion about the trauma these photos may inflict on the families, or their right to privacy. The dead are for us all. The dead have the right to speak. We have no right to silence them.

So much of storytelling, especially in the US and in English-speaking countries more broadly, privileges life. We tell stories about the living, about surviving. The dead are punctuations. Hiba and Ameenah are committed to tell stories about the existence of both life and death. They cycle through a photo slideshow of *shuhadaa'*, focusing on the children. They report the minutiae of vibrant lives, before the martyrs became no more than testimony. But the details are only hints, and there is only a blink of time for each slide. There is too much ground to cover. The faces in the photos become images with names that count only because they prove the numbers.

Ameenah delivers her own story of survival by rote. It is exact, given word-for-pause to the UN, at advocacy groups events, and in personal settings over dinner. I memorize her words as if they are my own. "One of the chemical missiles fell only 100 meters away from the front of my house but the air took the Sarin gas to the opposite direction. That's why I survived, thanks to God's mercy," and, "I felt faint, and I wasn't sure if it was because of the Sarin or because of starvation." Her delivery is usually fiery, though sometimes her words break in half while she takes a moment to practice breathing.

After introductions mentioning the Assad government, Hiba stands up. "Please," she says, smiling. "Do not call Assad and the Ba'ath party a government. They have no legitimacy with us. They are a regime; he is a dictator." She will continue insisting this at other functions, saying it sometimes in Arabic, sometimes in English.

Hiba and Ameenah have a solid grasp of English, at once fluent but halting as their testimonies refract trauma from Arabic to English, their minds building proper grammatical phrases and sifting through words to describe suffering that even native speakers would struggle to express. Hiba studied English literature at Damascus

University, but Ameenah is more willing to speak impromptu. Her sentences rush into and stumble over one another with urgency.

In the testimonies they give, the music of the language is absent. English is a tool: *Listen to us*, they say, *we will speak English for you if it means you will listen, and help.* Their faces reflect shock, disappointment and cynicism. But privately, over a dinner I host, they are still young, easily scandalized by this new world outside their small Damascus suburb. They giggle when we discuss provocative ideas about gender and the challenges facing young American Muslims. When I explain that I am equally Syrian and American, they pat my hand and tell me it's not too late to improve my Arabic.

Both wear white synthetic headscarves in two pieces. They have recently purchased ankle-length puffer jackets. They wear these not as outerwear, but as outfits, the way Syrian women of a certain religious inclination wear trench coats. Outside, in the New England winter, this works. Once indoors, they overheat but can't shed the protective layer. Underneath, they only thought to wear short sleeves, they confide in me as we look at the photos of Muslims in cultural dress. At dinner, when the conversation turns to their work in Moadamiya, they proudly describe how they covered their faces with the *niqab* to facilitate their frequent work there with men who adhered to that interpretation of religious modesty, even if their own segment of society did not. In photos years later, they wear outfits favored by American Muslim women, breathable tunics with slim-fit pants and flats, or long leather jackets with wide-leg trousers, knit caps, and turtlenecks sometimes replacing the headscarf.

Ameenah, fair-skinned, angular, her eyes small and set wide apart on a broad forehead, has a habit of knitting her eyebrows and scrunching up her nose and squinting so that she always looks like she is thinking, confused, experiencing a headache, and disdainful all at once. Hiba, her face round, her chin round, her lips full, her eyes big and brown and penetrating, disarms with the ease of her smile before she launches into political discussion presented with compelling gravity. She tells personal, difficult stories: about her father, detained for two-and-a-half years and still missing; about her dead fiancé, killed in a battle against the regime three months before their wedding; about her work as a nurse in the local field hospital which later ends

44

when she is shot at and injured in the arm by regime snipers while visiting her fiancé's grave; about her mother, who worries about her safety, a woman both proud and displeased by Hiba's work as an activist.

Both Hiba and Ameenah are raw and unfiltered, frank and unapologetic. Unlike the cosmopolitan and diplomatic sophistication of Raed and Razan, I see the typical Syrian women they will become: strong, determined, and severe.

◊

At the University of Chicago talk back in January, Raed and Razan focus not on who they were, but what kind of a life they lead.

The seminar, titled "Art, Irony, and Popular Culture," draws a crowd of upper-level undergraduates, graduates, and community members. We sit in a small room in Wilder House, quaint and domestic with bay windows and an old wooden banister leading to a second floor. But the space is outfitted like a classroom, with a screen, a mounted projector and audio system on the ceiling and corners, and a conference desk in the middle of the room. We fill the room, pens and journals out.

Lisa Wedeen, professor of Political Science, makes introductions and moderates. One of her books on Syria, *Ambiguities of Dominance*, was written long before the revolution and published before Bashar Al-Assad took power following the death of his father, Hafez Al-Assad. In it, she argues that under Hafez, the regime secured its power through absurdity, shackling rational discourse by encouraging citizens to regurgitate outrageous propaganda. Critique was silenced, hidden in the privacy of intimate gatherings or implied between the lines spoken in public by brave souls. Now, nearly three years after the start of the Syrian revolution, we sit, an American audience in a public seminar, listening to Raed and Razan speak bluntly. But while most of the news focuses on the breaking apart of Syria, Raed and Razan remind us not all breaking is calamitous. Instead, they tell stories of Syrians breaking the silence.

45

Razan speaks first, in near-perfect English, her vocabulary academic. She knows her audience. She describes what Syria was like before the protests, focusing on the university experience.

"There was no campus life. A gathering of more than eight people was considered dangerous to the State, and could not meet without express acceptance from the regime. This right here," she says, "would land us all in prison."

She once attended a secret screening of a critically-acclaimed film organized by a friend. The screening went as planned, but before the group could discuss this film, they were shut down and questioned. "My friend was smart," she says. "She played dumb. 'Oh, this is a subversive film? I had no idea. I just heard it was a must see.' It worked, that time."

Razan labors to paint a picture of peaceful revolution, to chip away at the misinformation she sees in American mainstream media. Hers is a revolution for basic rights and fundamental principles, not just for Muslims and by Muslims. In fact, she says, visible Muslim activists are not as effective as atheist, Alawite, or Christian revolutionaries since their Muslim comrades are conspicuous, objects of suspicion, easy targets.

"Then I saw a close friend die," she says out of nowhere.

She goes through her personal history quickly, as if to be done with it. Her name was flagged at the border; she was wanted for the typical charges against those who dissent: indictments of "membership to [sic] a secret organization which aims to change the economic and social status of the state," indictments of inventing "false news that could debilitate the morale of the nation," and for "weakening national sentiment." She was detained. After she was set free, she fled Syria. She landed in Sweden. Once abroad, her emotions caught up with her. She had survived physical harm, and now guilt threatened to annihilate her. She mourned her friends. A few months later, she started a group tending to the psychological needs of kids.

Now that Razan has endured repeating the story of her own survival, she slows down. She shares a joke.

"Back in Damascus, we used to poke fun at people who worked for the revolution with kids—they were doing the warm and

46

fuzzy revolutionary work. There's a hierarchy of activists: First it's the Free Syrian Army guys, who are considered the most hardcore, the most dedicated, putting their lives on the line to fight. Below them are the peaceful activists, then the aid workers, and then protesters. At the bottom are those who work with kids, like me."

No one finds this funny. It is humor that only makes sense to the kind of life Razan has lived. I think back to the grim reality of the orphaned refugee children I visited within Jordan, the ones with small smiles and open, grasping embraces. Razan's work is heroic, offering sustained love and hope. The parents of those children gave their lives for their children's futures. Razan gives the next generation the chance to imagine life beyond killing or being killed.

Morose jokes pepper Razan's talk. Once she is done, residual energy ripples through the audience, nervous, chatty and anxiously upbeat.

Raed is the next speaker, but after his introduction, he says nothing. Raed changes the tone just in the way he sits. He closes his eyes, his chair pushed away from the table, his hands folded together in his lap. He leans his head back. We watch him. We hear our hearts beat. We look from Raed to Kenan, who translates.

Raed will not be rushed. He opens his eyes to look around the room, pausing at each face to gaze back with unapologetic intensity.

"Put down your pens. Close your eyes, and please, just imagine with me."

Kenan's translations are fast and faithful. His voice follows Raed's. Raed's Arabic, murmured in deep baritone, nearly unintelligible, thick with tongue, heavy with the figurative character of the language, undergirds Kenan's concise English delivered in tenor pitch.

"You are at home. Think of home. Think of your things, the way you've organized your room. Think of your favorite place. In the next room over, visualize the people you love most. Now, go to the window. Look up. There is a helicopter. Something is falling out of it. It's rushing towards you.

"Now, please bear with me. Remember where you were on the 11th of September. Think about the planes. Watch as the planes hit the towers. Think of the people on the flight. See it in your mind. Is it there? Remember how you felt."

We open our eyes. Raed's eyes are already open, watching us.

"That was one day. A terrible, deplorable, tragic day." He pauses. "In Syria, people are experiencing that terrible, deplorable, tragic day, day after day. Every. Day."

He pauses again.

"Of course there are differences. But the effect—the terror—it is the same. If that day was an act of terrorism, if we use that word for that day, then should we not also call what is happening in Syria terrorism? And should we not call its source—Assad—a terrorist? If we don't use those words in those cases—if we don't call Assad a terrorist and his acts terrorism—then we need to retire the word."

Raed holds up three fingers. "Assad spread three messages of propaganda." He touches the index and middle. "He failed in two. He succeeded in the third."

"First, Assad tried to claim our revolution was a *Salafi*, terrorist movement. When the people on the ground proved him wrong—as you can see now, while he lets the radical ISIS run around, we stand to fight them at the same time we are engaged with the regime—then he tries the tactic of calling it a sectarian war. But come talk to me if you believe that. I will give you names. Names of Kurds, Alawites, Sunnis, Shiites, Christians. Revolutionaries. They work with us. None of us speak of sectarian hate.

"Unfortunately, the third attempt of the Assad regime has worked."

He pauses.

"Assad has made this a humanitarian conflict."

Raed sits up in his chair, his pen in hand now.

"And the international world fell for it. They've tried to manage the symptoms, without success. By creating a huge humanitarian crisis, Assad has diverted attention from the root cause of these symptoms: his regime."

Raed is deep in thought now, looking down at his own notebook where he writes what he is saying, drawing asterisks and underlining his sentences as he discusses them, scratching them out

HASHEM

as he finishes making the point. He makes dark, deep indentations into the pages, applying pressure to the point of his pen. "But don't worry about us," he says. "We'll keep working for freedom. We're stubborn and have got stale heads." Stale heads, Arabic for obstinate, somehow translates itself. Everyone laughs.

"Now," he says, "we need to move the focus away from humanitarian work and building awareness. What's needed is not charity, but development programs." Raed, like so many others, is ready to begin rebuilding. He will not wait for geopolitics. He describes one of the bakeries he has started. Like the rest of us, he knows the importance of numbers, so he explains that the bakery employs seventy-five people and produces twenty thousand loaves of bread. He describes a radio station that started as a warning system of imminent bombings and expanded to offer news, social, educational, religious, and women's programming. He employs women broadcasters and doesn't fear pushing the boundaries of cultural gender norms, even as ISIS consistently raids the studio and captures its staff.

Raed wants to involve everyone. "The revolution needs to be won on many fronts. We need to work with all groups. Governments. FSA. Expatriates. Anyone who will contribute. We need everyone. Everyone can help," he says.

Raed is an optimist and a maximalist, but most of all, Raed is a pacifist. He believes in the power of people, of persuasion, but most of all, of words. He ends his talk as a radical rhetorician, wresting the power of revolution away from armed combat and replacing it with armed language.

"After all, the root word of *kataib is k-t-b*," he says. The word for the revolutionary brigades comes from the root for "to write." The people will write the revolution.

He closes his notebook.

◊

There are the lives counted as numbers, then there are the ones that count because they are Raed, Razan, Ameenah, and Hiba. There are four hundred and seventy Razans dead as of 2016, almost thirteen thousand by torture. Over 6.3 million Raeds internally displaced, 5.1 million Ameenahs made into refugees, over one hundred and seventeen Hibas detained or disappeared.

Are you keeping count?

Melissa Green

Instructions for the Journey

Morning wakes me but I have not slept.

A cough, a bubble of spit caught in a cleft on my tongue,
the spindle from which a single silver thread will tremble,
cautiously, carefully drawing itself from the cave of my mouth
at Cumae, at Eleusis, at Herculaneum—that minuscule filament
I want to cover the earth with always begins like this:

a cough, a bubble of spit caught on my pen's bifurcated
nib, pushing—no, pulling—a tendril of syllables
across the snows of the tundra, a hairsbreadth track
the mind imagines my footprints might make, hieroglyphs
in a virgin trail staggering from west to east,

always lost but heading toward where I hope the light
might be breaking, a glimmer, a mist of rose, Aurora
breathing on the banked snow but not yet on me.
There is at least that holy blush to aim for.
Whatever I drop behind me and can't follow back

is language nonetheless, a mysterious Voysich Manuscript
where confusion and beauty have kissed.
Open, heart, though wolves' wild circling howls shiver
over the taiga. Trudge beside the icy river as if
you weren't barefoot but wore ermine boots and were fearless.

Don't stop to wonder if it's the Squanicook again, or Lethe,
or Euphrates' frozen sister, never mind you can't decode
the blizzard, focus only on the one astonishing flake.

Your breath condenses, the cloud is full of shards—
reach up to snatch a shiv from the air and carve a lone rune
on your wrist—there is your ink, the vast Siberian steppes
your page. You starved for this— infinity, you a solitary traveler
crossing unprovisioned over empty lightless snowfields.

Go. It will never be better weather. You will not be braver.
Tug at your lip for its filmy saliva—you are still alive!
There is only this: the silent spider's spinneret from which
you drag forth lint, one letter at a time, and if you are lucky
and endure, watch it lengthen into a word, a chord, a shimmering
        line

you'll leave like floss embroidering the snow, woven of sorrow,
defeat, tenacity, failure, hope, the glitter of starlight, dead
for ten thousand years. The four winds, ghostly highwaymen
with bunches of lace at their throat, will slice at yours;
sleet encase you in its carapace, a hoarfrost cocoon.

Laugh aloud if you can, then spin a strand of fine angora yarn
through your chattering teeth. *I am a spider*, shout out
to the glacier before your snow-blind eyes, *I will catch
the world in my iridescent net*. Your voice—or the echo of an
        echo—
may at last return to your tympanum to crack your heart, "Yes."

JOYCE PESEROFF

Not Far

from my door, near a boggy bank of the Concord River,
its cattails bent, the muddy stones slick in December,
is a cell, several cells, where men never see the sun.

And further, far from the growl of my new furnace, is a furnace
lit and re-lit by a warplane's vector, the pilot burning to powder
city blocks, houses wall to wall, the mother and father inside

churned like concrete, or blasted with shrapnel if they leave,
or by a smoothed-cheeked soldier with an assault rifle.
Or, light-headed with hunger, they fall under the treads of a tank.

Closer is a man sleeping in a shed with rats, holes in his sleeping
      bag
shedding feathers. Also a man in a tent, knife at the ready. He
      hears
the flow of the river stilled by frost that creeps from stones

to the channel, thickening until the passage closes. Air glistens
with snow that shrouds his tiny dwelling. No one would know
that under the mound he is breathing, not his sister, nephew,

step-brother, those he lied to and stole from, cursed and punched
      out.
Far from his scabby mittened hands, a boy jaywalks across a street,
bragging to a girl on his phone, shaking a box of candy

for the last piece. He's being followed, maybe by police, maybe
by the MS-13. He won't make it to the next block, see the sun
   again,
or a river, or his grandma's blue mobile home with a saint in the
   yard

far from Manhattan where lights blink red but no one stops.
A tenant hammering the tower's gilded door is admitted
through the poor door. Past the atrium, rats chase rats upstairs.

JENNIFER BARBER

The lamp in the borrowed room

has a white shade and a pale green base
with milky blossoms

down the front in a single spray,
almost Japanese,

each flower made of three
rounded petals, three arching stamen.

Among the blossoms are
plump white dots meant to be buds.

The light cast by the lamp is soft
across the nightstand

and the folded newspaper.
There are, I know, many hells

in the other-wheres outside this room.
I know the ceasefire failed

and the Red Cross buses were too late.
A floorboard creaks

when I walk from the bed
to the fraying armchair and back.

Jen Hinst-White

Fifteen Eggs

> *The 4-ton-atomic bomb, called Little Boy, contained almost*
> *1 kg of uranium-235 . . . 1 kilogram can be scaled as 15 eggs.*
> —Seiko Ikeda, *My A-Bomb Experience*

1.

M ake sure you see . . . " begins the docent.

Airplanes? Spaceships? Astronaut movie in 3-D—heaven on earth for two small boys? All of these today, surely. My sons are six and two. First time at the National Air and Space Museum's cavernous hangars. Soon we will walk, awed, into a space near Dulles Airport that feels big enough to house cathedrals. We will see the grounded Concorde, and scores of aircraft suspended from the ceiling as if in mid-flight, and the space shuttle Discovery sleeping like a white whale after a long migration. We will ride the glass elevator. We will play in a Cessna. I am content: this will be a day of children wonderstruck instead of trying to kill each other.

A docent with a gray mustache is smiling at us.

"Make sure you see the Enola Gay," he says.

A little jolt flickers in my stomach. I smile back, but I feel as if I've just caught sight of a stranger at my kitchen window. What is wrong with me? But the boys are off and running, and I need to keep them from climbing over the barriers, and the feeling slides away into whatever part of my mind it came from.

We spend hours at the museum, and we never see the Enola Gay.

2.

A few days later, back home in New York, I keep thinking about the airplane I didn't see. It troubles me. It feels like an omission. Did I not *want* to? Well, why shouldn't I? We need to see this history, the aircraft that dropped the first atomic bomb.

Does it remind me of that year, more than a decade ago, that I lived in Washington, DC? The work I did—the way we failed—the months of nausea—how I used to grind my teeth in my sleep—the things I cried over and couldn't do anything about?

Do I avoid that particular plane because of my little boys? The mother-sense does not bow to logic, and sometimes transcends it: you know the baby is about to roll off the changing table a split second before he moves. Does something in me refuse to bring my children near a machine that killed children? Tens of thousands of the one hundred and fifty thousand people killed in Hiroshima were babies and children: thousands died instantly at the moment of detonation; thousands more, maimed and burnt, dead within hours; thousands more within days from radiation sickness; thousands more within a few years from cancer. If I let myself think too long about this, the numbers turn into pictures: toddlers eating crackers, and seven-year-olds folding paper airplanes, and preteens playing with each other's hair. Call this maudlin—fine. It is no less true. Some children were evacuated from Japanese cities during the war, but far from all. In a city of three hundred and fifty thousand people, at 8:15 on any given morning, surely women were laboring in childbirth. Surely many were nursing babies.

But to avoid the plane—this is silly. It's not a monster; it's just machinery, and it's dormant now. It can do nothing.

Maybe I'm reading too much into this. Maybe my failure to see it was nothing deep and psychological, just a scattered day with little boys.

Either way, I should have done what the docent said and stopped to *see*—particularly because I knew someone who survived the atomic bomb: an elderly woman who *was* one of those children on the street in Hiroshima.

57

3.

The following are the words of Seiko Ikeda, from a speech she gave at age seventy-three, six decades after she survived the atomic bomb. This text was provided by Nihon Hidankyo, Japan Confederation of A- and H-Bomb Sufferers Organizations.

I am Seiko Ikeda. I am from Hiroshima, the city known as the city of atomic bombing and the city of peace . . .

That day on August 6th, I was bombed at 1.5 kilometers from the epicenter in Tsurumi-Cho town. I was 13 years old. As a student trooper, I was cleaning up the site of an evacuated building. All of a sudden, there was a strong lightning, 1000 times or even tens of thousands times stronger than thunder lightning, with intense sparks. With the sound of *ka-boom*, everything turned pitch black. I was blown away about 15 meters by the blast. When I came back to consciousness, I realized that my hair was all crimped and my clothes were burned. I also realized that the skin was peeled and hanging off my hands and feet, with the raw skin exposed. At that point, I was not ashamed to be naked in public and just cried for help. With their burnt bodies, people were crying and screaming, and they were walking in the same direction. It was like looking at a march of ghosts. The lively city of Hiroshima turned into a black, burning field . . .

The blast not only blew people away but also ripped the skin off the human body. It also made eyeballs spring out and internal organs burst out. Streetcars and buses on the streets were blown away, while wooden houses were leveled and buildings were completely destroyed.

HINST-WHITE

Then there was the radiation. This is only found in the explosion of nuclear weapons . . . The person who was bombed at 100-200 meters away from the epicenter experienced radiation levels of 17 sieverts, which is 17,000 times more than the harmless level of radiation a human body can take . . .

4.

I feared nuclear weapons years before I even heard Mrs. Ikeda's story, and I'm beginning to realize that, given my age, this makes me odd. I was born in 1980, the year of the first Millennials. My early years, then, were the Reagan years, when the arms race was at full tilt, but children my age and younger (including me) were still occupied with G.I. Joes and Cabbage Patch Kids when the arms race peaked. By 1986, the year I was in first grade, the United States and Russia had collectively built about seventy thousand bombs. This was—the fact has been famously repeated—enough weaponry to destroy humanity many times over, and friends who are only two or three years older than me, the youngest Gen X-ers, remember the anxiety of these years with clarity.

Within five years, though, the Cold War would end, and the specter of a nuclear war would recede. This timing was significant. For most of my generation, I think, the picture of terror was the fireball of the World Trade Center, not the fireball of a mushroom cloud. Even if we saw that earlier image, we didn't really *see*.

The six o'clock news was background noise to me. I only knew of nuclear weapons because my parents talked about them. A lot of this came in the course of our unremarkable daily life. They were not scientists or activists or professors or military or ex-military or Mennonites. We lived in an apartment near the Nassau-Queens border on Long Island; my dad commuted to the city; my mom took classes at the community college; our dinners sometimes included Spam. But alongside *Green Eggs and Ham*, our bookshelf held Dr. Seuss's *The Butter Battle Book*—a cartoon-colored parable of Mutually Assured Destruction. Sting's new song "Russians" played on our cassette player: *How can I save my little boy / from Oppenheimer's deadly toy?* What was Oppenheimer's toy? My parents answered any question

I asked. They explained to me things I wouldn't have noticed: we wandered the aisles of the mom-and-pop video store, all those shelves of clamshell VHS cases, and later my father told me about the plot of *WarGames*. "A strange game," concluded the super-computer, processing the dynamics of nuclear war. "It cannot be won."

In their closet was a soft red t-shirt with the graphic of a missile broken into pieces. The pieces were arranged to look like an angular dove, and the slogan read *You Can't Hug Your Child with Nuclear Arms*. It's the kind of clever-ish sloganeering that changes no one's mind, but it does say something about my parents: they saw the arms race as having everything to do with the fate of their children.

5.

My parents taught me to question everything—even them. I question them now, here, as I write this: was it right to talk to me about those things at age six? You could argue no. I remembered my dad telling me that an atomic bomb could vaporize human beings. Whether or not this was the correct way to describe it scientifically, there was truth to this: near the epicenter of the bomb's detonation, all that remained of people was their ashy silhouettes against the benches and buildings where they'd been.

Perhaps this was not something to share with your first-grader.

On the other hand, my parents also taught me that I could do something about the things I feared. "Did you know," my mother said one day, "that you can write a letter to the President?"

I had not known. I liked mail. We sat down at our Formica kitchen table, snug next to the pantry, and I wrote one. My mom interfered little and did not tell me what to say, except for suggesting I write *Dear Mr. President* instead of *Dear Ronald*. I remember nothing else about the contents except the sentence *Please stop buying so many bombs*. Beyond that, what do you say, really? *How are you? How is Nancy? Hey, I like jellybeans too?*

We wrote no other letters that I remember, nor marched in protests nor gave money to the cause, and I am certain that my solitary letter changed the *world* not one iota—but I know it changed me. This one action my mother took—teaching me to write a letter—stayed buried in me until years later, at a critical moment of my life, when it mattered a great deal.

6.

Fifteen years later, I was about to begin my senior year in college. In the interim, much had changed, both personally and politically. I was no longer preoccupied with nuclear war. In 1986, I was just learning to write letters; now I wanted to write novels. The Russian looming largest in my mind was Vladimir Nabokov, and he sat companionably on my bookshelf with Walt Whitman, the ultimate American poet. My mounting stockpiles were pages. My attention was not on war anymore.

I wasn't alone. Nuclear weapons never ceased to be a global concern, but they were casting a far smaller shadow on our national conversation. The United States unilaterally stopped testing nuclear weapons after 1992, and in 1996, the General Assembly of the United Nations adopted the Comprehensive Test Ban Treaty (CTBT), which prohibited all nuclear explosions worldwide. When India and Pakistan tested atomic weapons in 1998, the United States swiftly responded with sanctions. Progress was not unbroken: although the US signed the CTBT, it never ratified it, nor did China, Egypt, Iran or Israel. The US and other nuclear states *did* ratify, and then voted in 1995 to extend the 1970 Non-Proliferation Treaty—a treaty that included a legal obligation to eventually complete disarmament—but this commitment had no timeline.

All the same, the general trend was toward arms reduction. The US greatly reduced its arsenal, and global stockpiles were cut in half between 1986 and 2001. Even President George W. Bush—who argued, early and often, for the renewal of the United States missile defense program—at the very least paid lip service to US global leadership in arms reduction. "My goal is to move quickly to reduce nuclear forces," he said. "The United States will lead by example to achieve our interests and the interests for peace in the world."

Surely, I'd followed all this news with avid concern. Or not. I had one year of college left in the Green Mountains of Vermont, and I was planning, as Thoreau said, to "suck out all the marrow"

61

of it. On the first day of my senior year, I sat on a rock wall the students called The End of the World, jotting notes about my novel-in-progress until it was time to walk to my morning class. Day still early. Leaves still jade-green. Sky a gaping blue. Fresh air. Fresh start.

It was September 11, 2001.

Everything went dark for a long time.

First came the grief—the footage of human beings, hand-in-hand, leaping from the towers toward broken concrete, iron and ash.

Then, a month later, more grief: the bombing of Kandahar, the deaths of civilians and soldiers alike—humans are humans are humans.

My mother had taught me, with that letter at age six, to *do* something about the things that troubled me. But I had nothing to give to alleviate any of this suffering. I had no expertise. No power. No great sums of money. What I had was grief, and questions, and that was all—except for one tiny thing. I had an internship requirement.

I'd considered interning in publishing, journalism, literary agencies. Instead, I went to Peace Action, a national grassroots organization in Washington that sought foreign policy alternatives to war.

I knew this was a tiny thing. I was a mouse in the grand house of Washington. But I was twenty-one years old and I'd spent three years focused on myself, and I wanted to do one thing that was bigger than me.

I loved it.

The office was three blocks away from the White House. Everyone on the Peace Action staff was dedicated and whip-smart. My supervisor, at the worldly age of twenty-six, could organize a campaign or lay out an argument with the ease of a chess master gliding pieces around a board. On my first day, she put me to work researching and designing fact sheets on nuclear treaties.

This internship turned into a full-time fellowship after graduation. For one year, I would be the coordinator of Peace Action's student network. This was how I met Mrs. Seiko Ikeda.

7.

It was terrorism and the "war on terrorism"—not the specter of nuclear war—that brought me to Washington. But that red t-shirt in my parents' closet, *You can't hug your child with nuclear arms*, turned out to be an odd bit of real-life foreshadowing. At the bottom of that shirt, in small lettering, were four words: MICHIGAN NUCLEAR WEAPONS FREEZE. This phrase had always been a mystery to me.

I spent part of my first week at Peace Action reading through the organization's forty-five-year history. It turned out that the name "Peace Action" had been adopted only a decade ago. Before that, the organization was known as SANE/Freeze, and it was the merger of two giants of the anti-nuclear movement. Michigan Nuclear Weapons Freeze was one of its local chapters.

I had come to work at the same organization whose name was on that red t-shirt, buried in my parents' closet during all the years of my growing up.

Peace Action had a longstanding relationship with an organization of A- and H-bomb survivors in Japan. It also had a brand-new relationship with a young organization called September 11th Families for Peaceful Tomorrows, a network of families whose loved ones had died on 9/11. Even as US troops were still committed in Afghanistan, the Bush administration was beginning to make noises about a "pre-emptive attack" on Iraq. Peaceful Tomorrows believed their loss was being co-opted as the pretext for an unnecessary war.

Both of these organizations were founded by suffering people who wanted to protect others from violence, including retaliatory violence. One of the first tasks I was given was to organize a speaking tour so their stories could be heard. I soon found myself on a road trip with a woman who had survived an atomic bomb.

8.

What does a nuclear survivor look like? Is her face ridged with scars? Fingers melted together? Does she tire easily or limp? I wouldn't have suspected Mrs. Ikeda. She was seventy years old and had been through fifteen reconstructive surgeries. If you looked closely at her hairline, you could see the powdery edge of thick foundation, but this could have been any elderly woman.

63

She brought along a translator, Mika, and off we went in a rented economy sedan: three women, four states, seven colleges, eight days. Sometimes we were joined by a man who had lost his brother on 9/11, or other speakers from Peaceful Tomorrows. Sometimes it was just the three of us.

We rarely spoke of anything serious during the drives. When Mrs. Ikeda pulled some dried seaweed out of her purse, crackled the package open, and offered me some, I was scared to try it, and both women found this funny. I loved their running commentary: the things that tickled them (so many squirrels) or struck them as odd (the way American servers filled water glasses to the brim). Because of our budget, we ate at inexpensive restaurants—diners, truck stops, Denny's—and by day four, Mrs. Ikeda, this woman who had survived radiation, was feeling ill from all of the fried food. She and Mika were both relieved when we found a Japanese restaurant with fresh vegetables.

We drove, we drove, we drove. Most of the trees had only a few ragged flags of foliage left, but the early November days were bright.

It was at night that Mrs. Ikeda became serious. For seven nights in a row, I walked with her into lecture halls and auditoriums where she told the story, again and again, the bright flash, the blast, waking up with her skin hanging from her body and her clothes gone, and how she was burnt so badly that her father did not recognize her when he came to find her. She spoke of the weeks that followed the bombing:

> Being that I was at the boundary of life and death, neighbors thought that it was a miracle that I was still alive with all my injuries, having heard a rumor about my funeral coming soon.

> Two days after the dropping of the atomic bomb, Chie Okisue, a former classmate from the elementary school, came back to the village from Hiroshima with no injury, and the family was overjoyed. Nevertheless, in a month, she felt ill and had to spend her days in bed. When she combed

HINST-WHITE

her hair in the morning, a lot of hair just came off in lumps and she eventually lost all her hair. Then her chest and her stomach became very hard, and there were purple spots appearing all over her body. She started bleeding from her nose, mouth, and ears. When a doctor at last came to see her, her mother was crying for his help. The girl was telling her mother that she did not want to die and had so much that she wanted to do. She died of acute radioactive symptoms.

"Make sure you see—", said the docent.

9.

Fifteen years have passed since I went to work at Peace Action and took that road trip with Mrs. Ikeda. In the interim, much has changed, personally and politically. Here is my confession: Although I loved my internship with Peace Action, the joy was short-lived. Put in charge of a national network, working in the peace movement full time, I was miserable. I was an introvert, and I had not stopped to consider that organizing involves a lot of *people*. I came to dread marches; the night before, I would slump around our apartment droning *Nooooo blooood for ooiiiilll* as I folded the laundry. I spent most of my days wracked with nausea, and I woke from nightmares in which I personally was trying to dissuade Hillary Clinton from voting for the war. I knew that these little miseries were nothing compared to the experience of American soldiers stationed in Afghanistan—but on the other hand, it is not terribly useful to compare suffering. I was sick all the same.

Most of all, I became disillusioned. Millions of people were writing letters and calling their representatives, and on February 15, 2003, we saw the largest simultaneous protest in human history: ten to fifteen million people worldwide staged demonstrations against the Iraq war. But a month later, on the night of the vernal equinox, my boyfriend woke me from my sleep and said, "They started bombing Iraq. I thought you'd want to know."

The next day, the streets around my office, with their crowds of gray-suited people, looked exactly the same. The flower vendor by my Metro stop sold the same bright alstroemeria; the flags hung limply at the top of flagpoles as they had the day before. What did I expect—sackcloth and ashes? If there was any evidence that the world was different, I could not see it. It seemed wrong that I could go home and get General Tso's Chicken take-out, cracking open fortune cookies as bombs fell across the world.

I finished out my fellowship. I could have applied for another job at Peace Action. I didn't. We went back to Long Island, where my boyfriend and I had grown up. We got married and started a small business and lived in three different apartments and bought a little house, and I went to grad school and finally finished my novel, and we had a baby, who then became a toddler, and we contemplated having another; and that was how I measured the nearly nine years that passed before US troops were finally withdrawn from Iraq. I was so burned out on politics from that one year in Washington, and so hopeless that I could have any effect at all, that I stopped reading the news with any depth. Once we had the baby, everything else became background noise for a while anyway.

A hiss and a pop in that background noise: North Korea began testing nuclear weapons.

10.

I can't believe that this world can go on beyond our generation, and on down to succeeding generations, with this kind of weapon on both sides poised at each other without someday some fool or some maniac or some accident triggering the kind of war that is the end of the line for all of us.

This is not a quote from Mrs. Ikeda or the Nuclear Weapons Freeze; it's from a speech by President Ronald Reagan in 1983. Of course, Reagan was no dove; he was arguing for anti-ballistic missile systems. You don't have to share his agenda to know that the words still ring true.

Does Kim Jong Un, supreme leader of North Korea, qualify as a "fool" or a "maniac"? Certainly, he has been called volatile, unpredictable and brutal; has channeled huge sums into his nuclear aspirations while North Koreans starve; has been condemned by the United Nations for committing human rights violations worthy of trial by the International Criminal Court.

When North Korea began its series of nuclear tests in 2006, the Bush administration responded with sanctions and surveillance. As the tests continued over the next decade, the Obama administration followed the same course, with increasing severity. Just in time for the 2016 presidential election, some politicians began calling for a "stronger response" to North Korea—without specifying what that might be—but State Department officials warned of responding to rashness with rashness:

> It doesn't mean you get a hair-trigger and it doesn't mean you have to overreact. Part of [Kim Jong Un's behavior] is about eliciting reaction and how the world reacts to him. There's an awful lot of people at risk here through this guy's unpredictability and rashness, and I think woe betide the international community that overplays a hand and reacts too harshly too quickly. (*The Guardian*, "North Korean Nuclear Test Unites Republicans—Against Obama," January 6, 2016)

I am not an expert in military tactics or international relations. If there exists some policy panacea that will defuse the threat of nuclear warfare in this part of the world, I do not know it. I have no specific action to advocate; I also do not advocate for inaction. But I am a mother, and now I know why my parents took nuclear weapons—and the bravado of political leaders—so personally. When I was pregnant, more than one parent told me: "You'll love your baby so much you would die for him." In fact, I love him so much I suspect I would kill for him. But I've also become—on the deepest instinctual level—the protector of children not even mine. I watch over them in stores when their parents turn their backs. Films with stories involving children in jeopardy are excruciating. To this day, well past my son's weaning, if I hold a crying baby in my arms—anyone's baby—I have to fight the urge to nurse her.

Also, because I am a mother, I know that the quotation above is basic wisdom. I share a house with two human beings much smaller than me, in many ways at my mercy, and when they feel disrespected and powerless, they marshal all their resources to prove they can take me on. They are capricious. They act to "elicit reaction." They try to bait and manipulate. I love them dearly, but at this stage in their development, they will rush at me with violence to get their way.

If I do not operate by the wisdom of the quotation above—discernment and deliberation, cool head and thick skin—I am at their mercy. It is odd, the parallels between dictators and children. In either case, you need to decide—*before* a conflict—what your convictions are, and what you will and will not do.

Have we decided, as a nation, what we will and will not do? During the 2016 presidential primaries, Chris Matthews interviewed then-presidential candidate Donald Trump for an *MSNBC Town Hall*, and Trump shocked Matthews (and many others) when he said, "Look, nuclear should be off the table. But would there be a time when it could be used, possibly, possibly?"

Maybe it is alarmist to take a tossed-off statement at face value—to think that a United States president might reintroduce, with any seriousness, the prospect of another Hiroshima and Nagasaki. Or maybe words matter. *Possibly, possibly.*

It is complex, deciding what we will and will not do. It is not as easy and clear as the six-year-old's letter. *Please stop buying so many bombs.* But if we hope to make this decision with any wisdom, there is a step we cannot skip: we need to see the Enola Gay.

11.

It was happenstance, not politics, that brought me back to Washington. My husband had a work trip to Virginia, just outside the district, and I wanted to take our two sons to the Smithsonian museums. I wanted to ride the Metro with them. These were the things, when I worked in DC, that had brought me comfort and joy. I delighted to see my older child tracing his finger on the Metro map,

68

figuring out which trains we'd take to the Smithsonian stop.

After the trip, I found myself thinking about that missed airplane. I needed to correct my omission—to see. I wanted to know about the men who flew it. I wanted to know how it escaped the mushroom cloud. I needed to see pictures of the plane and the crew and the city and the citizens. I wanted to know why it was called the Enola Gay.

It turned out that the pilot, Colonel Paul Tibbets, specifically chosen for this mission, was allowed to select his plane off the assembly line—and also to name it. He knew what the plane would be used for. He named it after the person who had most encouraged him—his mother, Enola Gay Tibbets.

A plane named after a mother had dropped a bomb called Little Boy?

And why *did* they call it Little Boy? No familial reason. The name was pulled from the film *The Maltese Falcon*, as was Fat Man, the name for the Nagasaki bomb. Little Boy had a more diminutive design.

Coincidences, then, these names. They still haunted me. Words like *mother* or *little boy* will always strike flint in the human psyche where other words—fission, uranium—don't. I carried babies in my body, and I can't stop trying to read these correspondences like tarot cards, as if there must be meaning in them somewhere.

What will I find there? Maybe nothing. Or maybe something speaks out of our depths, like the king's fool telling the subversive truth, to prick us with the gravest kind of mischief—to christen our deadliest things with cradle names—to wake us up with the dissonance.

I needed to read Mrs. Ikeda's talk again. When I contacted Nihon Hidankyo, the organization she works with, they could not find it, and told me she was in the hospital with "an illness of the brain." They *were* able to find the text of another speech she gave, however, and this was the text I've quoted throughout this essay. I suspected it may have been her boilerplate address, because the stories in this text are those I remembered—but I did not remember everything.

Out of the 64 kg of uranium in Little Boy, only a fraction

69

underwent the fission that produced the explosion. That fissionable material weighed, as Mrs. Ikeda said, just under a kilogram—about the weight of fifteen eggs. In the original talk I heard, I don't remember her making this comparison. Maybe she didn't, or maybe it didn't stand out to me then. It does now.

Of all the things you could equate to a kilogram—a bag of rice, a small melon, a liter of water—why this? Again, maybe it's nothing deep and psychological. All the same, I cannot stop thinking about the fifteen eggs. Surely the image of an egg has been lodged in human consciousness for tens of thousands of years as a primal symbol of life. Fifteen is the number of eggs my boys consume in a week, between the two of them. Fifteen eggs is about how many I hide for each of them on Easter morning to seek out in the gray dawn light.

12.

I sometimes wonder if I wasted a year of my life trying to stop a war. I want to find *something* in that experience for someone else— maybe for my children. Maybe for myself. Maybe for you. Searching this out feels not so different from those Easter morning hunts in our winter-worn yard.

If I gather up all I have told here—my childhood fears; the way I unwittingly landed at an anti-nuclear organization; Mrs. Ikeda's story; all I learned about nuclear tests and treaties; my ferocity to protect my sons; Little Boy and the Enola Gay—if I sought in these brambles fifteen eggs, fifteen stories, fifteen useful somethings, would I find anything?

"Make sure you see . . ." begins the docent.

My oldest son, now six, sometimes strikes me as a grandpa in a child's body: lovably grouchy; often buried in reading or ruminating; yet under all of this is the warmest, softest heart. He is troubled, as I was at six, about the state of the world, though his fear is climate change, not nuclear war. I haven't purposely exposed him to that distressing reality. He's picked up tidbits from the radio, and seen an astronaut movie that included melting icecaps, and wanted to know about that house with the solar panels. I don't want him to fear. I tell him there's time. I tell him smart people are working to change things. I tell him—as my mother told me—that whatever might scare him, he can do something about it, even if it's something small.

It will be years before he's ready to hear about the specific horror of nuclear weapons, but when he is old enough, I will tell him, because I have begun to realize—with grief and fear—how many *adults* don't seem to know. What scares me about the Town Hall exchange between Chris Matthews and Donald Trump is not simply that the future American president expresses a willingness to use nuclear weapons—against a diffuse terrorist organization, no less, that can easily maneuver itself into civilian areas. It scares me that Trump never acknowledges, as Matthews does, the fact that nuclear weapons are in a class of their own, and not just Really Big Bombs.

How many American citizens feel as he does? How is it we forget that nuclear weapons are different? I suspect our national narrative makes it hard for us to see through other eyes—to look up at the bomb from underneath as well as above. Most of my high school history teachers have told us, with authority, that the bomb was necessary to end World War II—that without it, the war would have dragged on and killed many more. For some, that wraps it up, perhaps.

Does it feel unpatriotic to acknowledge the effects of an atomic weapon?

When the first script for the Smithsonian exhibit of the Enola Gay fuselage was presented in 1994, it provoked fierce controversy. The original text included a history of the final year of WWII and deliberations to drop the bomb, and the experience of the Enola Gay pilots. It described Ground Zero (do Americans remember that this was a phrase from Hiroshima long before its use with 9/11?). It briefly chronicled the beginning of the arms race. A number of outside groups and Congressional representatives opposed that script, arguing that the inclusion of this history was tantamount to an "ideological campaign" against nuclear weapons. Passion was so high that members of Congress threatened the museum with an official investigation and budget cuts. The revised script, after much negotiation, included exactly nothing about the bomb's effect on the people of Hiroshima.

So, we don't see. Even if I saw the Enola Gay, I wouldn't have read a story like Mrs. Ikeda's.

Is it not possible, are we not grown-up enough, to present all of these things at once?—to accord respect to servicemen and women, and to scientific achievement, and the complexities of history, and the difficulty of the decisions our leaders face—*and* honesty about the cost of those decisions? The Smithsonian controversy included lengthy debate over casualty numbers and the number of lives potentially saved by ending the war more quickly (the rationale for dropping the bomb). The focus on numbers belies the emotion around the question of whether or not the bomb was justified.

That's a moral question, not a historical question. If we will not look at the history alongside the artifact, we cannot decide that moral question. If we are secure in the belief that this bomb was justified then that is all the more reason to be honest about the cost. Perhaps dropping the bomb did, in total, reduce the number of lives lost. Let us, then, have the courage to acknowledge that doing so came at the cost of particular civilian lives, in a particularly unprecedented way—including tens of thousands of particular children. Just as mine are particular children.

13.

If I had five minutes to explain to an adult friend why nuclear weapons are different, here's where I would start: the scale of destruction from an atomic bomb is nearly inconceivable. Before Hiroshima, never had a single bomb killed seventy-five thousand people, most of them civilians, in one day. Today's B83 bomb is eighty times more powerful than Little Boy. The Soviet-era Tsar Bomba bomb at fifty megatons, was more than three thousand times more powerful. After a few months, Hiroshima had lost between one hundred and ninety thousand and two hundred and thirty thousand people. Making no comparison, but for the sake of understanding the numbers: the 2016 shootings in San Bernardino, CA, killed fourteen innocent people and injured twenty-two more. Imagine an attack that took the life of every single person in San Bernardino that day. It's a city of about two hundred and fifteen thousand.

72

To these numbers I would add the story of Seiko Ikeda and other first-person accounts by *hibakusha*—the Japanese name for atomic bomb survivors. These stories are easily found online. Go and see, I would say. Read just a few. The handful of *hibakusha* alive today survived the bomb as children and teenagers. This is not ancient history, but quite fresh in time, and what happened to these children is still a real possibility for us and ours. Even for those who survived, "the victims can never get rid of the radiation from the body and fear of death for the rest of their lives," Mrs. Ikeda said. "If there is a headache, there is a fear that it may be leukemia." *Hibakusha* were often shunned in Japan. Many never married. Doctors didn't know if the *hibakusha* could have children of their own. Mrs. Ikeda, it turned out, did marry and have children, and later, grandchildren; but many did not. Even survivors like Mrs. Ikeda had no way of knowing if their children would one day manifest the effects of radiation.

I'd tell them, finally, about the environmental shock of a nuclear war, and what that would do to humanity, which is not widely discussed anymore. In the 1980s, scientists warned that a large-scale nuclear war between the United States and Russia would result in a "nuclear winter" for all of planet Earth. In 2016, however, the same scientists found through simulations that it would only take a "small nuclear skirmish" to wreak sudden climate changes—not simply localized trauma, but for all of humanity.

Firestorms would produce volumes of sooty smoke greater than the worst volcanic eruptions seen in recorded history, rising as far as the stratosphere and absorbing sunlight to such a degree that the sky would be no longer blue, but gray. Global temperatures would drop to levels not seen since the Little Ice Age. Our protective ozone layer would be dramatically stripped away, exposing us to new levels of ultraviolet radiation. The ability to grow crops on most of the planet would be crippled for five years or more.

Nuclear weapons are different from other weapons.

14.

One day my children need to know these things—that these weapons are different, and that whatever small action an ordinary

73

person can take, we must take—but this is not *all* they need to know. Some vital pieces are missing. It is only fifteen years later, reflecting on my time as an activist, that I understand what those pieces are.

On that day after the bombing of Iraq began in 2003, I walked to work and felt guilty that my comfortable life went on while Iraqi civilians suffered. It was right to mourn, for if we turn away from the suffering of others, we forfeit our humanity, one blind-eyed day at a time.

The missing piece is this: we must also seize the pleasure of being alive. If we act for justice, it is because we want all humans to live in health, safety, plenty and *joy*. If we refuse to relish our own numbered days, including moments with no purpose other than delight, then we exhaust ourselves into eventual bitterness, and our own lives become a sort of joyless war.

I became disillusioned after my time in activism work. Millions wrote, and called, and marched, and used all the available channels of our democratic republic, and our leaders still took us to war.

The missing piece is this: if we work to make some change in the world and the world is slow to change, we will cripple ourselves if we call it failure, or worse, apply that word to ourselves. If my children find themselves where I was—their work apparently amounting to nothing—I will point them to our spaghetti pot. Fill it with water, I will say. Get a thermometer. Fire up the gas. The temperature will rise—until that water hits boiling point, and after that, no matter how much heat you add, you will never see that temperature go up another degree. In the heat of that flame, the water is boiling off, all the same. I will give them these lines, in the spirit of Oscar Romero, the famous Salvadoran archbishop who spent his life in pursuit of human rights—not written by him, but often attributed to him:

> We cannot do everything, and there is a sense of liberation in realizing that.
> This enables us to do something, and to do it very well . . .
> We are workers, not master builders; ministers, not messiahs.
> We are prophets of a future not our own.

I want them to know their tiny offering is good, and understand themselves as good, so they know that life itself—despite the anguish of nuclear weapons and the like—is also fundamentally good.

We must see the particular danger and the difference of nuclear weapons, and must acknowledge it and name it and speak of it. The missing piece is this: as we are seeing and naming what is unjust and destructive, we must also see and name what is good. Good can grow, but sometimes it needs naming and noticing to do so.

A thousand times, I place my palm on my older son's chest and tell him, "You have such a good heart. It is full of love." Why do I do this? One: it is true. Two: I want it to remain true. This is the kind of man I want to send into the world.

Does a practice like this matter?

My husband and I recently went to parent-teacher night at his elementary school. We noticed a bulletin board full of handouts, all of which said, "The best thing about me is . . ."

One kid wrote, "I am funny."

Another kid wrote, "I am good at soccer."

My son—a six-year-old boy—wrote this: "I am loving."

I am loving. All the times we named the good—it mattered.

15.

From "My A-Bomb Experience," by Mrs. Seiko Ikeda:

> I looked for a mirror, but somebody had hidden it from me. I looked everywhere and finally found a mirror. When I saw my face, I was in horrible shock. My face looked like something I had never seen. It looked dark red like liver meat and the skin was very hard. The left corner of my lips was turned over, and my chin was stuck to my neck. I could not believe what I was seeing. Since that day, my suffering became also psychological from the physical suffering.

About a half year passed from the bombing, and I started going back to school. But on the train, I had many people staring at my face, and I could not go anymore. Who should be blamed, where should I go to make my claims? I was devastated and thought about my death many times.

In such mental pain, what saved me the most were my father's words that I overheard. He was always with me and taking care of me. I overheard my father talking to a neighbor, saying, "She got completely burnt and suffers from a high fever. I can't even move her body. Next time if we get nuked, I am ready to hold her in my arms and die with her. But despite the scars, she is now getting better and better. We never know what a human body can do. I believe that Seiko can and will survive."

"Make sure you see," began the docent.

Make sure you see, I want to tell my sons. Make sure you see everything. The awful. The awe-inspiring. The exquisite. The horrific. With honesty. Make sure you see everything, and go and speak the truth about it. I will paint this on every egg in my armful of fifteen.

Fiction

KAREN HALVORSEN SCHRECK

Ghost Warrior

Nilsen's deep coat pockets held three dented tins of Spam, four softening Hershey's bars, and seven squashed sandwiches. He'd pilfered KP packs from the canteen—something he did most mornings, thanks to the ragged kids waiting on the other side of the barbed wire fence. He'd spotted them soon after his arrival, soon after he shot the man in Osaka. Once, early on, he made the mistake of passing cigarettes through the barbed wire, though he could have traded these for real loot on the black market. He'd already acquired an ivory Buddha, an engraved saber, and a black lacquer box, all thanks to his Lucky Strikes. A single cigarette for each object—that was all it took. So he slipped a pack of cigarettes through the fence, imagining the kids clean, chubby, rickets-free, thanks to him. They could swap Luckies for powdered milk, withered root vegetables, bruised fruit, maybe coats, blankets, shelter—who knew? Anything was better than the nothing they had. But one of them, one of the older, grabbier boys, ripped open the white package with its red target. A few of the other boys fell upon him then, and they devoured the cigarettes, paper and all, dried tobacco sticking like prickly caterpillars to their raw, chapped lips. Like that, bango, and the boys' eyes went glassy. One after another, they retched, lurching off to vomit, worse off than they'd been before. After that, Nilsen limited his offerings to food.

Now the kids lifted up their hands, and Nilsen delivered what he had. There was no grabbing these days. The kids had turned unnervingly polite, resurrecting manners they must have been taught before all fiery hell broke loose. The boys and girls, for there were always two or three girls, bowed low, heads nearly to knees, and murmured words Nilsen didn't understand. Such niceties seemed all the more strange given the otherwise feral nature of their appearance—

77

patchy black hair, lesions and bruises, skeletal frames. At times, the kids managed smiles. When they did, Nilsen felt something lift in his chest—a sensation that, before he shot the man, he might have called hope.

"Sergeant!"

The bellow came from some distance behind Nilsen, across the barren yard, nearer to quarters. He stiffened. He knew that voice, bullish and brutal. He'd heard it often enough.

"You! Nilsen!"

He turned. Major Gorman stood by the filthy, leaking pillow that served as a pitcher's mound for the makeshift baseball diamond that Minx, a second-string catcher for the St. Louis Cardinals, had set up yesterday. For one lunatic moment, Nilsen thought of opening his coat wide, trying to hide the kids and his fraternizing.

"Get your ass over here!"

Nilsen glanced back. The kids had high-tailed it. From this distance, through the lengths of barbed wire, they looked like nothing more than a tumble of sticks, scattered by the harsh wind. Jap wind, the men called it. Its bleak wail dominated every livelong day, along with the soot, debris, and acrid scent it stirred. The wind grittily filled Nilsen's eyes, ears, and nostrils even now as, turning into it, he got his ass over to Gorman. Other men, roused from cots or cards, watched his approach. Who didn't love a show at the expense of another, stewed in boredom as they were? A few gathered in front of quarters—previously a hospital, a relatively modern structure and all that remained of this neighborhood, almost all that remained of Osaka, except for the ring of buildings by the harbor's edge, and the single, long dock that cast its shape across Nilsen's bad dreams. On the second floor of the hospital, other men leaned out of broken windows. They grinned at him, pulling faces, thumbing noses. One chump—Cullen, no doubt—mooned the back of Gorman's head. Several privates—Nilsen's men—hesitated outside their pup tents near the baseball diamond, evaluating the situation, then ducked beneath tent flaps to hide from the wrath they might incur.

Everyone just wanted to stay under the radar, especially the Major's radar. Gorman had been transferred here only a week ago, but from the get-go, he was not liked. It wasn't a by-the-book

78

mentality that Gorman had. No. By-the-book was one thing, but Gorman saw infractions where there were none, and liberally dealt out punishment. Unpredictable, cruel—that's what Gorman was. Tightly wound, always threatening to blow the flimsy lid off things. The soldiers might have accepted him as a leader when they were positioned outside of Lyons, in beautiful, brutalized farm country where they crawled through minefields, dismantled bombs with shaking hands. Or on Corregidor, with all the bat-shit crazy that happened on that island, too much crazy to think about. In France and the Philippines, as long as you felt like the guy in charge wasn't on a suicide mission, or he fooled you into thinking he wasn't on one, you endured commands and reprimands without question. If you were a good solider, and most of the men were good enough. You had no choice. But here in Osaka, the war was over. The men had heard rumors of nights on the town in Kyoto, brimming jugs of sake and geishas galore. And they were the Army Corps of Engineers, after all. All of them were on special assignment, the cream of the crop. Time they got some respect. Or were, at least, treated fairly.

At a careful distance from the Major, Nilsen came to sharp attention. Scowling, his heavy-lidded eyes narrowed to a squint, Gorman snapped off a salute.

"Drive a jeep?"

"Yes, sir."

"Then you're driving me to town."

"Osaka?"

It was a mistake—that wavering in his voice—but Nilsen couldn't help himself. Not with the blistered plain that seemed to stretch to the end of the world, the miles of ash, grit, and pulverized bone they would have to cover to get to Osaka, and the harbor there, the dock.

Gorman hissed a string of foul words that boiled down to: Yes, Osaka.

Bile rose in Nilsen's throat.

◊

79

He retrieved a set of keys from the administrative office, then went to the garage. Gorman was already there, wearing a black fedora with a grosgrain band. He'd exchanged his heavy army issue jacket for a black trench coat. Tucked inside, a white scarf, its luster suggesting silk.

"Take it off." Gorman jerked his thumb at the heavy canvas that served as a jeep's top.

A single touch confirmed the canvas was stiff with cold. Nilsen no longer kept track of time—better it pass in a haze—but whatever month this was, it was winter in Japan. Maybe come summer, he would be informed of his exact discharge date; he would track time then. For now, the hours and their passing were tolerable only because of the relative quiet. The last gunshot he'd heard was his own. Since then the quiet had descended. He now wanted to eat and drink the quiet, bathe in the quiet and wear it, hold it and make love to it, never let it go. All the lines from love songs—that's what Nilsen wanted to do with the quiet. Everyday accoutrements, so recently restored, were also key to Nilsen's survival now. The narrow hospital bed upon which he slept, the thin hospital towels with which he dried himself after morning ablutions and night-time showers, the toilet into which he pissed and shat, the squares of thin paper, so unlike anything back home, with which he wiped himself clean. And the children at the fence. Them, too. They were almost like neighbors, with their visits, helping him withstand the time.

"Hey, Patsy!" Gorman barked. "Something on your mind?"

Nilsen set to work on the snaps and latches, and then wrestled the canvas top of the jeep over to the corner of the garage, where it lay in the shadows like the husk of some monstrous insect— one of those roaches that outlived everything, even, rumor had it, in Hiroshima and Nagasaki.

"Let's go." Gorman heaved himself into the passenger seat; Nilsen climbed up behind the wheel. Initially the engine was unresponsive—Nilsen turned the key once, twice, three times; maybe Osaka wasn't in the cards after all. But then something clicked, pistons fired, and what could he do but pull the jeep out of the garage? There they were, heading out, heading off. It might have been Camp Claiborne, Louisiana, Basic Training again, him and the boys on leave to Alexandria and the USO Club. Or better, far better, it might have been his now MIA friend Frank's 1937 Buick Century Convertible Coup, the two of them back in Indianapolis about to pick up those two girls. What were their names? Franny and June? Something like that. He remembered them in bits and pieces, a puzzle he couldn't put together anymore—the smattering of freckles, red lips, thin arching eyebrows, whorl of an ear. Faint fuzz of coppery hair at the nape of a neck, dip between collarbones, shadow of breasts. And Frank, driving fast, wrist propped on the wheel, laughing until the tears came, and not the least bit embarrassed, with his clean-shaven cheeks streaked wet.

Nilsen started at the sound of a big bone breaking—no, the crack of a bat as the jeep rounded the baseball diamond. Someone had gotten a game going, men playing like the boys they'd once been. Minx, of course, crouched behind home plate. And Gardziella on the sandbag that served as a pitcher's mound, winding up. Gardziella nearly lost his balance when he saw the jeep and who was inside. But Gorman didn't make a peep, and now the game was in the rearview; they were fast approaching the gate. Two of the pimply-faced privates swung the wide wooden doors open, as in the distance Minx triumphantly called, "Strike!"

They were outside the base now. But with no compass or map, with every road, tree, building, trace of humanity obliterated, and no man's land stretching flat and featureless in all directions, Nilsen had no idea which way to go.

"It's drivable. You want a papal blessing, or what?"

Gorman was glaring off to the right, so Nilsen accelerated in that direction, tires spewing dust and debris. The horizon line appeared to have vanished, lost between the gray sky and the gray earth, incinerated like everything else. Unsettling, that's what this was, driving without a horizon. They might as well have been speeding through a vacuum, up and down indecipherable, one and the same. Vertigo, that's what this was, the Jap wind buffeting, and the cold, cold, cold. Base was better than this. At least for Nilsen. Gorman, with his heavy head tipped back, was sniffing the air like a hound on the scent of something big. The Major seemed to be enjoying

81

himself, as much as he ever seemed to enjoy himself. "Now we're cooking," he said, and Nilsen gritted his teeth.

After a while—who knew how long exactly; too long, that was what mattered—a gray hump bulged ahead of them. A hill. Nilsen drove the jeep up and over it, and there, suddenly, the harbor, again. Only this time, no boats, no people to be seen. Only the dock itself, and the few buildings made of brick and stone, spared when the surrounding cottages constructed of paper, straw, and wood went up in flames.

Nilsen eased up on the accelerator. His legs were shaking now, his hands white-knuckled on the wheel. Gorman would sense his distress, and that wouldn't be good. That would make things worse.

But Gorman merely pointed a thick finger at the incongruity of a paper lantern suspended above one of the stone doorways, and said, "There." The lantern bobbed and twisted in the wind; miraculously, it appeared to be intact. Gorman yanked a pack of cigarettes from his pocket, knocked one between his lips and lit it. "You waiting for an invitation, Sergeant?" He exhaled a stream of smoke. "Or what?"

Nilsen drove on. Still no people in sight here, at least not adults. But the kids by the fence back at base must have someone—some mother or father or guardian—to whom they could return. There must be men and women somewhere. Maybe they'd gone underground. Probably. Dug down, burrowed in for the long haul, as long as peace took. After everything, it made sense that kids were the only ones who would remain hopeful in their desperation, naive enough to cast aside fear.

He parked the jeep beneath the bobbing lantern. This close, its previously hidden side revealed itself as pitifully torn, paper shredded, ribs of wood broken. It was like the moon, with its light side and its dark. It was like the face of a young man Nilsen had glimpsed the day of their arrival here, as he stepped from the dock to the shore. One half of the young man's face was lovely, the skin as delicate and smooth as a flower petal. But then the young man turned, and Nilsen saw the other half of his face—the skin mottled, twisted, and taut, with a lacquered sheen that was reminiscent of

SCHRECK

meringue. A burn victim. Once whole, now divided. The war did that to a man.

The harbor was a stone's throw away. Nilsen couldn't let go of the wheel or Gorman would see his shaking hands.

Gorman took a last drag on his cigarette, and flicked the butt up at the lantern's good side. There was a hiss, a black-ringed hole where contact had been made, a tiny tick as the butt hit the ground.

"How good are you at improvising, Sergeant?"

"I'm no musician, sir."

Gorman coughed out something like a laugh. "Well, follow my lead then."

They got out of the jeep. The Major strode to the shop and flung open the door. Wind chimes tinkled, an otherworldly sound, bright and cheery. The shop was thick with shadows, but Gorman walked purposefully to the counter. There was a cash register there, and a silver bell.

"Preeze ling." Gorman laughed that laugh again. "Picked up some Jap along the way. Couldn't help it."

Gorman struck the bell with the flat of his palm, struck it again and again and again. Nilsen's eyes had adjusted to the dim light, and he saw that the shop walls were flanked with cases and shelves—simple constructions of wood with glass panels, some of which had survived the bombing, others of which had been shattered like the medical supply cabinets back at barracks. Here—it might have been Marshall Field's or L.S. Ayres—each case was filled nearly to overflowing: cufflinks, tie tacks, bracelets, necklaces, rings, earrings, napkin rings, candle holders, and vases, most of it jade—green, of course, but also in shades Nilsen hadn't known existed. There were pearl and mother-of-pearl items, too, hand-painted porcelain, and crystal, silver, gold. Too much stuff. Too much beauty all at once.

Maybe it was the close air, or the bell's clamor, or maybe it was all the sparkle and shine, but Nilsen felt suddenly light-headed. He leaned against the nearest cabinet, trying to keep his balance, and stared down at what it contained: a slew of pearls, white, pink, and—incredibly—black. They looked delicious, as smooth and cool as the edible seeds of some forbidden fruit. Saliva flooded Nilsen's mouth; he swallowed.

Then something stirred at the back of the shop—a watery garden, no, a flowered curtain—and Gorman finally withdrew his hand from the bell. The curtain parted, and a man emerged, carrying a kerosene lamp. The light from the lamp shot through the shadows and bounced off the shop walls, glinting against the remaining panels of glass. Briefly, regarding the man, Nilsen froze in horror. But no. No. This man was stooped and wizened—older, far older than the man he shot on the dock. This man was bald with a thin white beard.

"Keep one eye on me, Sergeant, and the other eye on our friend," Gorman muttered.

The old man folded into himself and bowed. The tip of his beard ended just at the spot where his gray tunic dipped deeply into the hollow of his chest. Gorman removed his fedora, clapped it down beside the bell, and nodded abruptly in return. Then he gestured broadly, commandingly: show me what you've got.

The shopkeeper set the lantern at a safe distance from Gorman's hat, and, fumbling with a small set of keys, began to unlock the cases. From these he withdrew trays and boxes, which he set on display. Gorman uttered appropriate, appreciative sounds. *Oh. Ah. My, my.* Then he turned to Nilsen.

"Take a closer look."

Nilsen followed Gorman's order. The Major's thick fingers rifled with surprising dexterity through the objects, palpating stones and settings, clasps and chains. Ritualistic, Gorman's gestures seemed, when he lifted up a piece of jewelry he deemed particularly beautiful. Like a father or a lover, Gorman gently removed the battered Elgin from Nilsen's wrist, and draped something light as air, gold and glittering, in its place.

"A rare Seikosha. Tavennes movement," Gorman murmured. The watch had a thin, square face; its second hand ticked forward in a wink. "Worth fighting for."

From the corner of his eye, Nilsen saw the shopkeeper steeple his bony fingers before his mouth, hiding his expression. Despair, hope, eagerness, dread—the old man might feel any of these things, or all of them simultaneously, or some complex Jap emotion Nilsen couldn't begin to understand. Back in Indianapolis, things were always black or white, good or bad. Not here.

84

Gorman removed the watch from Nilsen's wrist and with a careless gesture, dropped it back into its velvet box. The band twisted in on itself, but the shopkeeper didn't flinch. He righted the watch in its box, and set it aside as Gorman examined the contents of another case. He drummed his fingers on the glass top as if suddenly bored, and inside, jade beads trembled.

"What do you think?" Gorman said.

Nilsen blinked, confused. "Nice?"

Gorman glared. He yanked off his white silk scarf and tossed it at Nilsen, who managed to catch it.

"Hot." Gorman unbuttoned his fur collar.

Nilsen didn't say anything to this, though he was hot, too, sweltering in his great overcoat, which emitted an overpowering smell of wet wool. His palms were slick with sweat; no doubt the silk scarf would soon be stained if it wasn't already. Nilsen draped the scarf across the counter, then shoved his hands in his pockets and dried them against the coarse lining. Bread crumbs snagged in his ragged fingernails, and there was a sticky patch, probably from a melted Hershey bar. Gorman shot him another smoldering look. Scarf on counter, hands in pockets—Nilsen must not be following the Major's lead; this must be a glitch in the routine. He should make amends, but how? He would never know the answer to this. Never.

Gorman wheeled around to face the old man. "Stop shitting me!" He slammed his fists down on the case, and it heaved, wood creaking. Nilsen's heart banged in his chest, but again, the shopkeeper didn't flinch, even as Gorman lifted his fists and slammed them down again. "Let's get down to business, shall we, Ghost Warrior?" Gorman's tone was brash, mockingly cajoling. "Don't play dumb. Bring it out. Bring it all out. You know what I mean."

The shopkeeper hesitated, furrowing his brow. Anxiety flickered in his eyes; Gorman's demands were apparently lost in translation. But then the shopkeeper's expression brightened, and he turned and disappeared behind the flowered curtain.

"Watch and learn, Sergeant." Gorman rolled his shoulders—a fighter preparing for the ring. "Watch and learn."

The shopkeeper emerged again, bearing a large roll of black velvet. He walked behind the cases to where Gorman and Nilsen

85

stood. Cradling the velvet in one arm, he gently pushed aside the other fine pieces. Crowded together like that, they were less alluring, a jumble of magpie treasure. The shopkeeper closed his eyes, then opened them again, his face a mask, his gaze flat and empty. He set the velvet roll in the space he had cleared on the counter, undid the black ribbon, and unfolded the cloth. Nilsen gasped. Gorman did not. Gorman held very still.

Diamonds covered the velvet so thickly that the black was more hidden than seen.

The Milky Way, Nilsen thought. But closer. Better.

Gorman said, "Loupe, please."

The shopkeeper drew a loupe from the depths of his tunic and handed it to Gorman, who fitted it over his eye, then bent to scrutinize the diamonds. This proved excruciating—the slow, methodical way Gorman checked each stone for facets and flaws. Sometimes he'd straighten up, grunting, shrug his shoulders, stretch his back. Once he asked Nilsen to dig his fist into a kink that had formed just to the left of his spine. Nilsen tried, but beneath Gorman's meaty flesh, the muscle remained rock hard. Still Gorman thanked Nilsen. Nilsen appreciated that. If the Major was grateful, who was he to object? Maybe he alone in the unit would witness Gorman's other side.

The sky was darkening by the time Gorman had selected his favorite gems, four of them, rectangular in shape, ice-white, shot through with prismatic color, all about the size of the Major's pinkie fingernail. Gorman tapped each of the diamonds once, gently, as if bestowing a blessing. Then, baring his nicotine-stained teeth in a grin, he handed the loupe back to the shopkeeper.

"Perfect," Gorman said.

For a moment, the shopkeeper looked stricken. Then he, too, smiled. A single, gray tooth poked up from his lower gum like a crooked tombstone. At the harbor, the man Nilsen shot had smiled, too. That smile wasn't directed at any American. It was a private look intended for the few other men gathered around him. A Jap look, Nilsen thought at the time. Cutthroat, bloodthirsty—or maybe the man had passed some gas. Kamikaze smile, gaseous grimace . . . who knew? Nilsen didn't. Not anymore.

What Nilsen knew was that he shot the man in the thigh. An old man, dressed in rags like the kids on the other side of the fence. The man had been in the wrong place at the wrong time; he'd looked at Nilsen in the wrong way and smiled. "A Jap'll kill you as soon as look at you." Nilsen had been warned. Disembarking in Osaka, Nilsen saw that man's inscrutable smile, and when the man failed to lower his gaze—the traditional Japanese sign of respect—Nilsen knew. The man had no respect. The man and the others—they'd lost a war. Nilsen had won it. A victor, that's what he was now. Then the man's hands twitched—sniper! Nilsen thought, and he went for his gun. Report, puff of smoke, smell of sulfur, and the man crumpled and dropped like a water bird from the dock into the harbor. A flock of Japs followed him. Splashing and thrashing, they'd dragged the old man out. The left leg of his gray pants was black now. The black was spreading fast. Nilsen turned away. He saw his men staring at him, open-mouthed. He cleared his throat. "Now that's something they won't forget," he said. And that had been the end of it, except for the nightmares, and the memory, plaguing every hazy moment of the limbo in which he now lived.

Still smiling, the shopkeeper bowed to Gorman, then fluttered down the long line of cases, the sleeves of his tunic flapping as he flew behind the flowered curtain.

"Show time," Gorman said.

The Major emitted an explosive sound—a sneeze, a blast of raw energy. Nilsen jumped—it scared the hell out of him—yelping one sharp "Ha!", very like the Japanese for hello, or good evening, or now-we-are-really-fucked. Gorman roared again, not even covering his mouth, spit spraying, and thank God no one else was in the room, no other Japs, certainly not the shopkeeper or any of the children, because the Japanese had a penchant for cleanliness. All the soldiers knew this. Even in destitution, in desolation, these people valued hygiene. The kids at the fence had gasped one morning when Nilsen blew his nose into a handkerchief. A skeletal boy plucked a soft tissue of paper from the pocket of his tattered pants, then passed the tissue through the barbed wire, and pantomimed blowing his nose and throwing the tissue away. Nilsen had followed the boy's lead.

Now Gorman exploded yet a third time, pitching forward over the jewelry case. Huffing, the man righted himself, dragging his coat sleeve across the black velvet. The diamonds scattered at their feet, a strange sight indeed beside Nilsen's scuffed boots and Gorman's patent leather shoes, the laces of which, Nilsen saw now, were trailing. Odd, in such a fastidious man . . . unless it was intentional.

Nilsen knew then what would happen next.

Gorman dropped to a squat. He began to shovel the diamonds into his shoes. Such a barrel of a man, working so fast with his beefy hands. "Sir. Stop." Nilsen didn't say this. He knelt down by the Major. Diamonds didn't roll like pearls on the tongue, or taste like the seeds of some forbidden fruit. Diamonds were what they were, jagged rocks that could break teeth, cut muscle and gum, but the taste of bone and blood would be the taste of communion. So long since he'd taken communion. Years since his last confession. Here was a diamond, roughly the size and shape of a bullet. There, two more, shaped like dice. All around, innumerable others, waiting.

Gorman nodded, delivering his order, and Nilsen knew there was no time to waste. Time, for once in this god-forsaken land, was passing too quickly. Following Gorman's lead, he scooped up a handful of diamonds, clawed at his laces, untying them, and stuffed the diamonds inside his boots. Again, he did this. He couldn't stop himself, like that day on the dock. Again and again, he grabbed at the stars.

And then they were standing, and the shopkeeper, weeping silently, was regarding the swatch of black velvet, where only a few diamonds remained. Nilsen stood very still, his feet and his ankles throbbing. The diamonds in his boots pricked and punctured his skin; thinking about this fact only made the pain worse. So he thought about the loot he would share. He would give diamonds to his mother, his father, his grandparents, and the many, beautiful girls he had yet to meet, and would meet, because he was still alive. He would fashion an engagement ring for that perfect girl from the most beautiful diamond, a tie tack and cufflinks for himself. His future was as bright as diamonds. He'd survived this war. He'd been chosen by Gorman on this day. Why him, of all the men? Nilsen decided not

88

to dwell on this question. Blood would soon be leaking into his socks and boots. This question was like the pain, best not considered.

The shopkeeper tucked a tuft of beard into his mouth and sucked on it as he wept.

"How much?" Gorman asked, referring to the four diamonds he'd originally chosen, nothing more.

In a broken voice, the shopkeeper mumbled something in Japanese.

Gorman shook his head. He tugged some coins from his pants pocket, slapped them on the black velvet. "My best offer. Take it or leave it."

The shopkeeper took it.

The beginning of the end, that's what this was, hobbling out of the shop and back to the jeep. Soon this would all be over, but first Nilsen had to drive, press the soles of his feet against the clutch, accelerator, and brake, against the diamonds in his boots. It took all his self-control to stay quiet and follow through on orders. He was glad for the cold and the wind now; these offered the only distraction, except for the headlights, bouncing along as they illuminated what Nilsen hoped was the way back to base. Gorman, for once, was no distraction. He stayed quiet too, staring vacantly at dark no man's land. Deflated, the man seemed. Defeated. Mission accomplished, the Major was given now to something like despair. If Nilsen's feet hadn't hurt so damn much, if the way hadn't been so hard to find, he might have been surprised. He would have kept it to himself, of course, but he might have been concerned.

Finally: the gate, guarded now by two different privates. And the kerosene lamps flickering inside hospital rooms like fireflies. They were driving past the silent baseball field when Gorman finally muttered something unintelligible. "Pardon, sir?" Nilsen said. Gorman turned on him then. Turned on him like an accusation, and yelled into the wind, "Spoils of war, Ghost Warrior. Spoils of war."

"Yes, sir," Nilsen said. Meanwhile, he was planning it all out in his mind. In a moment, he would park the jeep in the garage, and there, behind closed doors, he would empty his boots and wait for Gorman to give him a share. Back in the hospital again, in some secret place, a closet would work, he would use his pocketknife to slice open the lining of his coat. A slit, that's all it would take—a hyphen in the sentence that was his life now. He would funnel the diamonds inside, sew up the damage he'd done, keep his secret safe, hidden away. After that, he would fill a bathtub and take a nice long soak. For once cold water would be better. It would take down the swelling and numb the pain. He would emerge as clean as a baby, body and heartache eased. His future bright as diamonds.

This was who Nilsen was now, and Gorman knew it. This was why he'd been chosen. This was who he was now that he'd shot a man, he'd shot a man for smiling, he'd shot a man for nothing. And he'd do it again if he had to. He'd do it again to survive.

◊

The next day, ignoring the stares of other men, Nilsen carried his blanket, sheets, pillow, towel, washcloth, and a duffle bag, stuffed full, out past the baseball diamond to where the children once again waited. They watched, open-mouthed, as he threw the bedding and linens over the barbed wire fence. He shoved his hands into the duffle bag, then, and the bulging pockets of his stinking coat and his stinking pants, and passed them everything else he'd pilfered, so many sandwiches, Hershey bars, cans of Spam, too many to count, and, who the hell cared, packs upon packs of Luckies. The kids weren't just smiling; they were laughing, wretched bubbles of sound that might have seemed anguished or demented, if Nilsen didn't know better. The kids had to be happy. Had to be. "*Arigato*," they said, thanking him again and again, grabbing at what he'd brought, too excited and stunned to share. Nilsen waited, but it didn't come— that lifting in his chest. It would come, he told himself, with the passing of time. It would come. He waited. It would come.

Lee Sharkey

Concertina Wire

breathes in and out like its namesake. From *con* + *certare*, to contend with, alt., *cantare*, to sing. A wall you can carry. Can see through. Viz., a denial weapon. See: *crannog*, *abatis*, and so on.

Foot soldiers planted coils in no man's land at night to ensnare their mirror images. Animal eyes in moonlight. My thoughts grow *concertinaed*.

From the training manual: *the desirable properties of random entanglement*.

A small flock of women move in concert with the night over scrub desert and rocky inclines to a depression under a wall of wire. Their names are Fatma, Iman, Oum Drar, Nadia, Amal, Ghada, and Sumaya. Their names are Rukan, Leila, Hanan, Basimah, Bushra, Salma, and Azar.

Shiny intersecting spirals. Venn diagrams of parallel narratives. Let's say it's Fatma who lifts a loop of wire. One by one by one, they belly down, crawl under. A shred of sleeve snags in dragon's teeth.

From the training manual: *difficult to handle, particularly in darkness*. Footsteps in darkness. Rag and bucket as denial weapon. Every night the women come and go.

They see it. They see it through. The universe, I read, will speed apart until the night no one believes there were ever stars.

Theadora Siranian

Ouroboros

after Lee Miller's photograph of female collaborators,
Rennes, August, 1945

Dear Audrey, In my dream I'm back in Poughkeepsie,
standing naked in the snow. Every night
for a week. *I wanted another battle before Paris*
but I've just sat in this room, drinking cognac in the dark,
smoking black market cigarettes when *I could have been*
at the wars. I sit at this desk alone, wring stones
for enough blood to fill my pen. I never know what you
want from me—what to say about this world that loves
to burn. There should have been another sister at Rennes,
shorn and dragged along the boulevard, dumb animals
not intelligent enough to be ashamed. Their pale faces
expressionless, eyes dark as dirt in the sunlight. I used
to believe there's something deep blue and burning *inside*
a human being no one has thought of putting into
a machine, and I see now how wrong I was. It's our ability
for ignorance, our seedy love of it, that is the hungry
beast pushing the wheel of this war round and round.
Sitting here thinking about it is what's killing me;
I could be back at the front, seeing all there is to see
with these blood-filled, bloodshot eyes. *Love to everyone.*

Götterdämmerung

after Lee Miller's photographs of the Leipzig
Burgomaster family suicide, April 1945

Dreaming, the girl walks barefoot beneath
a sky obscured by dense fir trees.

She runs blue fingers along rough trunks,
slowly sifting the damp, almond-scented air
through her lungs, tongue candying.

Dead, *the girl had exceptionally pretty teeth*,
lying on the family couch, mouth just parted,
parents slumped and stiff across the room.

A hundred miles away, in Berlin, blonde
children carrying baskets drop small glass

capsules into the palms of the audience
as the orchestra tilts, roars, then breaks
and the curtain falls on the flames.

Ida Faubert

Sonnet to Pierre Loti

–Translated from the French by Danielle Legros Georges

O marvelous artist, O creator of dreams,
To my soul your solitary soul spoke,
And I followed you, a sweet and sad exile,
In the far-flung lands where you went restlessly.

I knew the *spahi* who lay heaving on the shore;
I felt him die in my deserted heart,
And took in his good-bye, his veiled gaze,
In the grave and calm hour of the rising moon.

O pilgrim of Angkor, I followed you.
I saw the great lotuses, the pagodas of gold,
The deep eyes of the saddened belles

Who weep in silence and sigh soundlessly,
Dreaming of a joy they will never achieve.
Loti, I resemble your Disillusioned Ones.

Note: *spahi*, members of the French cavalry units recruited from
North Africa who took part in the First and Second World Wars.
Note: Pierre Loti, a French navel officer and writer.

Nonfiction

J AMIE Z VIRZDIN

On the Revolution of Revolutions: Nicaraguan Women After War

The Interview

It won't do to have Comandante Dos show up for an interview and make her wait. You don't make Dora María Téllez wait. I try to breathe deeply in calm cycles, but it isn't easy: I'm about to meet a former Sandinista guerrilla commander who led the attack on the Nicaraguan National Palace, threatened to murder fifteen hundred hostages, including children, and negotiated Sandinista demands with the dictator Anastasio Somoza Debayle over the course of three fraught days. I'm an astronomy teacher, not a reporter, a new moon in a full moon world, but I need to ask the Commander a question. I'm dying to know the answer, but she's the one who faced death to find it.

It's late afternoon on May 8, 2017, and I'm sitting in Café Las Flores in Managua, Nicaragua, trying to watch both the front and the side entrances at the same time. Like a Galilean pendulum, I swivel my head from one glass door to the other, still trying to appear calm, languid, and professional. I might be failing in this effort.

This particular Café Las Flores is near the Movistar office building—if you're Nicaraguan, that's all the direction you need. Addresses are often described using landmarks, even landmarks that might no longer be there. Outside the front door, I see the busy Carretera Masaya. Water trucks, grungy taxis, black-belching but colorful hand-me-down buses, pickup trucks with cargo beds stuffed with local pineapple or *plátanos* or people, enormous flatbed trailers loaded with hexagonal paving blocks ("Somoza Stones") placed precariously near the unguarded edge, rusting roadsters, roaring dirt bikes, Pizza Hut delivery motorcycles, Tip Top delivery motorcycles, horse carts, and expensive white or black SUVs—all these race by, with the exception of the horse carts. It's taken me almost two years of wheel-gripping, horn-honking, lane-swerving driving to feel confident on these roads. My students at the Pierre and Marie Curie School know that without the movement of atoms in stars, there is neither heat, nor order, nor light; without the Earth's movement around our Sun, there is no life. To move is to live, I tell them. But the phrase holds new meaning for me on Nicaraguan roads.

The upscale wooden furniture store next door undoubtedly made a deal with Café Las Flores, because all around me are sleek wooden tables and chairs, accented with green and white cushions. The smell of the wood mingles with the coffee. I haven't ordered anything, however; I'm just awkwardly swiveling my head from door to door in a way that would embarrass even Galileo. I ask the barista—again—if the private room is ready. She tells me it'll be ten minutes—again—and when I crane my neck even more to get a glimpse of the private room at the back, its sliding door opens, and my heart rate increases as if I'd slammed a double espresso: other people are still in there, and they don't look like they're finishing up anytime soon.

The type of clientele here is middle-upper class, well-dressed, with light-brown skin. A smattering of young professionals work on their laptops, undoubtedly drawn here by the tractor-beam promise of free Wi-Fi. I get a few questioning looks from my neighbors as the minutes tick by. I know this nervous white American is destructively interfering with their softly caffeinated vibe.

I've now talked to three people about getting the back room ready. She's not here yet, and I must remind myself to breathe properly, to keep blood and oxygen cycling evenly. I have an important question I want to ask her, and I must keep my shit together. I must not fan-girl over an ex-guerrilla commander.

Astronomy Night

My question arises during an astronomy night earlier in the year, a perfect Nicaraguan night in February, a perfect night for a revelation

96

on revolution. I'm in the physics lab teaching the fourth graders of the Pierre and Marie Curie School about the creation of our Solar System. They listen, legs swinging back and forth beneath their black chairs, as I tell them how the Sun was born 4.5 billion years ago from dark swirling curtains of gas and dust. When that bringer of life burst onto the stage, the 1% of leftover matter coalesced into planets, which still spin like solemn chorus line dancers around their lead star.

Antonio and Gerardo, who teach astronomy with me, take over. Antonio, the high school physics teacher, describes the differences between the rocky planets and the gas giants, and Gerardo, the high school math teacher, talks about other stars, how our Solar System is only one of many star systems revolving around the supermassive black hole at the center of our Milky Way Galaxy. The children fire back with their own questions in Spanish, and if Antonio and Gerardo can't answer them, they turn to me and I have to ask them to repeat the question. In this more or less bilingual atmosphere, we oscillate between English and Spanish as needed.

Antonio and Gerardo take the first group of students to the roof, to the small, white dome where we set up the school's 10-inch reflecting telescope, a classic Dobsonian. I entertain the last group of kids with Phil Plait's *Crash Course Astronomy* videos on Venus and Mars, and at last the students rush upstairs for their turn at the telescope.

I am tired—in addition to our daytime classes (I also teach high school science writing at Pierre and Marie Curie), we hold special astronomy nights for the whole school, preschool through twelfth grade, and we've only just finished with fourth. Still, I am deeply satisfied. I love sharing the grand chronicle of the cosmos, even though the story of life-giving heat, order, and light is riddled with cold, violence, and darkness.

Something about an intimacy with the sky and a knowledge of its patterns also grants me a sort of priestly status, whether I want it to or not. Students, particularly teenage girls, have come to me in the comforting darkness of astronomy night asking about depression, motherhood, careers, religion, sex, and suicide. These Nicaraguan girls are already grappling with *machismo*, an aggressive and

97

exaggerated sense of masculine entitlement that extends far beyond Latino cultures. I hear these girls, and I hug them, and although I don't have solutions, I help them hitch their dream wagons to the nearest star, hoping they will free themselves and their children from the horse mill of history.

I ascend the stairs to the roof, stoop to enter the low door of the white dome, and watch quietly by the open slit of sky as the students peer through the telescope at Venus and Mars: the goddess of love and the god of war. In the northern sky, the two planets seem to create a diagonal stairway to heaven with the thumbnail of the waxing crescent Moon as the lowest rung. Mars is a disappointing fuzzy red dot, even through the telescope, and Venus is a similarly unspectacular bright white blob, the Sun reflecting off its toxic clouds. Neptune and Uranus are also wandering nearby this evening, too far away for the Dobsonian. Saturn and Jupiter, my two favorite planets, won't be out at all tonight, according to the convenient app on my phone that predicts these heavenly cycles.

Gerardo and Antonio are better at connecting with the younger students than I am, speaking in the familiar *voseo* of Spanish as they readjust the telescope and answer more questions. But that is as it should be, given that in another year or so I'll travel with my husband to his next post in the US Foreign Service. I leave the cacophony of the dome.

There are enough streetlights around Las Colinas, the neighborhood in Managua where the Pierre and Marie Curie School is located, to silhouette the trees surrounding the property. Approaching a group of students chatting near the waist-high white wall surrounding the roof, I see that some of the students are staring at their phones, which were more strictly regulated downstairs. I want to bring the students back to the present, to this physical moment in time.

"Have I taught you what the ecliptic is yet?" I ask them brightly.

Heads shake no as eyes stare at screens. I don't want to command them to put the phones away; I want them to be seduced by the stars, to look up of their own volition.

98

I launch into an explanation and make sweeping gestures across the sky. The thin plane of the planets, which we draw horizontally with concentric circles in our lazy diagrams of the Solar System, actually marches almost vertically across our night sky in real time. The space-time gravity well keeps Earth and the other planets swooping around in giant elliptical paths so that every year we end up where we began. But the Sun is moving too, I tell them, just as Gerardo was saying: it too is locked in orbit around the supermassive black hole that keeps our Milky Way Galaxy together. I point to the southern horizon where that great fire-ringed eye, Sagittarius A*, watches us from the center of its gravitational web. Eyes are up now, screens are dark.

When the students leave, I help Gerardo and Antonio dismantle the telescope and return it to its closet, where it will be shielded, sort of, from the fierce heat of the day. We return the dome to its starting position, turn off the power, and shut the small door. We sit on the roof under the stars: an astronomer's reward. Gerardo is drumming on the ground, Antonio is softly strumming his guitar (they play in a band together), and I am thinking about stories.

In teaching and talking and drinking with Nicaraguans, I hear story after story about life under Somoza, life during the Sandinista Revolution of the 1970s and the Contra War of the 1980s, and life under the current administration of President Daniel Ortega. Ortega was part of the original underground movement against the Somoza regime; fighting alongside Ortega, Edén Pastora, Thomas Borge, and many others revolutionaries was Dora María Téllez, the woman who would eventually be known as Comandante Dos. I am most curious about her story, how she feels about revolution, how she deals with machismo. Nicaragua is a small enough place that there's a good chance I can ask her myself. She may have something to say that could help my astronomy-night girls in ways I can't.

Tonight, the two senses of the word revolution, both astronomical and political, suddenly merge in my mind like an eclipse. I know what I want to ask Comandante Dos.

99

The Hostage

We're still on the roof when I say out loud that I want to interview Dora María Téllez. Antonio casually tells me that his mother was one of her hostages in the National Palace. I'm in shock. Nicaragua is a smaller place than I thought. I beg for the full details, and Antonio hands the guitar to Gerardo.

As Carmen was reluctant to meet with me personally, this is her story as told through her son.

On August 22, 1978, Carmen Zavala (name changed) went to the National Palace Library to collect data for her statistics project. She was a student at UNAN-Managua, a local Nicaraguan university known for its revolutionary thinkers. After hours studying in the library, Carmen went to her aunt's office on the first floor, expecting to wait for her aunt there until the shift ended. What Carmen did not expect was that she and her aunt would not be leaving the National Palace at all that day.

While Carmen was waiting, she saw a Rena Ware salesman collecting money for the pots he had sold to other workers in the office. Carmen joked, "Don't bother paying him—the war is going to start soon." Just then gunshots were heard ricocheting through the palace. Carmen and the others locked the office doors, and all eyes turned to Carmen in incredulity. Over and over she had to tell them that she didn't actually know the war was coming.

No one ever entered the office. At first, the other people in the room were frantic, but by the afternoon they had calmed down. At one point Carmen lay next to the door, and through the crack between the door and the floor, she saw heavy boots walking by. Carmen wanted to go out and talk with the guerrillas, but the other office members wouldn't let her.

The day dragged on. Carmen and the others resorted to eating the office snacks: crackers and olives. Then night came, and people slept, or tried to sleep, on the office desks.

The following day, the women and children were released; men were kept the full three days, until the Sandinistas had reached an agreement with Somoza.

Carmen was initially concerned but not horrified like the others. She was a firm supporter of the Sandinista cause—a willing hostage. Somoza had been amassing wealth and businesses for himself for decades, and when a massive earthquake toppled Managua in 1972, Somoza stole a large portion of the foreign aid and sold it off, including the very blood plasma donations that would have saved thousands.

"Somoza was killing his own people without any reason," Carmen said. She didn't understand why the United States was still supporting Somoza even though they knew he was killing people and making them disappear. Today she still supports the Ortega administration; she feels she has had more opportunities after the war, and women are considered for jobs they were previously barred from. Carmen now has a good position working as one of the directors of a company.

"The Sandinistas did what they had to do," she said.

The Commander, 1978

As Carmen waited for her aunt inside the National Palace, the Nicaraguan National Assembly was in full session on the second floor. Two Jeeps carrying Sandinistas dressed in National Guard uniforms pulled up on either side of the Palace, a stately, four-level neoclassical structure flanked by giant-order Doric columns. At the side entrances, they announced that the boss, Somoza, was coming. The National Guard was fooled by the trick, and the Sandinistas rushed the building. Although there was still resistance both inside and outside—which accounts for the shots Carmen heard—the two Sandinista groups managed to lock the doors behind them, and they all headed upstairs. One group of Sandinistas took over one wing on the second floor; the other captured members of Congress. Twenty-five rebels, led by Edén Pastora, Hugo Torres, and Dora María Téllez, captured the National Palace in four minutes.

Somoza relented to their demands after three days of humiliating negotiations with Téllez, paying a ransom of five hundred thousand dollars, freeing fifty-eight imprisoned revolutionaries (including Daniel Ortega), broadcasting a Sandinista manifesto, and

101

allowing safe passage of the Sandinistas to Panama. It was a major turning point in an already brutal battle. The photo I find most interesting is the one taken after "Operation Pigsty," where Téllez is striding confidently next to Edén Pastora, her M-2 carbine slung over her right shoulder and a gas mask hanging from her neck. You can tell she is smiling behind the red-and-black handkerchief tied around her nose and mouth.

As the Sandinista/Somoza conflict ramped up over the next year, Téllez led the final six-week assault on León, her home city and the intellectual capital of Nicaragua. It was the place where, as a twenty-one-year-old medical student at UNAN-León, she had first been asked to join the resistance. She'd been told she was needed in the mountains—a sure death sentence. Revolutionaries rarely lasted more than six months if they were sent to the mountains. Nevertheless, Téllez immediately responded she would go, and without saying goodbye to family, she prepared one backpack. Her recruiter came back saying that it had been a test of loyalty. She would not go to the mountains: she'd stay in the city and fight with words, writing newsletters and other communiqués for the Sandinistas. Téllez never dreamed she'd eventually fight her own people on the streets of her own city.

On July 17th, 1979, Somoza fled the country—to be assassinated in Paraguay a year later in "Operation Reptile"—and the Sandinistas stepped into power and into the abandoned mansions of wealthy Somoza supporters. Although they began a slew of reforms in literacy, health care, education, childcare, and unions, the seizure of property and possessions by the new government soured the victory. Not even a year had gone by when the Reagan administration, fearful of the spread of Communism, began funding the Contra War, which ultimately cost sixty thousand lives, $178 billion, and an untold cost on Nicaraguan infrastructure, its economy, and its psyche. It was in reaction to US interference that Daniel Ortega took office, proclaimed a state of emergency, and suspended civil rights. The same prison Ortega was tortured in—he still bears the scar of a kick to the face—has been renamed but is still in use.

Téllez became increasingly disenchanted with how *sandinismo*—the ideology of General Augusto César Sandino, a 1930s

102

resistance leader holding George Washington status in the eyes of the Nicaraguan people—evolved over the decades that followed. She became an open opponent of Daniel Ortega, the fellow revolutionary she so valiantly saved from Somoza's inhumane prison. After Nicaragua's 2016 November elections, she called Ortega's re-election fraudulent and undemocratic.

"I don't fight against a person but against a system. Against the model of a dynastic, family dictatorship," she told Fabrice Le Lous of *La Prensa*. "And now I fight against the same model of dynastic and family dictatorship. You change the name but it is the same."

Gyres

I'm not the first to connect the astronomical and political definitions of *revolution*. Carlos Fuentes, one of the foremost Mexican thinkers of the twentieth century, says in his essay "Revolución" that political revolutions involve "an element of both rupture and return," with an almost inevitable "return to its point of origin."

In college, I was particularly fascinated with the poet William Butler Yeats and his philosophy of gyres. Yeats proposed the idea that history spins through two interconnecting spirals, one representing growth and order, the other decay and chaos. As one waxes, the other wanes. In his book *A Vision*, Yeats carefully divided history into these cycles, incorporating aspects of astrology into his theory. Yeats believed that each new cycle would be heralded by a crisis point, although no future crisis point would be an exact repeat of a past point. I've begun to see the cycles of repression and revolution in Nicaragua in this way, and I wonder what kind of new crisis point is spiraling closer.

What most people don't know is that the astronomical definition of *revolution* is intimately connected to the secondary sense of political upheaval; it is, in fact, the predecessor. Vernon Snow, in a 1962 article entitled "The Concept of Revolution in Seventeenth-Century England," says that the word *revolution* "evolved through the centuries from a simple, rather obscure, Latin word denoting the periodic return of a moving object (or person) to the point of origin, to a widely used and complex doctrine of political action."

103

The scientific definition came first. Copernicus came before Locke. While the first use of revolution in its socio-political meaning is unknown, in 1605 the historian William Camden wrote, "All things runne round; and as the seasons of the year; so men's manners have their *revolutions.*" Thereafter, Snow says, historians used *revolution* to refer to cyclical political change and then political change in general.

Via e-mail, I ask Dr. Victoria González-Rivera if the status of women today is better or worse than it was before the Sandinista Revolution. González-Rivera is a PhD professor in Latin American History at Indiana University and author of the book *Before the Revolution: Women's Rights and Right-Wing Politics in Nicaragua.* "There is no way that women's overall situation in Nicaragua or anywhere else, for that matter, can go back to what it was in 1979," she responds. "Some of the changes were brought about by the revolution, some were brought about because of the Contra War, others would have taken place regardless."

I ask Juanita Jiménez Martínez, a Nicaraguan human rights lawyer, the same question. Her answer is that the position of women is better in some ways: women are better able to be protagonists in their own lives; normative frameworks for gender equality are stronger; and there's a greater awareness that abusers must be held accountable by the government. However, Martínez also said that *machismo* is "deeply rooted" and "modernized," and sexist violence shows that women are still treated as inferior beings. In asking Nicaraguan women this question for the last seven months, I get a constellation of answers.

Are we doomed, then, to forever cycle through Yeats' gyres of repression and revolution? Can we ever escape the gravity of the human condition? The Oxford English Dictionary lists a third definition of *revolution*, an obsolete one that yet seems particularly meaningful as I've researched, discussed, and puzzled over this topic:

> Revolution, n.: The action or an act of turning
> over in the mind or in discussion; consideration,
> reflection discussion, debate; judicial review.

It is in this sense that I, too, wish to join the revolution. In thinking of the scientific revolutions of Aristarchus and Galileo

ZVIRZDIN

and Copernicus, I find it utterly bizarre that hundreds and hundreds of years later, we have Flat Earth Societies that have obstinately set Earth back in its original place, content with concentric circles and closed minds. The same can be said for men's manners, despite the increasing pushback from women. But I want to believe that it is in the constant and careful reflection and discussion of history and ideology and humanity that this retrenchment, this cycle can be escaped.

The Ex-Commander, 2017

Journalist Stephen Kinzer, author of *Blood of Brothers: Life and War in Nicaragua*, describes Téllez as "short and stocky, with close-cropped hair. Unlike other Sandinista women, she rarely used makeup and wore no jewelry other than a man's watch. Her female friends described her as warm and even sensitive, but in public, dressed always in uniform, she seemed very tough."

Thinking of Kinzer's description of Téllez as I wait in Café Las Flores, I wonder which version I'll meet forty years later, the warm one or the tough one. There is so much that has happened, and yet Téllez is still fighting the same revolution. The blood of sisters bleeds on.

Téllez enters through the side door. She is still short but more wiry than stocky. Her hair is gray-white like my grandma's, her purple-checked shirt and black fanny pack are as far from threatening as I can imagine. She has no jewelry, and her skin is smooth but for a small mole on her left cheekbone. She greets me cordially but does not come in for the traditional kiss on the cheek, and I'm glad she doesn't. The back room is, amazingly, ready as promised, and I can stop reminding myself to breathe. The room contains a simple long table and chairs partitioned from the general murmur of the café by a sliding door. We order coffee, ham sandwiches, and a side of vegetables and hummus.

Naturally, the first serious interview I ever conduct will be entirely in Spanish. (Not intimidating. Not at all). I start off by bumbling around the topic of women after war, and then her small phone interrupts us.

"It's a nun who stayed at my safe house during the war. She's quite old but I've always taken care of her," Téllez says. She invites me to keep talking. The pause has given me time to collect my scattered thoughts, and my chest feels abnormally inflated as I finally ask my question.

"While I've been here in Nicaragua, I've had the pleasure of teaching astronomy and science writing at the Pierre and Marie Curie School," I begin. "We've talked about the orbits of the planets, their revolutions around the Sun. In a revolution, the object returns to its original position." *Get on with it*, I think, and I blurt out, "I'd like to know if the state of women in Nicaragua suffered this same type of revolution, returning to a *machista* position, to violence, injustice, to the oppression of women." I took a deep breath. "For you, what is the state of women today? Is it better, worse, or the same as the position of women before the Sandinista Revolution?"

"It's not easy to respond to this question," she replies. The nun calls back again. The balloon inside my chest deflates.

"She's eighty-four years old and she's like a mother to me . . ." Téllez says apologetically as she puts the phone down. "It's difficult to respond to that question because the situation of women depends on an enormous quantity of variables: education variables, work variables, social variables, political variables . . . it's very complex." I have my pen poised over my paper, expectant. "But I'll take one of them; let's take education. I feel women are doing much better than forty years ago."

She explains that in the 70s, under the Somoza regime, education was restricted for girls, that they were expected to stay home and do housework. Today women are arguably in a far better place when it comes to education than they have been in the past. "This is an important change," she says, in part because of the Sandinista focus on literacy and in part because the war sent young men to fight and die, and high schools and universities had more positions open for women.

"When the men came back from the war, could women keep their jobs, or were they fired?" I ask, thinking of Rosie the Riveter.

"There was never work for all those people; unemployment has always been a big problem here," Téllez responds. "What other variable could we take . . . let's pick a different variable. Measuring violence, for example." She explains that although rape and sexual abuse claims have increased, "this epidemic always existed, but no one would report it. So, the fact that it is coming to light is a positive thing. In fact, the laws penalizing sexual abuse and rape have changed a lot in the past thirty-something years." She pauses now and again to dip a carrot in the humus, chewing thoughtfully. In the past, she explains, rapists in Nicaragua didn't hide, because the culture thought of rape as something natural and didn't condemn it much. The raped one would traditionally hide because she was considered dishonored. Rapists are the easiest criminals for the police to capture, she says, "because they don't run." She mentions Daniel Ortega, and I know she's referring to the alleged sexual abuse of his step-daughter, Zoilamerica Narvaez Ortega. It is hard to fight for the rights of women when the leader of a country violates those rights himself. I'm thinking of Trump now, of a US President who has shown that his desires for power and pleasure come before his concern for his people.

I ask her if she ever experienced sexism as a commander, or if there was a real revolution of gender equality during the fight against Somoza.

"*La guerra siempre es machista. Las guerras . . . todas son machistas, ¿verdad?*" Téllez says immediately, powerfully. "War is always sexist. Wars . . . they're all sexist, right?" She slurped loudly with her straw on the last of her iced coffee. "I was not really a victim . . . but like the world over, women are considered less capable, that they can do fewer things, that they have less strength or less resistance. The very concept of war assumes that it's not for women . . . but neither is war for men. Wars are for no one."

"What do you think of the things Donald Trump has said about women?" I ask.

"I believe he's misogynist. Really, I see him as misogynist. To me Trump has an authoritarian personality and archaic thinking—incredibly archaic—very *machista* . . . dominated by dogma, not by evidence." To my mind comes the image of the rough beast from Yeats' poem "The Second Coming"—a grim, grinning beast slouching back in time.

107

We've finished our coffee and our food, and I ask her what *sandinismo* means to her. She again answers immediately, forcefully: "First, national sovereignty, self-determination, anti-interventionism; second, defending the interests of the working classes." Third, she says, is the concept of equality, the concept of opportunities. "And there is a fourth aspect, democracy, which was integral to the *sandinismo* of Sandino. It is essential to us." She has her mission, and to me it sounds very much like an American one—a terrible irony, given all the times the US has prevented them from achieving Sandino's dream of governing themselves.

It is dark outside; the stars are beginning to shine through the clouds. I thank Téllez for her time and we stand to leave. She says she would love to come to an astronomy night sometime, and I tell her I'd be delighted. It is a moment, as we shake hands, when all three definitions of *revolution* come together: the Nicaraguan political revolutionary and the American astronomer, historical enemies, coming together to reflect on and discuss the nature of the universe we find ourselves in.

Crisis Point

On August 10, 2017, Karla Patricia Estrada Rostrán put on dark blue lycra jeans and a black and yellow blouse, anticipating a merry time laughing and talking with friends at the Santo Domingo festival that day. The only cloud blocking her bright day was that her ex-military husband, Francisco Ariel Mercado—from whom she had separated multiple times on account of his abuse—insisted on accompanying her. Karla left her house near UNICA, a Catholic University a short walk from my house, and she set off down the road with Mercado. Karla was thirty-four years old, a year older than I am now. Her long dark hair framed a perfectly oval face, dark brown eyes, high cheekbones, and sensuous lips. She was tall and slim, with a rose tattoo on her lower back and a small ring, set with a white jewel, on her finger. She walked past my neighborhood to the festival, where colored flag banners zigzagged across the street and vendors were already selling ice cream, tortillas, small wooden toys, neon-colored strings of candy, alcohol, and boiling cauldrons of *nacatamales*, a favored local dish.

ZVIRZDIN

I know this because I was there too, on an early-morning walk with my husband and my son. Later that day, after work, I had planned to return and see the "bringing back" of *Minguito*, a small, wooden statuette that personified the patron Saint Dominic, miracle-granter of faithful Catholics.

Each August 1st, *Minguito* is taken in a boisterous and joyful procession downtown, and on August 10th he is returned to the Las Sierritas parish church. Karla met up with her seventeen-year-old daughter Jenifer inside the church, both of them happy and laughing. The pews had been taken out, alcoves boarded up, and sawdust scattered all around. People around them had painted themselves with grease or even gasoline to make their skin darker, recalling their indigenous ancestors. It rained for a good part of the day, but that didn't stop the celebration or the fireworks later that afternoon. By the time the fireworks went off, I had become so engrossed in my work that I missed *Minguito's* return—and Karla's abduction.

At some point that evening, Mercado took Karla away from the celebration. "He must have been *endrogado*," said a family friend. One of Karla's daughters, Natalia, who is almost nine months pregnant, told police that Mercado never wanted Karla to go anywhere. If he couldn't have her, he didn't want anybody else to. Karla's brother, Elmer, said Mercado always beat her and threatened her, and her mother said Mercado often kept a military-issued bayonet at his side. Karla had already gone to the police three times to report domestic abuse, but each time Mercado had been allowed to go free.

Karla did not return home the night of the 10th, and when Mercado came the next day, a little after 9:00 AM, he told his three daughters—Dayeri, Natalia, and Jenifer (ages fourteen, sixteen, and seventeen, respectively), that he was leaving for a military job near Costa Rica and wasn't ever planning on coming back. Jenifer told me he was crying as he scratched at his hands. He gave them the house keys and left.

Karla never came back in one piece. On August 17th, a decapitated body was found in an overgrown lot in Las Colinas, just around the corner from the Pierre and Marie Curie School, the school where I had stared up at the planets during astronomy night and thought about the revolution of revolutions, the place where I had heard how Dora María Téllez took Carmen Zavala hostage. While Karla's head could not be found, her violated body was identified by the rose tattoo on her back and the little white-jeweled ring on her finger. Her black and yellow blouse bore the marks of twenty-four knife wounds. The news is full of the story now, since her daughters didn't want to bury her body without her head. "I'm calling on my dad to please, tell us where my mom's head is," Jenifer told *La Prensa*.

But yesterday, August 24th, inside a dark gray coffin with silver casket corners, Karla's body was driven by a gray Nissan truck to the Las Sierritas church cemetery. She was interred one crumbling cement wall away from where she had come two weeks earlier to enjoy the return of *Minguito*.

This morning, overcome by this news and the news that we've had eight violent femicides in the last three weeks in Nicaragua, I want to visit the family myself, express my grief, and offer what Americans offer best: money. I tell my twenty-four-hour guard where I am going, leave my barbed-wire compound, and set off down the road. It doesn't take long for the US Embassy's Roving Patrol guards to catch up with me. I'm a nervous white American again, as I was in Café Las Flores, but this time I'm also angry. I argue with the guards in the middle of the road. I know I can't go to the vigil tonight, I tell them. At least let me do this. This is my neighborhood too.

I finally receive permission, and with my undesired armed escort, we find Karla's house, her mother, and one of her daughters. I wait outside the little green house while other family members go in to see if they will talk to me. Plastic white chairs line one side of the low cement wall that encloses the property, and a pink shirt and blue pants hang from the limb of a stunted tree to my left. A wheelbarrow, its wheel caked in wet gray mud, lies upturned next to an abandoned Styrofoam plate, soggy napkins, and some clear plastic bags. Fake green ferns and giant plastic sunflowers stand guard in plastic pots near the open door; the door's rusting metal gate provides a perch for a scraggly green and yellow parrot. The parrot quietly watches me with one red-ringed black eye.

Luz Marina, Karla's mother, appears at the doorway, hunched with age, fever, and grief. Get her a chair, someone says, and I take a plastic white chair from against the wall, wipe off the water from yesterday's rainstorm, and set it down on the dirt. She's burning up, an aunt says, feeling her forehead. I ask Luz Marina if she wants to go to the hospital. She shakes her head no. I pull a wad of cash out of my bra and tuck it into her palm.

"This doesn't fix things, but I hope it will help with the funeral," I say. She grips the money tightly and draws it under the folds of her shawl. Her daughter, Jenifer, rests against the doorframe. I tell them who I am and that I want to say sorry, to repeat the obvious—that this monstrous thing shouldn't have happened. I try to ask what Karla was like, but I am having a really hard time forming the past tense in Spanish, not wanting to cause them more pain. What did Karla like to do? I finally get out. Luz Marina doesn't answer.

"She liked to cook for her friends," Jenifer says.

"Her favorite colors were purple and black," a cousin chimes in.

"She was a happy person, often smiling, often laughing," the aunt says from behind me. The parrot hanging on the gate was Karla's pet. His name is Paco. Karla was excited to see Natalia's new baby, her first grandbaby.

As we are talking, a brown and black puppy waddles over, jumps up to put his paws on Luz Marina's knee, and, licking the air, looks into her face. I see Luz Marina smile. One of Karla's nephews wanders in and sits near the plastic sunflowers. Surrounded by caring family members in the cool morning air, it doesn't seem possible that such a colossal tragedy has happened. I thank them for their time, and I tell them I will write about Karla so she will be remembered, so things like this don't keep happening. It is one thing to discuss revolution in an upscale coffee shop; it is quite another to see the fallout happen to women in your neighborhood. It feels like a crisis point for our local community.

I ask Luz Marina's family friend if she feels that things have gotten better since the Revolution. "No," she says simply. "We were not as afraid to walk in the streets at night. Now men are killing their family members. Nobody is safe, not the little boys, not the little girls, not the women, not even the elderly."

Mercado is still at large, as is Karla—many Nicaraguans believe that because she was buried without her head, she must wander the neighborhood as a phantom until things are set right. At the vigil tonight, near the blue UNICA gate, in the place where Karla Patricia Estrada Rostrán used to live, no one will be at rest.

The Return

Mercado was found a week after I visited Karla's family. He had sent a WhatsApp message to his pregnant daughter, who turned in the phone to the police. The police were able to track Mercado to Nandaime, a town an hour away from Managua. As Dora María Téllez told me, rapists don't run.

Like Minguito, Mercado was taken in a grand police procession to El Chipote, the same terrible prison where Anastasio Somoza Debayle tortured Daniel Ortega. Mercado was locked in a maximum-security cell. A Nicaraguan man told me that the police probably beat and tortured him to force him to reveal where he had put his wife's head. Three days later, Mercado revealed that he had buried Karla's head in a black plastic sack some sixty-five meters from where he left her body, in the field next to where I talk with Nicaraguan girls about their troubles and their dreams.

"This man makes us ashamed to be men," the Nicaraguan man told me. "That son of a bitch deserves what he gets." It is hard for me not to agree with him.

"Now I can be tranquila," Luz Marina told Ernesto García of El Nuevo Diario, "because she is now going to rest in peace with her body and her head in the same place." Karla's head has been returned, but my sense of security and hope have not. I'm still fearful that the revolution of planets foretells the ultimate futility of political and social revolutions, including positive, lasting change for women.

As I mull over—revolve—this dark thought in my mind, however, an astronomy lesson comes back to me. It's the lesson where we talk about the difference between astronomy—the study of the stars—and astrology, the pseudoscientific belief that the motions of stars and planets govern human affairs and determine our fates.

ZVIRZDIN

Maybe I should take a chapter from my own astronomy book, I tell myself. I choose to reject astrological thinking.

The very end of my interview with Dora María Téllez also returns to me: After shaking hands, Téllez's hand is now on the sliding door, and the hum of the café turns back into a steady buzz of pleasant voices.

"Getting back to your original question . . ." Téllez says suddenly, and I curse myself for turning off the recorder too soon.

"In reality," she continues, "a planet doesn't ever return to its exact spot." Stars move, galaxies move, space expands. I nod, dumbfounded. She's right. She says goodbye with a warm smile, and I watch as Comandante Dos leaves the café. She walks in a straight line, with purpose, out the side door.

Ruth Mukwana

The Minister

The Minister arrived in Truck Town in his Hummer, the color of the Ugandan military's uniform—brown, green, black—flanked by his henchmen who carried Kalashnikovs across their chests. His arrival always evoked excitement in Truck Town, the kind of excitement a cherished daughter conjured every time she visited her family. Half-naked children ran to touch The Minister's car, no longer afraid of the men with guns. Old men in small groups, sitting on the verandas of their houses, drinking *waragi* and smoking tobacco, nodded in admiration; one of their own had succeeded, which kept them hoping for better things, better days.

Not Big Mama, though, who owned the only bar in Truck Town. She was called Big Mama not because she was a large woman. In fact, she was slender, tall with a giraffe neck and a hint of dimples. She was called Big Mama because she was tough.

Big Mama was wary of The Minister and his henchmen. The money he now threw around, the charisma he now exhibited, the nice things he did, like picking up babies and playing with them, the dark tailored suits he wore, none of it made her forget the things he and his henchmen had done during the war or pretend that things were going right in the country. It disturbed her that instead of shunning him everyone was now worshipping him. All she wanted to do was force him to acknowledge the things he'd done, for if he did, perhaps she could heal and not drown in *waragi*. She failed to confront him: He'd turn up, and she'd see the guns.

The Minister walked around the town, a small crowd of children and men following him and laughing at everything he said. Even when he said jump, they laughed as they jumped. He knew the town well, having grown up there. The son of a truck driver, he only went to primary school, for there was no money for his higher education. He remained in the town doing small jobs here and there, and because of that the town people called him Small Boy, a name that never sat well with him, especially after he became a teenager. Then the war started. The Small Boy became a Captain. He was fifteen years old.

◊

At the bar, The Minister found Big Mama behind the counter drinking her fourth bottle of Nile Beer as she counted the money she had made during the day. Her drinking had worsened after the war, and every time she saw The Minister, she drank more. She felt his presence before she saw him. Her hands trembled, her heart raced before she remembered that the war had ended. She folded the money and put it inside her bra.

"Minister," she said, "how good of you to grace us with your presence. Shall I bring the usual?"

"Yes, yes, the usual. But can one of the girls serve us, eeh?" He winked his good eye at a girl dressed in a tight, black dress cleaning plastic tables. His left eye had a patch. Shrapnel from a bomb.

"The girls are busy," Big Mama said.

"Busy? For The Minister?" He raised the eyelid on his good eye, and Big Mama looked away from his distorted face. "We're hungry tonight," he said. She turned back toward him and saw him lick his lips in a way that made her recoil. She stared at his large suit, which hung off his body and reminded her of the days they used to call him Small Boy. To her, he'd always be Small Boy.

"No, not for The Minister," Big Mama smiled. "The nightshift has just started. They're getting ready. They'll come out soon," Big Mama said, and went off to fetch the glasses of *waragi* and slices of lemon.

◊

During the war, when they came to the bar, the young boys and girls called him Captain and each other Ninja. Big Mama used to

115

watch them struggle to carry Kalashnikovs bigger than them, drunk on power and war. As she listened to them, they sounded as though they were chatting about games.

"Captain, did you see his eyes before you shot him? Did you see them, big eyes, eeh, about to explode out of his sockets?"

"And he pissed on himself."

They laughed. "A grown man, Comrade, pissing in his pants!"

"Oh how he begged for his life . . . please, please don't shoot, don't do this. Take the money, take everything, please."

"Oh, but Captain is tough, he shoot him in the head, right in the head. Psst . . . blood. To the Captain," they shouted and gulped the *waragi*.

Big Mama would flinch as she listened, but she let the girls serve them *waragi*. They were fighting the rebels, fighting for peace. Sometimes she barked at them to stop. Then, they were still children. They listened to her.

◊

The bar had started to buzz with people, and The Minister invited more to join his table. Red, yellow, and blue bulbs dangling from black wires were switched on, exposing brown brick walls covered with soot and bullet holes. Bob Marley songs mixed with the loud conversations in the bar. They breathed in the smoke from roasting meat. The Minister's loud and boisterous voice carried throughout the bar and could be heard praising the government and calling out for Uganda Waragi for everyone. Regular *waragi* would not do.

After knocking back another bottle of Nile Beer, Big Mama returned with tin candles, a bottle of Uganda Waragi, and small glasses on a metallic tray, which she placed on the dirty-white plastic table. She put a thin slice of lemon in each glass, twisted the cap from the bottle, and poured the clear liquid into the glasses until they overflowed. Once they were all full, she handed each man a glass, the clear liquid spilling on her hands. She remembered how, after what had happened during the war, she constantly thought about putting poison in their drinks. But then the rebels were defeated.

MUKWANA

Jubilations everywhere. Rebuilding the town was planned, but never commenced. Then, putting up with The Minister and his henchmen seemed a small price for peace.

During the first few years after the war, Big Mama focused on the future. It was best to forget the past, everyone said, no need to re-open wounds. But, The Minister would come in his Hummer and the wounds would start to itch and she had to scratch them.

Big Mama satiated the illusion of peace with alcohol, and the second she was sober, the price for peace weighed her down.

"How about our roasted meat? And the girls, why aren't they serving us?" The Minister asked, his voice cutting through her thoughts.

"Minister, you're already served," Big Mama said.

"We want their company, eeh?" The Minister said.

"They'll come as soon as they're ready," Big Mama said. She thought about drinking something stronger. She needed to make herself bolder.

"That one," he pointed at the girl serving drinks at another table. "She's ready, isn't she?"

"Patience, Minister, they'll come soon," Big Mama said.

"And the music, do something about the music, eeh, put something more, more . . ." he danced with his shoulders and put his hands up in the air as though the words were lingering there.

"Upbeat," one of the henchmen said.

"Yes, upbeat," The Minister said.

"How about the money for the drinks?" Big Mama asked.

"Later, I pay you later."

"Now, you pay now. Last time you didn't pay," she said and stretched her right hand out until it was in front of him.

"Ah, I didn't pay. Well, one for the war. I fought the war, for all of you," he winked his good eye and pointed his index finger at everyone around the table.

"Minister, you did, indeed you did, but I have to buy food, pay rent, keep the business going."

"I'll pay you later," he said.

They glared at each other.

◊

The war that had started in a small village dragged on and engulfed the whole country, turned neighbors into enemies, tore families apart. The children became young soldiers who carried the Kalashnikovs confidently, the guns no longer weighing them down. Their faces wore hard lines and their stories became more violent, more personal. Women being raped, bottles pushed inside their vaginas. Children made to kill their parents so they could join the war, and those who couldn't fight were left limbless. Villages were erased, farms set on fire, to flush out the rebels, the soldiers said. Big Mama pleaded with them to stop telling the war stories. They didn't.

Truck Town became a ghost town. Big Mama's bar that used to be awash with customers, loud music, and girls that were paid to entertain, became empty. A handful of regulars turned up, but most of them left as soon as the young soldiers came, for they'd get drunk and do random things like command whomever was in their sight to climb on a table and dance on his head, drink a bottle of beer in thirty seconds. Sometimes they'd cock their guns at someone's head, threaten to shoot, and laugh at the look of terror in their victim's eyes. At other times, they went outside and fired their guns into the Ugandan darkness.

These things used to frighten Big Mama, but she'd drink her *waragi* and pray for the war to end so the children could go back to being children, until the night the bar ran out of *waragi*.

That night, they arrived earlier than they normally did. As soon as they entered the bar, Big Mama knew something was wrong. It was the way Captain paced up and down the bar, the way he cocked his gun at the slightest sound, and the way he drank the *waragi*—too quickly and straight from the bottle. They were silent. The bar was quiet. No tales of horror. Just drinking and waiting: Big Mama for them to leave, and they, for the night to turn into day. And then, Captain asked for another bottle of *waragi*. One of the girls, Irene, went to get one but came back empty handed.

"Bring something else. Gin. Whiskey, anything," Captain said.

MUKWANA

"There's nothing left."

"Nothing? What do you mean nothing is left?"

Irene shrugged.

"Is that how you talk to me?"

"It's finished," she said.

"Let's go look." He grabbed her by the arm as he kicked chairs and tables out of the way and took her into the store at the back where the others pushed crates on to the floor breaking empty bottles until one of the Ninjas called out to the Captain; he had found a bottle of *waragi*.

"You lie," Captain said. "Why you lie to me?" he asked holding the bottle in his hands.

"Captain." One of the others cocked his gun.

"No," he shook his head and walked over to Big Mama who was behind the counter. "She lied to me. Why? Let's go," he said and kicked her. Before Big Mama could comprehend what was happening, before she could throw herself at them, before she could fight for Irene, they had left. She never saw Irene again, and she feared to ask; she had heard them boast about the killings so many times. Her guilt was immediate.

◊

Big Mama sang along to Bob Marley's "Get Up, Stand Up," her balance slightly off as she returned to the table with the tray of sizzling roasted meat. She continued to sing, her face breaking into smiles as she listened to The Minister listing on his fingers all the things the new government had done for its people:

"We have built schools, hospitals, roads. Everyone has electricity," and then he stood up and shouted, "Government of Change, oye, Government of Change, oye," his fist raised in the air, his good eye wide open, and the people in the bar that had now filled all the tables and chairs, roared along with him.

Even Big Mama joined and shouted until everyone else had stopped and all their eyes turned upon her. She burst into laughter, "Minister, you're not serious?" she said. "Only a week ago, my auntie died of malaria because the only clinic we have in this town had no tablets. Government of Change, oye," she shouted.

The noise slurped out of the bar. Not even the sound of breathing could be heard. Even "Get Up, Stand Up," came to an end. The silence turned into fear paralyzing everyone in the bar, reminding them of the children with guns.

"Eeh, baby steps, this is a big country. We start in Kampala and then we come to the small towns and villages," The Minister said.

"But then, Minister, stop talking like this government has done much apart from steal, steal, steal money. The money for the schools has been stolen. The money for the hospitals is gone. The money for the roads, vanished!"

"Big Mama," The Minister's face no longer jovial. His voice steel. With his good eye half closed, his right hand moved down to his pockets and he felt for his pistol as he clenched his teeth.

"Oops, am sorry, did I misspeak?" Big Mama's voice was high pitched. She walked over to him and held him from behind, "Our Minister," she sang, swaying from her right foot to her left, "doesn't like to hear anything bad about the corrupt government. Our Minister, he used to be Small Boy . . ."

The Minister turned his head around and faced her for a second and then straightened himself in his chair. He picked a piece of meat and threw it into his mouth. It burned his tongue. He spit it into his hands, blew on it, threw it back in his mouth and started to chew. "Let's eat," he said, "this one is drunk."

Everyone released their breath and Bob Marley's "Africa Unite" started to play.

"Big Mama," The Minister called as she walked away. He waited for her to turn towards him and said, "I want the girls to serve me."

Big Mama slowly walked back and stood in front of him. "They're not going to serve you tonight," she said. "They're busy, busy, busy."

The Minister leapt to his feet, slammed the table sending the food and glasses flying and ending up on the clothes and shocked faces of the people seated around the table. In one step, he was at the next table. He grabbed a girl pouring drinks for a group of young women, dragged her and stopped in front of Big Mama, his pistol on the girl's temple. The henchmen, following their leader, raised their Kalashnikovs.

Big Mama stared at him, but all she saw was the vision of Irene as she was hauled out of the bar. She thought about all the things she could have done to stop him from taking her away and remembered the many ways she had thought about avenging her.

"Oh no," she said. "The Minister is angry again. What's the matter this time? Oops, The Minister doesn't like questions. What's The Minister going to do now? Kill again?"

"Big Mama . . ."

"Yes, Minister, did I misspeak again?"

The Minister let go of the girl and pointed his pistol at Big Mama.

"You should never disrespect me," he said and pushed her down. "I didn't fight for this country to be belittled by the likes of you." He yanked her up and made her kneel in front of him.

Big Mama knelt, her back straight. The pistol in her face sobered her. Her heart pounded fast, and she closed her eyes tightly as though that would deflect the impact of the bullet. She had survived the war, and now she was going to die a senseless death. She could apologize, ask the girls to serve him and his henchmen, and perhaps everything would go back to normal. Except, she knew it wouldn't, it couldn't. During the war, she was frightened. One girl could disappear so others could live. Big Mama wanted to live but instead of living, she was dying slowly. If only she could tell them that she never asked anyone to fight for her, to destroy her life. If only. They chose to pick up guns, and now they were carrying on as though that was justification for continuing the torture. She heard the gun click and held her breath and thought about death, and visualized a long road of light and blood, and felt Irene's mercy.

Jill McDonough

But Yet

That summer poetry class at the university I said over
and over knock it off with *but yet*. It was their most
pointed transition statement. They said it so often, imbued
with such heft, I started to love it. I warned them about this
friction: *I know you're serious. But yet I laugh.*

One cried once. Not because I'm a jerk, not because *but
yet*. He was reading his poem on PTSD, or trying.
Next thing you know he's trying to get his shit
together while we all hold very still. Just there
with the chill of chalkboards, cement blocks. All on his side.
First day, he said since he got back sometimes
he just tears up, so don't freak out if he does.

So when we see him crumple, I say *okay,
let's take ten minutes*, take him outside to stand
in the sun while he hitches *I'm sorrys*, tries to take
a decent breath. It's not in my lesson plan
but I pull him to me, hold his big body
in my arms, saying *shh* until he can stop
sobbing. Then I squeeze quick, say *you trying to get
me fired?* and he laughs. I step back, say *so not
appropriate* and he's better. For now. But yet.

Martha Collins

Blue

the river almost blue, the sky bluer,
the boat on the river, the river cool
as the stone steps to the seven-storied
stone pagoda, and behind it the blue

car that fifty years ago took the monk
from here to the streets of the large city
where he opened the blue door and sat
while gasoline spilled over his body

and did not move while his body burned
to black (except the heart that would
not burn) beside the blue car that is now
behind the pagoda beside the river

Hue, Vietnam

Marjorie Agosín

Footsteps at Night

—Translated from the Spanish by Alison Ridley

At night,
The footsteps of men with faces like hyenas,
The footsteps of vultures,
The footsteps that come looking for us, to rob us of life,
The footsteps of the Nazis,
The thieves of lives,
The thieves of art,
The footsteps . . .

I want to leave this city that banished you,
That robbed your garden of poppies and stole your smile,
But you stop me from beyond the grave.
You tell me to wait,
That a new day always dawns.

Trembling, I search for you.
I cross the threshold of death
With its dark avenues.
I quietly entreat you to let me return
To my other country,
To the country of life.

You detain me in the darkest of fogs,
And I remain in order to find you.
I grasp the handrail of the staircase of the house that witnessed your
    escape.

Now I know what you do not want . . .
You do not want me to run away.

Radiant Vienna, Savage Vienna

–Translated from the Spanish by Alison Ridley

They set fire to the garden close to your house.
From the balcony you felt the leaves dancing, the passage of time.
Unfettered by time, stories survive in the absence of words,
The light shines brilliantly,
The tenuous rains arrive,
Around you wellbeing and love for your city,
Carriages passing slowly by your house,
The fragrance of chestnuts,
The dreams at dawn.
You loved that life,
And you faced each day without hesitation.
Such was your city,
Your street,
Your balcony.
Splendid Vienna,
Sinister Vienna,
Vienna that yearned to welcome only dead Jews,
Savage Vienna,
Pilfering Vienna.

Treacherous Vienna

—Translated from the Spanish by Alison Ridley

Dark Vienna,
Somber Vienna,
Vienna where the dead howl,
Vienna where at night you can still hear
Echoes of the deceased, of the living.

Vienna where they pounded on your door,
Stole your voice,
Took your son away.
He scoured the dark sidewalks with acid.
Everyone laughed at the laboring Jews,
At the Jews in that city that robbed them of their name and
    their light.

Vienna awash in murderous hands,
Awash in eyes blind to the pain of others.
Repressive Vienna,
Adeptly deceitful Vienna,
Elegant and treacherous Vienna.

In that somber Vienna
You sewed stars of David.
Your hands were like stars.
They reached up to heaven.
They were diaphanous.

AGOSÍN and RIDLEY

The Photography of

VIRGINIA DWAN

Selections From Her Book

Flowers

Laura Laing

Your Leaving

I don't remember your leaving.

I remember your coming home—the argument I had with your parents, the bubble I felt around myself while among joyful families, the Shoney's breakfast we shared before coming home to have sex on the kitchen floor. I remember the jubilant look on your face, your blue eyes glowing, like lasers, over cheeks burned by the African sun. I remember the eight-inch knife you slid under the driver's seat of your car. I remember the night sweats and bad dreams and that you were losing hearing in your left ear.

But I don't remember your leaving.

I remember the weeks leading up to your departure, fuzzy memories of the night you came home to tell me that you were going. We sat on the sad little patio of our condo, on beach chairs with unraveling seat straps, smoking Marlboro Lights, even though we had quit two years before. Darkness covered us like a blanket, and we were numb. You were headed to war, to Somalia, a country so broken it had no government, but this fact was slippery, a puzzle with a complex, indecipherable solution. The president ordered you to make peace and gave you an M-16 rifle and flak vest. You said it was like being invited to dinner, only to climb with a weapon on your back through a broken kitchen window, rather than stand under the front porch light, ringing the doorbell.

I remember the five months you were gone, when I felt both empty and content, filling that emptiness with my own choices: watching hours of television, going out for Mexican food with friends, teaching math to my students. I remember how the seven-hour time difference made you seem as far away as you actually were. I remember sending you care packages, like you were a college student spending weekends in a chemistry lab. In those five months were Labor Day, your birthday, Halloween, Veterans Day, Thanksgiving.

There's grittiness to these memories. They are sand in my eyes, irritating, never fully washed away. This is forever; this is permanent, impairing my sight without blinding me. The before and during and after has altered the present and future. Yet, I don't wonder how we would be different if you hadn't gone. Because you did go. And I stayed. We traveled along parallel lines for those five months.

◊

We watched *Platoon* at a theater where we could drink pitchers of beer and smoke. It was the summer before our senior year in college, and you were an ROTC Army cadet, all hoo-wah going into the darkened room, where we found seats together at a long table. The floor was sticky and the air thick with smoke. I thought we were so cool, but I was terrified. I had never watched a war movie.

From the first scene, I felt gutted. That damn soundtrack— Samuel Barber's "Adagio for Strings"—reached into my belly, pulling one slick and shiny nerve at a time. You grew quieter and quieter, your bravado deflating with each horrific scene. I hid my eyes as much as I could, gulping Bud Light and pulling cigarette after cigarette from the cardboard box. You lit each one for me with a plastic Bic you kept in your front jeans pocket. As the credits rolled, we sat slumped in our chairs, unable to move.

We left groggy—from the beer and the brutality of the images. I couldn't cry or rage against the ways in which the characters were made to feel in the heart of violence, how they became feral and unfeeling. I was like Charlie Sheen stumbling from the jungle, wounded, inhuman somehow, unsure of what to do with what I had witnessed. War required a barbarism that I couldn't muster, and I couldn't imagine you ever feeling.

You went back to your ROTC lessons, and I became inured to a dissonance—your sunny disposition and the ruthlessness your chosen career seemed to require. *Platoon* introduced to me images

137

of what you could do and what you might experience, war scenes that I understood were possible but couldn't reconcile with who I knew you to be: kind, gentle, generous to a fault. I knew I would never fully understand, and so I accepted the inconsistency, waited for you to show me how the variables—you and the Army—created a solvable equation, as you practiced hand-to-hand combat and learned to shoot. My work was different than yours.

◊

I never expected to be an Army wife. I never expected us to stay together after college graduation. In the last month of our senior year, when you turned to me and asked, *Should I join?* I gave you the most honest answer I could. I told you to think about what you might regret. You chose the Army over a graduate degree in mathematics. There's no way to know if that was a good choice, if avoiding regret is a good measure.

Two weeks later, moments after you were commissioned and the day before we both graduated, you posed for pictures with your father—you in dress greens and regulation-height pumps, he in his dress blues—and I watched from behind the camera. We stood in the May air, three years after consummating our secret love, thinking we were facing the reality of our choices and our fate. You were so happy to please your father, to follow in his footsteps as a commissioned officer. You wanted desperately for him to be proud of you. Maybe you knew how much you had already disappointed him, leaving little clues about our love, and how that disappointment would lay in a thick and heavy smear across the next four years, even before he asked, tearfully, why you rejected men. But this moment, captured in photographs, was a happy time for you. I was fearful. You were no longer playing soldier. You were one.

◊

I began my education in war that fall, when you went to Officer Basic Course at Ft. Eustis and I helped you study for your tests. I learned that hydrogen cyanide gas smells like almonds and mustard gas like garlic. I learned that each platoon has a designated chemical warfare tester, a soldier who acts as a canary in a coal mine. We argued about the ethics of this practice, and you reminded me that one death is preferable to many. *That is true,* I thought. *But what if that one death is you?* One of your instructors spent his years in Vietnam collecting dead American bodies from the jungle. He was intent on imparting the seriousness of what you were getting into. My imagination played movie clips of the second-hand stories you told me, and those images follow me like a caustic mist.

It had been more than fifteen years since the Vietnam War ended. You and I had become adults in that time—a period of relative peace, of tearing down walls, of ending Apartheid, of economic growth—but because of you I was skin close to war's gut-churning grief and anxiety. Because of your gender, you could not sign up for combat, so you joined the Army's transportation corps, learning to lead soldiers in convoys and unload cavernous Navy ships carrying the supplies of battle. You were preparing for an ancillary role, one close enough to combat to receive danger pay. We had no idea how long the Gulf War would last, whether you would finish your training in time to ship off. But this war was short, a reprieve we silently celebrated.

Three years after you graduated from OBC, you did leave for a war masked as a peacekeeping mission. After losing his impetuous battle that would have let you serve openly, a victory that would have made me visible, President Clinton sent you to Somalia, where you were a platoon leader, the officer in charge of security on the Port of Mogadishu. I didn't even know which side of the continent Somalia was on.

Before this, I thought you were safe. I thought your gender would keep you from harm. I thought this liberal president would keep our country out of conflicts. I thought you had skirted danger. And so we smoked and talked and planned for hours on our patio. In the darkness, we interlocked our fingers between the chairs. In our other hands, cigarettes glowed hot and red as the fear pulsing through our veins.

You arrived in Mogadishu at the end of July, almost two months after twenty-four UN soldiers from Pakistan were killed in an ambush by the Somalia National Alliance. In response, the military unleashed airstrikes, pummeling Mogadishu and the surrounding area. The port was still on high alert, carefully screening each Somali who entered the gates. Watching the black-as-tar men in skirts walking across the asphalt holding hands, your soldiers learned the Somali word for *faggot*. They shouted it from the guard towers. You didn't tell them to stop.

You learned to say *waan ku jeclahay, naag*: I love you, woman.

You called me every single day from a satellite phone in the operations office. This was illegal, of course, but you didn't care. The line was probably tapped, but we soon abandoned my masculinized code name, speaking openly and freely. You needed to connect with me, and I was glad for that. No news was bad news. Sometimes you told me funny stories, and sometimes I could hear people joking around in the background. You said you were losing weight because of the diarrhea and that the Somali women were beautiful. You didn't tell me about anything dangerous, not at first. There were things you couldn't say and things you didn't want to say.

On August 8, four US Army military police were killed, when a command-detonated landmine exploded under their vehicle.

◊

On August 19, you called me at 5:00 AM, before my alarm went off. You told me not to worry; you were safe. On a convoy across the city to headquarters to get the mail, your truck was hit by a command-detonated landmine. The blast clipped the front of your vehicle, sending it into the air and landing on the other side of a massive crater. Sniper fire followed. When it was all over, everyone was safe—except for a couple broken bones and shrapnel wounds. You called from the medical center. Your parents, who lived one town over, got a different call, an official one from the Army.

That day, the news hit national and our local media, and the next morning, your high school senior photograph, provided by your parents, was on the front page of the *Daily Press*. I would have given them a candid shot: you in your camouflage uniform, leaning forward with your elbows on your knees, staring directly into the

140

camera, smiling. Instead, you wore a classic black drape and delicate, opal earrings, your eyes focused up and to the left, as if looking to heaven. I came home from school that afternoon to find messages from friends, telling me in frantic voices that the photo made them think you were dead.

The newspapers and television stations didn't call me, but your parents did interviews. Days later, they were on the front page, talking about the family's military tradition, telling the world that they were proud of you. Then they were on the six o'clock news, being interviewed from their living room. Your father said that women should serve in support roles, like yours, but not in combat. He didn't seem to understand that all of Mogadishu was a combat zone.

I pulled into the nucleus of our small community and waited to hear that you'd be coming home. Besides cuts on your face and arms, you were not injured. The Army gave you a Purple Heart and made you stay. Over the next year, the hearing in your left ear would deteriorate.

◊

The night of October 3rd in Mogadishu was a gorgeous, sunny Sunday for me. You were shrouded in darkness, and all hell was breaking loose. Two Black Hawk helicopters had been shot down in the middle of the city and the port was receiving fire. You described the scene to me: helicopters flew low and loud, and bomb tracers looked like fireworks streaming across the black sky. I imagined you in a messy military office, looking through a giant window into the abyss.

We talked for an hour—me, curled up on the sofa, the first piece of furniture we bought together—as the battle raged around you. I don't remember being afraid. If you could talk, you were OK. But then you told me to hold on. You said you needed to give your rifle strap to your buddy, because she had used hers as a tourniquet earlier. *Don't you need it?* I asked shakily. The scene was suddenly less like an Independence Day celebration; the bomb tracers weren't fireworks at all. But I couldn't let the enormity of your situation sink in. I couldn't think you were in danger—even after the landmine.

My only protection was knowing that you would come home alive. My mode of survival was to disconnect from reality, to acknowledge and then dismiss the danger reaching out to us.

◊

In mid-October, I planned to fill our front garden with purple and yellow pansies. In our mild Mid-Atlantic weather, they would last through the winter and spring, for your inevitable homecoming. I consulted friends and books. I chose a local gardening supply center forty-five minutes from our house. I'd never spent money on such an extravagance, and I was nervous I would fail, waste my resources.

On a Saturday, I bought bags of fresh soil, fertilizer, four flats of pansies and six pots of purple cabbage. I upgraded our second-hand water hose and sprayer. I bought a wide-tooth rake and a shovel to mix the hard clay with store-bought soil. After preparing the ground, I spaced the plants carefully, measuring their depth based on the experts I had consulted—regimented rows of baby pansies and cabbage interwoven with rich brown earth. Then I picked off each pansy blossom, one by one. I wanted the plants to send energy to the roots, so that they would grow strong and spread into a lush mass of leaves and flowers.

For weeks, I watered daily, added fertilizer, and broke off new buds. The stems and leaves grew, filling the bed. In mid-November, I stopped deadheading the plants, letting them bloom. The result was exactly as I had planned. A subtle welcome home for you, in the colors of our university, a way of saying, *You are not in Africa anymore.* Our own victory garden.

◊

You came home three days before Christmas. Your father, the retired Air Force colonel, arranged to meet your plane at Langley Air Force base, with your mother and older brother. Your mother told me this on the phone, days before your arrival, but she didn't invite me. I invited myself by asking when I should be at their house. The event was for *family only,* your mother said. I called them back after hanging up, after pacing in our tiny dining room for ten minutes, talking myself into asking for what I deserved. Your father answered the phone, and I told him they were being unfair. I said that you would want me to be there. He stuttered, stalled, eventually got the words out: I was not welcome. I pushed harder. He didn't budge, and I finally relented.

The next day, I wrote your parents' names on two fat strips of masking tape and affixed them to the bottoms of my shoes. I stomped through my classes in order to hold back the tears, letting my fists uncoil.

◊

Your plane landed as scheduled before dawn. You and your soldiers walked down the stairs into the darkness. Your mother, father, and brother hugged you, ate pizza with you, and talked to more reporters. Then they got back in your father's Cadillac to drive the mile home. You got on a bus and rode to the Army base.

I followed the directions you gave me for where you would be dropped off. The lights of the squat, cement building streamed into the night. People were everywhere—wives, children, parents, and soldiers. Men in flannel shirts and blue jeans hoisted television cameras onto their shoulders, pointing them at crisply dressed reporters holding microphones. Children wore their Sunday best. Parents held signs emblazoned with their sons' and daughters' names. The atmosphere was of quiet celebration. These were experienced military families in a military town. They, like me, were bracing themselves for the person who would reenter their lives.

I was alone. No one, not a soul, spoke to me while I waited on the curb, back far enough from where the bus would park and release its passengers.

When the bus arrived, the news people rushed to the door, flipping on spotlights for live and recorded shots of the homecoming. There was a cheer and then things got quiet. The families, including me, stayed back. One by one, the soldiers, with their sand-colored

143

uniforms tucked into jungle boots and sleeves rolled up, stepped down from the bus to the asphalt road. The bright camera lights forced their open pupils to dilate quickly, painfully. The trip home had taken more than a day, but no amount of time could fully prepare them for the jolt of winter or the faces of their families. Each time a soldier's feet landed on firm ground, a family celebrated, while he looked out into the bright lights of the cameras, searching for his people.

You were one of the last to disembark. I remember that you were so tiny, a foot shorter than everyone else, your uniform hanging on you like sagging skin. Mostly, I remember your eyes, which were so much bluer than I'd recalled—your sunburned cheeks, a contrast I didn't expect. Everything but your eyes seemed out of focus to me.

We hugged briefly on that curb, and then you went inside the little building with news reporters. You did a few short interviews—local girl survives landmine blast, stays in combat, and then comes home. You were in Army officer mode, and your responses came easily. I don't remember seeing the film on air.

Families left, one by one, with their soldiers in tow, looking forward to and, I imagined, for some also dreading a few weeks of rest and relaxation. After you finished with your interviews, you joined me outside again. You lit a Salem and offered me one. I had quit again back in August, before I started the school year, and so I refused. I never liked menthols anyway.

The sky had lightened considerably, despite clouds fat with rain. By the time we got to Shoney's for breakfast, the rest of the world had awakened. We ate in a two-person booth among shipyard workers—passing in the morning, from night to day shift.

◊

My war education continued for months, years, even after you left the Army. I knew you would be different. I had a sense of the effects of trauma; in preparation for your homecoming, I had learned a bit about PTSD. I expected the nightmares. I expected you to sleep for dozens of hours at a time and then stay awake for dozens more. I expected you to tell me that you couldn't, didn't want to talk.

144

I became a canyon, echoing your words and actions—softer, more gently—bringing them into the hot sun so that you could bear witness to who you were then. I became attuned to subtle shifts in the air around you. I watched for your wandering thoughts, a glint of light that caught your eye, the sharp sound of a backfiring car. I held you while you sobbed in fear. I washed sweat-soaked sheets. I left the knife under your driver's seat, afraid of how your eyes might turn wild with panic if I acknowledged it. You had become paranoid and somehow invincible; you believed you were in harm's way and that you could ward off danger wielding a blade.

Most of you was the same, intact. A doctor discovered the piece of shrapnel lodged in your ear, a little pearl crafted from layers and layers of scar tissue. He removed it, and your hearing was instantly restored. You drove home gripping the steering wheel in terror, as 18-wheeler trucks screamed by your open window.

We moved together more slowly, sat in silence more often. We avoided the din of large crowds and came home early after outings with friends. You were both a wife and had a wife, and so we nurtured each other, but in the shadow of your trauma, I became smaller and smaller, putting your needs ahead of my own.

I was deeply afraid, which made me completely determined.

◊

There was no way to fully understand what could and would happen while you were gone, while you were there. Not just the diarrhea and landmines and rats and bullets, but the way those five months in 1993 rearranged us for the rest of our lives—me at home and invisible, you at war trying to be invisible. The way that half year changed you on a molecular level, made you different in ways we cannot comprehend even today, much less point at and say, *Yes, there. There is the evidence.* The transformation, my adaptation to your anxiety, was insidious, like a snake swallowing eggs from a bird's nest: quiet, clean, irrefutable but difficult to pull into focus.

I don't remember your leaving, but your absence carved a hollow space inside us, a space we are filling with a teaspoon. For the rest of our lives, you will be coming home.

Fiction

KRISTIE Betts LETTER

Witnesses

The purple triangle indicated Jehovah's Witnesses.

All of us with the purple triangles still talked of Katherina Waitz, the Roma trapeze artist. She, of course, had a black triangle and she, of course, had slipped through the barbed wire. She did it before the morning call, when the sky was just leaving black, and not one of us saw a thing. Our religion kept us honest, with zero escape attempts even though we had been here the longest. We had no idea what shape she made her body into to get away from even the dogs. The guards wanted to punish everyone, but our confusion looked like theirs. They still haven't found her, as far as we know, and we hope they never do.

They brought in Marya after most of us had been here for more than a year, and some of us for almost three. They found her near-feral in a forest and she still had wildness in her eyes. Besides resisting capture and being Polish, Marya's only crime was her Roma blood. Her black triangle did not bode well. The Nazis worried that the Roma would sully their breeding stock.

The blonde devils in charge of Ravensbrück showed the goal of this kind of purity. Their blue eyes flashed as they knocked sick women to the ground before kicking them.

We weren't allowed to pray aloud, but we all learned to say the words without moving our lips or lifting our eyes from the mud. They threw Marya toward us that night after shaving her roughly. Bugs were the reason they gave for the shave, but they cared little for our cleanliness. They did it so that beautiful girls like Marya felt diminished. One of us helped her up the planked stairs into the

146

squat building teeming with all of us who had been humiliated.

Every bed was overfull, in dormitories meant for a fraction of the women now piled into the bunks. Marya stood, faced the somber crowd and raised a hand to a bleeding cut on her scalp.

Fela approached Marya first and put a gentle hand on her shoulder. Fela must have been the age of Marya's mother and her hair had grown out to her shoulders.

"You can sleep over here," she said and lead Marya to the corner.

One of us gave her a piece of bread saved from a shift in the guards' kitchen and someone else made sure she had water. We shared a blanket but had no more than that to make her bed on the floor.

We hoped Marya had trapeze experience.

The black triangle indicated the "asocials" which included the Roma.

Heinrich Himmler planned our camp as a place for deviant women, our deviance being our religion, which deviated from the strict rules of the Reich. As Jehovah's Witnesses, we did not vote, we did not recognize worldly government, and would not raise our arms to Heil Hitler. Our first act of resistance was our hidden Bible. They took away our Bibles when we arrived but, despite our honesty and our commitment to the path of righteousness, we managed to save one, hiding it beneath the floorboards.

At first they put us in the sand pits, shoveling endless sand, which would get in our wooden clogs and wear the skin from our feet. After a time, they worked the Witnesses in positions of trust. We were reliable. We also took it upon ourselves to care for the new ones, and to write down a list of names of those they took away on trains.

"Try to sleep," we told Marya. She lay still on her thin blanket, but we all knew her eyes were open.

They called us to line up when the darkness was cold and complete. They often made us stand for more than an hour, hitting and spitting when our rows of five were anything but perfect. This *appell* was the hardest, the roll call that woke the camp and froze us to the core. The wind from the lake blew through our cotton uniforms.

Marya stumbled that first morning after her arrival, still not confident in her body.

"Don't make eye contact," Fela said. The new ones didn't know to attempt invisibility when the guards walked the *appell* line. Fela prayed for the women to fool the guards and then had to pray for forgiveness. Time left lots of room for prayer.

"Why?" Marya turned her head to look at the guards starting on the far west side of the lineup.

"It just invites them. You don't want that. Stare at your shoes."

Just in time, Marya stared down at the wooden shoes far too big to warm her cold toes inside them. She had no way of knowing that the guard with the shiny blonde braids was the cruelest, or that the man walking behind her chose the *kanichen*, the rabbits for the human experiments.

Fela had been in Ravensbrück the longest, almost for three years. She had refused to Heil Hitler in the most polite way. In the Jehovah's Witness way. Like all of us, she was kind even to the officers arresting her and taking away her Bible. Now, we all tried to thank God for the beauty on the other side of the barbed wire and for the service Fela could provide.

The purple triangle indicated Jehovah's Witnesses.

"I have to help the children." Talking about these children helped Marya agree to sit up, eat soup and stand for *appell*. She told us a story of the children she had been protecting. Like a Pied Piper, she had been leading a group of them.

We hoped we would lead her to become a Witness. She had the strength for it.

"Is it true you can send letters?" Marya's face was less gray. "I have to tell someone to go help the children I left behind when they captured me. They are still in the cabin in the woods."

A few were allowed to send letters, to add gloss to the fiction that Ravensbrück was simply a workplace, a refuge for women. Fela was one of these. There were strict rules and limits: six lines maximum and no mention of dogs, of death, of illness, of starvation,

148

of mutilation, of barbed wire, of babies not allowed to live, of the Jews and their permanent transfers, of bugs, of shaving, of the cold, of privation, of stinking holes, of bodies no longer able to function normally, of loose wrists, of collapse at *appell*, of the stench from the illness, of executions, of escape attempts, or of the suicide resistance.

We needed the politicals and we needed the criminals, whose green triangles meant they were clever, brave or both. They all had the contacts and three million ideas for how to sabotage Nazi efforts. We, however, were the ones trusted enough to be able to send letters.

Fela was allowed to write one letter a month. "We can send this letter about your children," she said. "But we must figure out the words to say."

Wiebke and two other red triangles joined the conversation. "I can get a letter to my aunt in Poland. She can take it to your village," Wiebke said. Our purple triangles would soon be turned red if we were caught committing the treason of political defiance.

We kept our covenants with God and hoped He would forgive us deception in order to save the lives of a dozen innocent children. No one could bear the thought of them alone.

"But at least they aren't here," Marya said. "At least they aren't here."

If the Germans found out where the Roma children were, they would round them up and send them to the children's camp. Several mothers at Ravensbrück had children at these camps and their faces said enough. "They cannot find them. We have to help them. Please, please, please." Marya wasn't a woman of God, but we knew at that moment she would give her soul to save these children. "You have to help them."

"Shhhh," we cautioned. Ranting and raving about the need to save someone led only in one direction. Quiet voices were key, as were no movements that would trigger a dog's suspicion.

"We have to help them," she repeated more quietly.

Red triangles indicated political prisoners.

Fela and Marya used urine to write at the bottom of the letter, dipping the wrong end of the pen into a steaming cup brought by Wiebke. In ink, they wrote carefully of being near a lake doing work in Germany. In urine, an invisible ink Fela's aunt would know to make visible, they wrote where the children were as exactly as Marya could describe a cabin in the woods.

"They won't look for our message, they will just think the letter smells of the latrine," Fela nodded. "This is a good plan."

"We can get the letter to those who can help in Poland," Wiebke said.

"Thank you for helping me," Marya placed a small kiss on the woman's cheek and turned to embrace Fela. "I know this is not what you do."

"Helping children is what I do," Fela nodded.

"What if they don't figure out what it means? What if they don't figure out where the children are?" Marya's fear made her freeze for a moment.

"This is our only hope."

One of us grabbed Marya's arm. "They will know. They will. We are sending it to someone who understands." The red triangles had connections in Warsaw, and a green triangle could get the letter to a group in Berlin. We couldn't fight, since our God would not allow it, but we could bear witness.

Thank God for the connections between the triangles.

The yellow triangle indicated Jews.

To help the Roma women was difficult, but even more difficult was to help the Jewish woman. They never got the good job assignments, and the arms of the guards came down on them twice as often and three times as hard.

Even the infernal dogs, Alsatians, seemed more willing to bite a yellow triangle. How did they know?

They never kept the Jews for very long. They "reassigned" them to the other camps and whispers indicated what happened during these reassignments. Fela started the list, which we kept hidden in the office, of all places. We listed all the Jewish women sent to Bergen-Belsen or Auschwitz. Their names were all we could save.

The prostitutes from Aachen told us what happened at the other camps. "They kill them all there," a teenager with several scars told us. "Everyone dies at Auschwitz."

"A lot of illness? Typhus?"

"No. Murder. In large groups."

"That's impossible."

But, despite our faith's privileging of truth, we knew we spoke a lie. Here is what was possible: We were fed soup in the morning, bread at night with the soup water. When the food trains ran slowly we had no bread. When we had semolina, we gave our portion to the sickest, since they often couldn't finish the cabbage. We tried. But, we had seen women not wake up because they didn't want to. We had seen the dogs kill a young woman whose baby had just died. Dozens and dozens had been taken by illness, dying in their own sick when we couldn't keep them clean. We'd seen beautiful blonde guard braids spattered with prisoners' blood. We knew it was possible that Ravensbrück would kill us all. But they had been feeding Fela for three years, so we had to hope that all that soup wasn't for naught.

"How can they do that?" we asked. "Just kill?"

"They took allegiance to that man."

A prostitute shrugged.

"I don't even know if he's a man. What if these are end times?" Our fingers reached for the small Bibles no longer in our pockets.

"A thousand years. A thousand years." We knew Christ would come for a thousand years of peace, but we prayed for those years to start now.

◊

Marya's wooden clogs made her stumble. They didn't bother much with sizes and Marya's were twice as big as her feet. We would have to help her fill them in with leaves or cloth. If we left the shoes too large, they would get stuck in the dark mud after a rain.

"Where is the lake?" she said. "I saw a lake when we came in by the Furstenberg station." We had all been through this station, past Furstenberg church, whose beautiful spire could be seen from the camp gates.

"The lake is on the other side of the barbed wire," we told her.

The next day, Fela pulled a photograph from her pocket when she got back from her job remodeling leather and cloth from coats and bags confiscated from prisoners who could surely use the warmth and protection now. The workers had to recut coats they longed to wear. In Fela's job, she also cleared out the possessions left behind in pockets. When they brought the women in from the trains, Fela watched the coats carefully to match them to owners. She returned the photograph to a black triangle who cried in joy to see the photograph of the child.

The black triangle indicated the "asocials" which included the prostitutes.

The day after she arrived, Marya touched the black triangle sewn on top of her blue-striped uniform. "What does it mean?" she asked.

"Asocial," we said. "They identify people by their groups." We didn't tell her that the categorization included more than just her people. The asocials were the Roma, yes, but also the prostitutes and the women who loved each other. A few others were there because they were so poor that they were beggars or homeless before the war. For them, Ravensbrück wasn't so different, except they couldn't drink alcohol as a numbing agent.

Liesel stopped and rubbed her thumb over Marya's triangle. "Looks like we match."

"Are you Roma?" Marya's confusion showed in her dark brows.

"No, asocial." Liesel had worked as prostitute in Berlin. "That doesn't seem quite the way to describe me. Asocial." She laughed.

Another one with a scar that ran from her eyebrow to jaw nodded. "The men find me quite social."

◊

LETTER

The cold was biting, but still the roll calls went on for hours. We would all press our shoulders together to help even the weakest stand. The criminals helped us. The shiny boots kicked and the whips lashed out for any perceived infractions. The female guards wore black capes, like large evil birds. The pretty guards were the same. On a particularly lovely day, the blonde guard Emma Zimmer kicked a prisoner in the face for having pretty curls.

As Marya's hair began to grow, it curled. "We must make your hair flat," Fela said.

"How?"

"We can use just a little mud to weight it."

Marya sighed.

"Emma Zimmer is a sadist," we reminded her.

"A what?"

"A monster. Inhuman. She's barely older than you."

Indeed, the woman had soft gold hair in perfect braids. Her blue eyes matched the blue sky. All beauty is not beautiful. Soft woods and sparkling lakes surrounded Ravensbrück, a mismatch between the scenery and the horror.

Marya let us slick her hair with mud so that the natural curl wouldn't be mistaken for vanity.

"Why do the Nazis hate everyone?" Marya had grace and a sophistication in her movement, but at times she seemed a child.

"Nazis are full of hate." Fela spoke softly and glanced behind her. "This is not God's way but the devil's."

"How can we kill them all? Can we kill the guards here?" Marya swept her arm in an arc.

"Killing is not the answer."

"But they want to kill us!"

"A sin is not an answer to sin."

"Are the other places better? This place is horrible."

"They don't come back from the other places."

The red triangles indicated political prisoners.

Some prisoners were kept completely out of sight. Fela said that Genevieve de Gaulle, niece of Charles de Gaulle, was kept in isolation, with better provisions, because Heinrich Himmler thought he might want to use her as an exchange prisoner. She had more food than the rest of us, but without anyone to whisper prayers with, how much food was worth the sorrow?

Whether or not Marya realized, we kept each other going, holding up the nearly-unconscious at *appell*, and strategizing to save our own lives.

The political prisoners sometimes were just like the Jehovah's Witnesses, caught in a web they never saw. Some wanted to plan destruction at every turn, despite the toll on the bodies in the wake. One of the red triangles almost caused us to turn on each other.

"We should plan an escape. If everyone works together there are so many more of us," Wiebke, a red triangle with a white scar down her cheek, said. "We could overthrow them." Her small mouth set in a severe line.

"We can't do that," we said. Our faith forbids any form of war.

"You purples just accept everything. You're complicit in this." Wiebke's voice strung out to almost a shriek.

"We're here because we don't agree."

"If you don't help your companions in adversity then you love Hitler." Her smooth political talk had fallen into near hysteria.

"He is the antichrist." And this we believed. In order to get to the one thousand years of peace, we had to endure this portion fueled by the devil.

We had a hard time finding forgiveness in our hearts for Wiebke, but God helped us.

◊

Witnesses refused to work at the Siemens factory because our religion prohibited us from making rockets. We would bake or clean for the guards who ruled with such cruelty and we would feed the dogs we'd seen tear flesh. But we couldn't build machines used to kill. They can murder us, but they cannot make us build war machines.

So they put us to work cleaning the officers' houses because they relied on us not to steal. "They trust the Jehovah's Witnesses even as they castigate us," we said.

The others sometimes took action. They dragged Leni, a red triangle, from the camp when they realized that she had sabotaged Siemens V-2 rockets in the factory in hopes that it would make Nazis lose the war.

"I sabotaged at least a hundred," she said. "I hope they explode all over the Nazis."

They tied Leni to a pole in the square and made all watch her execution. To Leni's credit, she kept talking the entire time. We made sure not to turn away, as many of the other women did, because we wanted Leni to see the love of God that shone in our eyes, so that she could take this with her on her journey.

We could have sworn that Emma Zimmer's smile broadened in delight when the shots rang out.

Green triangles indicated criminals.

We heard the slaps at the other end of the *appell* long before we could see her clearly at our end of the line. Emma Zimmer's teeth showed in her smile the next morning when she got close enough.

"*Guten morgen,*" she said to us.

"*Guten morgen,*" we replied without looking into her cornflower eyes.

"I wanted to use the dogs," she said. She leaned in. Behind her pretty white teeth, her breath reeked of sausage and rot. "The dogs would have been a more fitting end for that woman. Next time one of you decides to stage a little rebellion, you'll find the teeth at your neck."

In a movement so rapid we didn't see it coming, she slashed at Wiebke's neck when she said it. Wiebke lifted her hand toward the red lines, but Emma Zimmer slapped her hand away before it reached her chest.

We were more silent than usual that day.

◊

Usually, the green triangles meant they were clever, brave or both.

"We can tell them about the factory," Wiebke said. "Siemens is making rockets using our slave labor. That's valuable."

"We don't tell lies. We don't try to escape."

"It's not a lie. We're telling the truth," Wiebke said. The marks on her neck stood out against her pale skin.

"We accept our fate here. That's why they trust us to work in the kitchens or their houses." After our early abuse, the Witnesses had settled into a wary trust. We, of course, were still criminals with a contraband Bible.

"I don't care about escape. I have to send letters."

"We can send letters, but we must be careful." We knew what we could not mention. "We can't mention the factory."

"I know what to do. We have a system," Wiebke assured us.

We sent a short letter asking after various relatives to Berlin. We addressed Wiebke's aunt but addressed it to a place Wiebke had never been. Once Wiebke wrote her short sentences, Wiebke squatted in front of us and produced a steaming cup of urine.

No bodily functions had privacy or sanctity here.

Wiebke dipped a stick into the urine and began a painstaking process of writing about Siemens Electric Company V-1 and V-2 rockets being assembled by prisoners at Ravensbrück between sentences asking after Wiebke's various cousins.

Leni's death had inspired her.

The purple triangles indicated the Jehovah's Witnesses

We were offered an opportunity to leave Ravensbrück. All we had to do was renounce our religion and proclaim Adolf Hitler our divine leader. They'd made us a convenient document articulating all of it. We just had to sign the declaration card.

They took us in individually to present this deal. "We are thinking of your families, of your children."

What a work of the devil, to discuss the children.

Each of us remained strong but we wondered about Britta, who loved her twin sons, and about Fela, who pined for her daughter.

Because we all refused to sign away our faith, Dr. Sonntag chose Fela for a rabbit, a *kanichen*, and mangled her leg to examine the effects of the gas gangrene. Anni the lesbian doctor had cared for Fela to make sure she didn't die as many other rabbits did, as Dr. Sonntag tested ways to cure gas gangrene and compound fractures by inflicting them on his chosen experiments.

Anni cleaned the wound each day after Dr. Sonntag released Fela and her twisted leg from the infirmary.

Each of us wanted to remain strong but wondered when we saw the twisted mess of Fela's calf. We understood that Fela's bones now hurt so much that she could hardly bear it even with her prayers. But whatever temptation to betray our faith, none of us fell.

"That's Dr. Sonntag," Fela said to Marya, when the bald man again walked the *appell* line. "You must never make eye contact. He's the one who did this to my leg." Fela pulled up her skirt to show the blue-white mess of scar tissue on her right calf. Marya looked at Fela's leg and made a sound in throat as if she would vomit. She almost fell, but we pressed in with our shoulders to hold her up.

"It will save soldiers," Dr. Sonntag had explained. Of course Fela's lovely strong leg would not be saved in the process. Now Fela wanted to save the others from becoming rabbits.

◊

The next morning the trouble took a different form. Emma Zimmer led a man with a bulbous nose across the line of women at *appell*. He stared at the young ones. He put his thumb on the mouth of a girl. "Jewish?" he asked.

"Yellow triangle is Jew," Emma Zimmer said.

He kept walking. He stopped in front of Marya and lifted her chin. "Do you want to come to work for me in Berlin?"

She shook her head and angled her face back down toward her wooden shoes. She made a keening sound. Emma Zimmer slapped her across the face and the sound stopped.

The man with the lumpy nose moved down the line. He pulled two young women with crowns of blonde hair away from the rest. He led them toward the gate.

157

"If they ask again, you might want to go," Liesel said to Marya. "They can't let the whores starve to death. No fun for the soldiers if the women are skeletons."

"But why don't they just take all the prostitutes who are here?" Marya asked. Liesel wore the black triangle, but wasn't Roma or a lesbian. Too late, Marya realized what that meant. "I'm sorry."

"I'm not hurt," Liesel said. "I worked. But they want just the young ones. I'd go in a second." She snapped her fingers. "I hate the Nazis, but I hated the other men too."

The black triangle indicated the "asocials" which included the lesbians.

The next day at *appell*, Emma Zimmer honed in on Marya, whose hair had begun to curl as it grew back from the violent shave. The mud couldn't quite keep it down. She smiled and her eyes, blue as the devil's ice, stared into Marya's. "You are pretty. Are you sure you don't want to leave this place to work for the nice German boys?"

"Work how?" Marya knew this answer.

"You must be nice to them." Emma Zimmer smiled wider, and we could see her wrist twitch.

"I can't. I'm pregnant." We all might have gasped. Fela suspected, but all of us hoped that this dilemma would pass with God's will and thin soup. Not much could grow at Ravensbrück.

When Emma Zimmer's wrist leapt up to Marya's neck, she screamed. We don't know what she thought would happen with her revelation—a reprieve from the brothels?

"Come with me," Emma Zimmer said, her smile gone. She led Marya to the infirmary. We stood in our groups after we were released for work, looking toward the door. We didn't want Marya to go to the Revier. Sickness led quickly to death at Ravensbrück. This infirmary didn't heal the ill, but took them more quickly. Plus, the laboratories for rabbits were in the adjacent building.

Only Anni could help Marya now. Anni was a famous doctor before the Nazis, and she had the ability to help heal bodies that others thought beyond repair, using only the poor bits and pieces we could gather in Ravensbrück.

Only Anni wore the black triangle; her love, Inga, had the red triangle for her political work, but had recently discovered that the one person for her soul was this woman imprisoned beside her. Inga and Anni's love for each other kept them from suffering quite as much. We knew that our God frowned on such practices, but in Ravensbrück, this love had beauty.

"Marya needs help," we said. "Can you go to the Revier?"

Anni was allowed to assist the nurses at Ravensbrück, even though her knowledge far outstripped theirs.

"She doesn't want to keep living," Anni told us.

"Can we see her?"

"They won't let you in. I will try to bring her to you," Anni said.

"I will help you," Inga said, putting her hand on Anni's arm. We could see why they made each other stronger.

The next day Anni held Marya up to help her home from the infirmary. Her skin was the gray-white of our soup.

"She is very ill. There is too much bleeding," Anni told us. "She needs strength." We had saved soup with semolina, and Britta had a bit of sausage from one of the guard's houses. Perhaps meat could make Marya's blood strong again.

Marya's dark eyes had trouble focusing. Anni wrapped a clean uniform around Marya's stomach and tied it tightly.

Shh." Fela put a cloth on Marya's forehead. "I got you some soup from the bottom. It is very thick. You must eat it." Lost children were the wound that hurt everyone the most.

Somehow Fela convinced Marya to hold the tin cup. Without focusing her eyes, Marya lifted the cup to her lips.

When Marya fell asleep with the tin cup dangling on her hands, we asked Anni questions. "Will she live?"

"If the bleeding stops. She won't be able to have any more children."

Someone began to cry. It wasn't the first time.

"They never would have let Marya's baby live."

"Why?"

"Because she is Roma."

We all shivered.

The purple triangle indicated Jehovah's Witnesses.

Three days after Anni brought Marya back, Fela stumbled to *appell* with a high fever. We all knew what was happening and we all pretended we did not.

Fela's face reddened to brick, even though her feet were still cold. She moved them in her wooden clogs as if they were sleds she dragged with her ankles. Three of us had given her our blankets the night before when she couldn't stop shivering.

"It's God," she said when we led her back to her cot.

"What?"

"Tell Marya."

"Tell her what?"

Fela made a gesture like the sweep of Marya's arms, a graceful arc. We wanted Fela to be a Roma trapeze artist, ready to slip through barbed wire.

But she closed her eyes and went back into her congested breathing. She didn't speak again.

We wrote her name in perfect letters on the list we saved.

Judy Labensohn

Homecoming, 1982

I stood in the kitchen, neck crooked right, yelling at Les in Lebanon on the other end of the receiver. Ori writhed in the cradle of my left arm, his mouth attached to my left nipple. He sucked and paused with the rise and fall of my voice, and I was pissed that son and father were pulling me in opposite directions.

"You're close to the border," I shouted, my inflection converting the statement to a question. "Sharon said we're only going in forty kilometers." The late summer sun pounded on the window over the stove. Jerusalem, the city I loved, lounged in its Sabbath peace like a content partner after sex.

"What border?" Les screamed back. Motors rumbled behind him, and men shouted "*Yalla yalla*. We all have families on the home front." I imagined dust and sweat mingling with the smell of homesickness.

"The northern border," I shouted. Did Ori need a burp? Should I try to hook him back on the right side? The spit-up diaper wasn't near the phone. If I went for burping, he'd spit up all over me and the floor.

"So why am I looking down on Beirut?" Les yelled back, mad.

How the hell did I know why he was looking down on Beirut? I had enough on my hands. Maybe Sharon lied. What did I know? This was only my second war, my first as wife and new mother. As I maneuvered Ori onto my shoulder, the receiver dropped.

"Shit."

"What are you shitting about?" My husband's voice rose from the floor and filled the kitchen. I imagined his voice flying through

161

the shared August heat from Beirut to Jerusalem as I squatted to pick up the receiver without dropping Ori.

"I dropped the phone," I said. "What time is it?"

"How the fuck do I know, Kate? I haven't slept for seventy-two hours, and they're sending me into Beirut tomorrow."

I hooked Ori onto the right side, and he sucked peacefully. I asked Les why, what would he be doing there.

"Driving an armored vehicle," he said, his voice softer now and edgy. "I'm the guy who's collecting the wounded soldiers."

I heard "shoulders" and mentioned mine ached and asked when he'd be home. I sort of wanted him to come home already, after two months in Lebanon. But only sort of.

"A moving target," he said.

He sounded scared. Did he think he might die tomorrow in Beirut? Maybe he was calling to say goodbye. I had never heard him sound scared. He was always self-assured, excited to be defending the Jewish state, fulfilling his Zionist dream. Les scared? "You'll make peace for Galilee," I said and felt dumb as soon as the stupid name of the war that wasn't even called a war, but an operation, left my mouth.

He asked how Ori was, his voice far away, as if he were lost in the cedars above the city, ignoring the pushy loud soldiers vying for their turn on the phone.

"Fine." I didn't want to go into details, cry on his shoulder.

A loud boom sounded somewhere. Ori opened his eyes, let go of the nipple, looked at me for clues and when there were none, cried. I looked out the kitchen window to see if the explosion was nearby in Jerusalem. But, of course, it was Lebanon, near Les. "Was that a bomb?""

"No, sweetheart. It's July 4th at the Beirut Country Club . . . Give the little bugger a kiss from his *abba*," he said and hung up, as I remembered to say Good Luck.

◊

There was probably a Zionist protocol for this role of soldier's wife and new mother, but I didn't know it. Nobody taught it at *ulpan*.

There were no "How to Cope" columns in the easy Hebrew weekly. I knew I was supposed to put the needs of the soldier and the State of Israel above my own, but I couldn't when my first baby was three months old. I was so absorbed in his every breath and burp that everyone else seemed secondary, even my soldier husband waiting on a Lebanese hilltop for the order to invade. I was so ecstatic that I was succeeding in nursing, that Ori was actually gaining weight from my milk, despite my doubts and fears during the pregnancy. I had no energy for anyone beyond my breast.

Rubbing Ori's back, I decided to write Les later while Ori slept. I would tell him that I loved him and hoped he would take good care of himself in Lebanon, because we needed him at home. I would describe Ori's frequent smiles, shits, the hands that made bells ring, his miraculous mouth. I would let him know how much I loved nursing our son, holding him on the rocking chair during the day, singing "Hush Little Baby," and cuddling him at night. I'd tell him how during the eighth week, when I was taking a shower, milk shpritzed from my nipples. He'd like that. And yes, I wanted him to come home, despite his one failed visit in July.

◊

On that Friday afternoon, Les dragged himself into the apartment with his M-16 strapped over his back and a week's growth of beard. Ori cried when the scruffy face smelling of tank oil, dust and cigarettes touched his.

"My little soldier," Les said.

"One in the family's enough," I said.

"That's what I love about coming home," Les said, looking beyond me. "All the loving support I get for defending this fucking country . . ."

I couldn't understand why he was calling Israel "this fucking country," if he loved it so much. He loved the army, feeling part of the macho in-group, the know-it-alls, even though he had only been in the country six years and served eighteen months as a new "older" immigrant. He knew more army slang than most of the guys who had served the full three years.

That Sabbath was a disaster—me needing attention, Les needing more and Ori getting it all. No grandparents or aunts around to help. Friends' husbands also in Lebanon.

My only pleasure, other than Ori, came from my blooming geraniums on the roof garden and my only support from the neighborhood shopkeepers on Bethlehem Road. During the long summer afternoons after Ori woke up from his nap, I would water the garden and then strap Ori into the Snugli and carry him down the sixty-four stairs to Bethlehem Road. Those afternoons were my happiest moments when Les was in Lebanon.

First I'd cross the street to show Menachem HaLachmi how the little *fresser* was growing. Menachem would hand me a rugelach, knowing I loved the chocolate, almond pastry. He'd stretch his hands over the counter and give Ori's cheek a little pinch. "*Ezzeh motek. Ezzeh hamud,*" he'd say.

Then I'd stop at Zion Yehuda's shack, where he sold rubber bands, shoelaces and scarves. "*Sh'yehiyeh barie,*" Zion said. I wished him good health too and asked when he was retiring, since the permanent sign on the shack advertised a close-out sale. "Soon, soon," he'd say.

Ezekiel Grossman, the bald Bulgarian butcher, was not the caring type, so I just nodded to him as we walked by. He nodded back. At least he never overcharged me when I bought a fresh chicken.

Shmulik Shem-Tov, the Tunisian laundry man, always held his iron with one hand and patted me on the shoulder with the other, asking about Les in Lebanon and wishing me Good Luck. His son served in the regular army, also in Lebanon. "It's no picnic this war," he'd tell me, "even on the home front."

The Moroccan owner of the grocery store, Eliahu Ben-Eliahu, was usually too busy for more than a smile and a dill pickle. His wife, her head always covered with a pink *shmatteh*, sat on the barrel, guarding the pickles. Ben-Eliahu's son was also fighting in Lebanon. Eliahu and his wife aged ten years during the first six weeks.

The storekeepers must have seen in my eyes that I was needy. They understood the nursing mother needed to be fed. I found love and caring on Bethlehem Road. Even Zachariah Levy, the falafel man, who was not generous by nature, put in an extra ball when

I ordered a full pita. This, too, I took as a sign of camaraderie and caring.

◊

Nobody ever knocked at the door during the war. Any knock would have made me think of the two soldiers and accompanying social worker coming to deliver bad news. So once, when I did hear a knock at five in the afternoon, I panicked. I was in the bathroom holding Ori's back under the running faucet. I grabbed his towel and ran to the door holding the baby folded over my left arm. Through the peephole I saw Schwartzkoph, our downstairs neighbor. He was a retired bus driver who talked about his days behind the wheel as if he were Ben-Gurion himself, driving the young country to glory. Now that he was retired, Schwartzkoph spent whole afternoons cleaning his Volvo's motor on the sidewalk in front of the house. What did he care if young mothers had to walk in the street? He had been a Jordanian prisoner of war for seven months after the fall of the Old City in 1948. The rest of the world could go to hell.

I opened the door. He started yelling. Ori wiggled around to see the voice.

"*Tizahari*," he shouted. "Be careful. You're dripping all the water from your geraniums onto my windowsill. *Tizahari*. You think my wife likes to clean the windows every day because of your flowers?"

I couldn't believe my ears. We were in a war. My husband was fighting in Beirut. I was home alone with a new baby, and this asshole was complaining about water on his windowsill? Clutching Ori even tighter, I walked past Schwartzkoph onto the common tiled roof. Les and I had converted it into a roof garden. None of the neighbors cared. Schwartzkoph followed me outside, repeating his warning—"*Tizahari*. You and your American flowers."

With my free right hand I touched the heavy asbestos flower containers on the ledge of the roof, the ones with hot pink and purple geraniums cascading over the sides. I turned towards him and asked him if these were the flower pots he meant. "*Elu? Elu?*" I raised my voice.

He nodded.

"These? These?" I repeated, working up a steam.

He nodded again, stepping back.

"These right here? Are these the American flowers you mean, Mr. Schwartzkoph?" I touched the blooming flowers with my free right hand. Ori wiggled and tried to look at this woman who twenty seconds earlier had been his loving mother.

"Yes," he said, "of course, those are the ones I'm talking about."

Then with my right hand, I shoved the heavy flower boxes onto the floor of the roof.

"Never again, Mr. Schwartzkoph," I screamed. "Never again," I yelled, "will I dirty your fucking windows. Do you hear me?"

The pots broke into a million pieces and the flowers lay scattered and wounded on the floor of the roof, their roots still attached to the soil. Ori cried.

"Is this what you mean, Schwartzkoph? Is this what you mean?" I screamed at him over and over.

He froze, then retreated a few more steps. In the doorway he stood and stared at me. I could hear him thinking, *This is a woman at the end of her rope, a crazy woman, over the edge, holding a baby.*

After he left I didn't know if that madwoman was really me or if I just played the role to get him off my back. Ori, crying uncontrollably, didn't seem to know either.

◊

Four months after he had gone off to volunteer for the war, Les called one morning at 9:00—during Ori's second feeding. He was in Kiryat Shmona, eating a schnitzel that the Moroccan women of the town prepared for the soldiers going in and out of Lebanon. Soon he would be getting a ride to Tel Hashomer to get his release papers. For good. Did I want to come pick him up?

Something in his voice sounded pathetic, ashamed, vanquished.

The last thing I wanted to do was drive down to Tel Hashomer Hospital near Tel Aviv in the heat, with Ori in the back seat. For

166

weeks I had avoided fixing the air conditioning in the car. I wasn't about to rush to do it that morning and then drive down there.

When I didn't jump at the opportunity, Les understood.

"No more Lebanon," he said, his voice half-dead.

I felt sorry for him, for what he had been through—though I didn't know what he had been through—and for my lack of response to his call for help. He sounded tired, exhausted, but so was I.

As always when he called, other soldiers were clamoring around him to use the phone. I heard him swear at them to shut up so he could hear me.

"Are you happy I'm coming home?"

This was so out of character. He never asked if I was happy about anything. "Of course," I said. It was partially true. I was glad he was finally out of physical danger, or would be soon. Driving anywhere in Lebanon became more dangerous the longer Israel stayed. Twelve-year-old boys were shooting RPGs at Israeli convoys. But during his four months away, I got used to full-time, on-demand nursing. I was apprehensive of any change in our non-routine routine. Yet, at times I did miss Les.

All day I straightened up the house, making sure the toilet bowls sparkled, the sinks shone. Ori followed me around on his stomach and elbows, giving me quizzical looks, as if to say, *Who is this woman cleaning the house?*

By the evening news, Les still hadn't arrived and hadn't called. I sat down with Ori in the rocking chair in the living room. During the burp, I sang our favorite lullaby.

Hush little baby don't say a word
Papa's gonna buy you a mocking bird

As soon as he was asleep on my shoulder, there was a knock on the door. Ori twitched his body, but didn't wake up. I carried him to the entrance hall, his head resting on my shoulder, and opened the door.

Les stood there, unshaven, wearing a wrinkled plaid shirt slightly opened at the chest and green army pants, filthy with dust and grease. Around his neck hung his silver dog tag chain, the tag itself hidden by his shirt. His army knapsack was strung over one shoulder and over the other he carried an M-16. He stood surrounded by a heavy silence, dazed, staring at the Hebrew sign on the door with our names on it, as if those names and this house were foreign.

In his right hand he held a single red rose. Eventually, he extended his right arm and handed me the flower. I took it with my free hand. For a moment we held the rose together, our eyes locked. Then he let go and I drew the bud to my nose. The smell was sweet and familiar and reminded me of places a million miles from Beirut, from Jerusalem, from the whole warring Middle East. I had grown up in such a place. The fragrance invaded my body and I surrendered.

"Just a minute." I turned around to take Ori to his own bed for the first time in four months. I put the rose down on the changing table and then I lay Ori down gently in his bed, so he wouldn't balk and wake up.

Les hadn't moved. He stood there, waiting. "Come," I said, opening my arms. "Welcome home."

He walked past me slowly, lay down his weapon and knapsack in the entrance hall.

I lowered my arms.

Released from the accoutrements of war, he seemed to lose his balance for a second, but then he cleared his throat and flattened his mustache over his lips with his thumb and forefinger. My husband was home, for good.

"Thank you," I said.

"For what?"

"The rose. You." I opened my arms again. He fell into them. We stood there in the entrance hall for a long time, my holding him, he too tired or dazed or who knows what to hug me back. The longer we stood there in this unbalanced embrace, the heavier he felt. It occurred to me that he might fall asleep in this position.

"What's to eat?" he said finally, voicing these words by rote.

I had made a special goulash for his homecoming. He sat down at the head of the dining table and seemed pleased to be served. He touched my hand when I put the full plate in front of him. I bent down and kissed his forehead. It smelled of cedar and sweat.

After dinner, he went into the bathroom and stayed. For hours. Before I went to bed at eleven, I knocked on the bathroom door.

"Don't do that," he clipped.

"Do what?"

"Knock."

"I did knock."

"Don't do that," he said, raising his voice.

I had had fantasies of our first night together, staying up talking about Ori, his war experience, passionate kissing, love.

I don't know when he came to bed, but when he did, I heard an unfamiliar moan and heavy breathing coming from the floor below the radio on his side of the bed. His crawling into our bed sounded like a military operation, some clandestine maneuver.

When Ori awoke at 3:30 AM to nurse, I went to him with eyes half-open and carried him to the rocking chair in the living room. We sat there for an hour, dozing, nursing, and singing.

If that diamond ring turns brass
Papa's gonna buy you a lookin-glass.

I slowed down and sang softer.

If that lookin-glass gets broke,
Papa's gonna buy you a billy-goat.

After each verse, I felt a deep sadness pulling at me from inside.

If that billy-goat don't pull
Papa's gonna buy you a cart and bull.

It was a sadness like no other, a feeling of total devastation, ruin and loss.

If that cart and bull turn over,
Papa's gonna buy you a dog named Rover.

169

By the last verse my tears flowed like milk.

If that dog named Rover don't bark,
Papa's gonna buy you a horse and cart.

The last lines were barely audible.

And if that horse and cart fall
  down,
You'll still
  be
  the sweetest
  little
  ba-by
  in
  town.

I pulled Ori tighter to my chest. The moon made frightening shadows on the living room walls, shadows that reminded me of soldiers hiding behind closed doors and large men dressed in black, brandishing swords.

Then I thought of the hug I had given Les in the entrance hall and how he couldn't hug back, how he hid in the bathroom the whole night. I wondered what he had done in Lebanon. I wanted him to tell me and to hug me like before the war. These thoughts and memories filled me with longing and sadness.

◊

The next morning Les sat on the edge of the bed and stared at his paratroop boots.

"They need polishing," he said softly. It wasn't clear if he was asking me to polish them or just stating a fact.

"I have to go back to Tel Hashomer." His voice was an eerie monotone.

"Why?" I asked, sitting on the edge next to him.

"To return all the equipment. I didn't finish yesterday." He looked at his feet as he spoke, his tone torpid.

He was tired, said he hadn't slept the whole night, wished I wouldn't sing to the baby in the middle of the night. It kept him up.

I tried to give him a hug, but it felt like I was hugging all the men in his armored troop carrier, as if Les were carrying all those who had survived and those who had been killed, carrying them all with their flak jackets and weapons and helmets in his stiff body. There was no soft place for me.

◊

We got into a pattern. Every night after I put Ori to sleep, I washed dishes and he read the paper. At nine, we watched the news, Les gritting his teeth and cursing every time Minister of Defense Arik Sharon appeared on screen. Then we read more newspapers, each ensconced in our black and white tents. At eleven, I went to sleep and he went into the bathroom. At two or three, he'd come to bed. One night when I was coming back from nursing Ori and he was just getting into bed, I leaned over to him and whispered in his ear. He brushed me away as if I were a mosquito.

"Don't do that," he snapped. I touched him gently. Slowly we started to make love, but as soon as my breathing became strong, he pushed me away and told me to shut up. "Never make those sounds in my ear."

◊

One Sabbath afternoon in November, Ori and I were playing peek-a-boo on the living room floor. Les snuck into the living room from the roof with a piece of the hose I used to water the few flower survivors from the Schwartzkoph incident. Les had cut off a foot-long piece and held it on his right shoulder.

"Be careful," he whispered, ducking under the dining room table.

Ori looked at him and started to laugh. I was happy Les was joining in our play.

"Shut up," Les yelled. With his left hand he aimed the pretend M-16 all over the living room. "Bang. Boom," he shouted. "I'm going to kill you."

Then from his nose and throat he made noises like a wild boar. He held the hose still and aimed it at us.

Ori's laugh turned to a cry. I picked him up and we crawled and crouched behind the couch.

"*Abba's* playing war," I said. I patted his head and started humming "Hush Little Baby." Then I pointed my forefinger at Les from above the couch and said "Bang, bang."

"Shut the fuck up," Les shouted. I peeked from behind the corner of the couch to look at him. He was lying on his stomach, looking through the hose and taking aim.

"I see you," he said. "Bang."

"Peek-a-boo," I said, but by now Ori was crying louder and clutching my neck.

"It's just a game," I said, shaking.

"Make him shut up," Les yelled. "Make him shut the fuck up." Then Les crawled out from under the table and stood up. I was afraid he was going to walk toward us and throw the hose at us, but he threw the hose on the floor and ran out of the house, cursing so all the neighbors could hear, "Goddamned son-of-a-bitch, why isn't there anything to eat in this fucking house."

I held onto Ori as hard as I could. I wanted to be sure his *abba* wasn't coming back with something more dangerous than a hose. My voice withdrawn and taut, I sang . . . "You'll still be the sweetest little baby in town."

After a few minutes of calm, we stood up. I carried Ori out to the roof garden. Was Les there or had he gone downstairs, taken the car?

I stood at the edge, clutching Ori, and looked down onto Bethlehem Road. The car was still parked across the street in front of Menachem's bakery. When I raised my eyes, I saw Les standing behind an electric pole near the curb. He seemed to be carving something into the pole, either with a pen or a penknife, but it didn't work. He threw his implement into the street. He tried to hide, peeking out every now and then from either side, looking up at the roof, to the left

172

and to the right, checking to see from where the fire—or salvation—might come. I looked straight at him, but he never acknowledged me. He wrapped both arms around the pole and started heaving. The terrifying sound of his moans reached the roof. Part of me wanted to go hide in the living room and lock the door. Another part wanted to race down the stairs and put my arms around my husband, push my body into his back, hug the pole with him and then turn him around and direct his head to my chest, wanted to hold his head in my hands and tell him it would be alright, that everything would be alright, the war was over, I would take care of him, we would find our love, we could do this, I can save you, I wanted to say, and as I imagined the words I would tell him, Ori started crying louder, now from hunger mixed with fear, and Les unraveled himself from the electric pole and with his arms dangling at his side like dead branches, started walking away down Bethlehem Road, towards Zion and Ezekiel, Shmulik and Eliyahu, and I wondered if the war was still going on in their homes too and how long it would take to end.

Ru Freeman

To Do List

Palestine is a sacred place
visit
the hills where the old scrolls were found
visit
this disappearing site
visit
the old mosque
& carry away the last coin
that will buy you nothing
take
the last key for no door that can open

Go where the earth has buried your home
sit beneath the tree planted over the cornerstone

visit
now while you still can
speak
in the language of memory
its diacritics dissolving into *resolutions*
visit
plant your feet, take root

In your widespread arms
hold the sky
Crush olives in your palms
let the juice run pickled down your cheeks

return the stolen water & let it reach Gaza already salted
bless the air escaping through your lips
Visit.
Begin this world.

Lily Bowen

Hoàn Kiếm Lake

Luc Thuy, my father says,
motions to the water.

It is March and the city
is gray and green.

Now it is Hoàn Kiếm,
of the restored sword.

Across the street a man
is relieving himself into the lake.

I envision a stream reaching all the way
to *Tháp Rùa,* the very center of the city.

Close your eyes, my father says.

As he leads me across the traffic weaves,
a school of fish. Cars and mopeds seem as distant

as water buffalo, as the rice paddies and villages,

as a woman wringing her hair out in the streets,
as a vendor slicing open a lychee,

as candles lighting on a soldier's family altar.
My father smiles at me on the other side,

you'll never get used to it, he says.

RENNY GOLDEN

Blood for Blood

for Oscar Romero

Your voice in Usultán, where ceiba trees open
green umbrellas above the cross-staked graves;
in Chalatenango, lush with mango trees and bones;
in Morazán, where poor farmers gave their lives
to a promise you, and they, both made:

> *If I am killed, let my blood be a seed*
> *for this suffering people.*

Blood and seed to break rock: these tattooed boys
with hearts so far from grace—
their muscled backs with black roses

and daggers, their spirits lost and hungry.
Your blood, Oscar, for fleeing mothers boosting children
onto boxcars, vigilant for the coiled and savaged.

Your blood for *campesinos* who walk into a desert
furnace that will burn them to ash.
Your blood for girls cut down, wildflowers
strewn in fields, gang raped, discarded.

Now as you are lifted to glory, your people
light candles and sing: *When the poor believe in the poor,*
then we will have our liberty—as if M13 and M18
might hear the words because the blood they spill

is yours, their stranglers' hands at their own throats,
because none of the blood will wash away, because
of promises made in a madhouse in the 1980s.

Erica Goss

At the Museum of the Western Allies

I picked my way
through exploded shells

stared at maps
of the occupation areas

measured my body
against military fatigues

stroked the warm wing
of the Candy Bomber

shivered at a segment
of the Berlin Wall

entered the dining car
of a French military train

ogled photographs of children
posed in front of rubble

shrugged at crumbling brown
newspaper headlines

but when I saw the contents
of a CARE package, the rusting cans

of meat, cheese, fruit, vegetables, coffee,
sugar, butter, condensed milk, cornflakes

I leaned against the glass display case
to hide my tears as my mouth watered.

At the Graveyard Where My Mother Used to Play

I've come across the world
for my inheritance, but for once
the dead are silent. No clue
in the November sky.

I need to feel something
but these are the graves
of strangers. The day seems
poised, a storm coming,

tension in the air.
Which direction
did my mother look
when she saw a man

who seemed to be her father
trudging home from war?
I point my camera west,
snap a photo

of the street, a few cars,
blurry green trees,
because that's where
I would have looked

just in time to see him
round the corner,
a small man with
beautiful posture,

lonely pockets
and the longing
to always be
somewhere else.

GOSS

Fiction

Daphne Kalotay

The Archivists

Michigan, March 12th. At the teak desk in her living room, the grandmother writes to her granddaughter:

> My Darling!
> Thank you for the flowers! The petals are the exact color blue. I will have Sable take a picture. For dinner we are having roast duck. Also soup, potatoes, asparagus, and the chocolate cake. Don't worry, we have two ducks!
> Love,
> Bunica

The flowers, blue hydrangeas, are a gift for her birthday. Big, plump periwinkle clusters, like outrageous pompoms. The vase arrived with a shiny pink ribbon tied round in a bow, but the grandmother found it inelegant and removed it.

Her daughter, Lea, is already in the kitchen. There are the two ducks to roast, plus the vat of soup to start simmering, not to mention the side dishes for Sable, her grandson's wife. A vegetarian.

Having completed her letter, the grandmother rises from her desk. With the aid of a cane fashioned after a stalk of bamboo, she makes her way to the narrow, fluorescent-lit kitchen, where Lea is arranging the ducks side by side on the broiler pan. No heads or feet, just the cold plump bodies, firm and slick. The grandmother stands at the kitchen doorway to watch her daughter truss the stubby legs with twine. She likes to make certain everything is prepared the right way.

◊

In an under-heated dance studio in New York City, a retired ballerina stretches her leg from passé into développé. Over her thin leotard she wears loose sweatpants and a little bolero-style knit sweater tied in a knot at her breastbone. "Not quite so high," she explains, her leg fully outstretched, toes pointing at the air in their tight leather slippers. It feels good, the strong reach of her leg, the arch of her foot, muscles extended in a single, focused intention.

The young star she is coaching, a dancer with her hair in a high blonde ponytail, repeats the movement. Too eager. Her effort is visible, beads of sweat crowning her forehead, her leg jabbing the air rather than piercing it. The combination she is learning—choreographed a quarter century before her birth and intensely difficult—has not been danced in three decades.

The retired ballerina's name is Brynn. She is sixty-eight years old and works in Houston as a consultant to the Ballet. *Off to NYC, and into distant memory,* she wrote last night to registered fans on her blog, while waiting for her flight to New York.

She has promised her doctor to do nothing that will in any way strain her bad knee.

◊

The two trussed ducks are slid into the oven. The grandmother secretly worries two won't be enough. She has this same worry every year. The fact that there are always leftovers in no way eradicates the residual hunger cautioning her to worry once again.

Clinging to her cane, she tugs open the refrigerator door and peers at the crowded shelves, searching for the turkey scraps for the soup. Wings (just the tips, less expensive) and a neck.

Lea says, "Let me get those," and lifts the styrofoam trays, ferries them to the sink, rinses the cold, slick turkey parts under the faucet. In the stock pot, wedges of parsnip and carrot sizzle against sweating layers of a quartered onion. With a wooden spoon, the grandmother nudges the vegetables to the edges of the pot, to make room for the turkey parts. Lea drops the neck and wings in and lets

184

them splutter for a bit, then covers everything with water and sets the lid partially across top. The grandmother turns the flame higher.

◊

In a laboratory a few miles northeast of Los Angeles, two research associates are beginning the day's work. It's 9:30 AM. The study is at an early stage, data collection, simple, repetitive.

The first subject to arrive is a twenty-seven-year-old girl. "Woman" the first researcher—also a woman—grumbles to her colleague, a man, who sees nothing demeaning in referring to women as girls.

"It's infantilizing," the female researcher explains.

Her colleague explains that he would never use the word *girl* for anyone who isn't actually young. For women too old to be girls, he prefers the term *ladies*.

Practicing the deep, full breaths she has been advised to engage in such moments, the female researcher heads down the hallway to the room where she will collect the *girl's* data. Before entering, she taps a quip into her smartphone, about men who call women girls. As much as her Twitter account is a diversion, it is also a record of her daily thoughts, activities and news. To not record something would mean, she believes, to lose it.

◊

The solo the young blonde star is to learn was choreographed in 1969, in protest against the Vietnam War. All wars, the choreographer later clarified, and told of his mother's beloved blue-eyed brother, who died in a labor camp.

The dance, "Forced March," was first performed on a sweltering July evening at the Jacob's Pillow Festival in Massachusetts. In the *Times* the next day, a critic wrote of Brynn's "dignified carriage giving way to fury and heartbreak" and of the way she "seemed to radiate perseverance in the face of infinite pain."

Photographs from that date show a young, round-cheeked Brynn in a black leotard with a thin white belt at her waist, the

185

expression on her unlined face resolute. Though brief, the dance required prodigious strength; by the end, the floor of the stage was wet from her perspiration. For the entire fourteen minutes that she was dancing, she was worried her pancake makeup would run.

From that night forward, each time she performed it, she told herself it was her very last dance. She felt it her duty to use up everything she had, sweat pasting her leotard to her skin, veins pulsing, bruises emerging on her knees where she sometimes fell too hard. Just a limp wet rag, that was how she felt by the end. It was a wonderfully satisfying feeling.

"I looked online," says the young star. They are taking a break, drinking water from big plastic bottles emblazoned with the company's logo. "I guess it's true no one ever filmed it. I wonder why. I found lots of recordings of you, but none of this one."

◊

The grandmother's other guests have begun to arrive. First her son, Benjie, and now her grandson Dave, his 6-month-old baby, and his wife, Sable, the vegetarian.

Everyone is cooing at the baby—an oblivious creature packed into a car basket. Dave and Sable used to live on the east coast but with the baby moved back to Michigan to be closer to family. As the grandmother is embraced by Sable, her cheeks soft and cool, Dave sets down the manifold bags that accompany the baby on even the shortest of travels.

Already Sable is complimenting the grandmother's fine color, how lovely she looks. Somehow her flattery always seems genuine. In fact, the grandmother has always found herself fascinated by Sable—her easy manner, calm and untroubled, that air of steady contentment. Even now, a new mother, Sable appears relaxed about the baby and seems to have gotten enough sleep (which Lea always claims to find suspicious but the grandmother secretly admires).

"Happy Birthday," Benjie is saying. He holds out the gift he has brought: a glazed ceramic pot containing a bright blue hydrangea.

◊

KALOTAY

The research associates are collecting data concerning a gene connected to the regulation of stress hormones.

That is all they have been told. They do not yet know that their subjects have come to this study via archives begun twenty years ago. They do not know that the archives, founded by a famous film director, are video testimonies recorded for an institute now located here at the university. The testimonies describe starvation, brutality, and death. They speak of life in ghettos, in hiding, in camps. In forests, in alleys, on the run.

Instead of archived videos, the laboratory researchers read swabs of DNA. The institute began collecting samples in an effort to reconnect dispersed families and identify bodily remains. But the researchers have been employing the samples toward a different end: an ongoing study of intergenerational effects of extreme trauma. Specifically, that the stresses of the Holocaust have altered the DNA not only of Holocaust victims but also of their descendants.

"Epigenetic inheritance" is the term. Environmentally-caused modifications of genetic material, via chemical tags that attach themselves to DNA. In previous studies, Jewish Holocaust survivors and their offspring were proven to share the same epigenetic tags, while the control group (Jewish families living outside of Europe during the war) did not.

This new study will test the theory that epigenetic tags are passed not only to children but to grandchildren.

◊

The blue of the second hydrangea—the one from her son—is very close to that of the first but slightly more violet. The petals, bright and absurdly healthy, could be leaves from some oversized blue clover, or the wings of a strange blue butterfly.

The grandmother has her son set the planter on the teak desk. Meanwhile, atop the round glass coffee table, the bouquet from her granddaughter in California makes a sort of altered reflection, periwinkle blossoms spilling luxuriously over the lip of the vase.

187

The plant from her son has a small white tag dangling over the edge of the ceramic pot: *Hydrangea* written in looping script. The grandmother leans closer to read the tag.

Hydrangeas require plenty of light and daily watering.
A hydrangea is a symbolic way to say
"Thank you for understanding."

She looks over to the coffee table, at the vase bursting with hydrangea blossoms. Those periwinkle ones, from her granddaughter, are the right ones.

◊

Brynn massages the area around her bad knee. So far, so good. She just needs to remember to ice it when she gets back to the hotel.

For a few years, the "Forced March" solo was her signature piece, created for her when she was not yet twenty. Danced for the first minutes in silence, with live drumming gradually layered in, the piece begins slowly, meditatively, building to a frenzy and then ultimately calming itself. Among the photographs on her website is one of a young, fearless Brynn hurtling herself across the stage while a stern-faced drummer plays impassively behind her.

It was flattering, an honor, to have a dance made for her, even if she had also been fending off the choreographer's advances for some time. After she left the company for a troupe in San Francisco, the dance was retired from the repertoire and never performed again. When the choreographer died, a few years ago, Brynn spoke lovingly, if with carefully chosen words, at his memorial.

Her work with this new star is part of a project to archive "lost" dances. It began as an Internet campaign and has since received national attention. Brynn finds the online platform—GoFundMe—crass. It seems these days anyone can ask for money for anything and, astonishingly, receive it.

Once revived, Brynn's piece will be publicly performed, recorded, and added to an electronic archive. *Dances long forgotten,*

188

the GoFundMe page explained, *will exist once again, recalled, performed, and shared into perpetuity.*

◊

"I will explain," the grandmother tells Sable, who has not yet heard the story. Leaning closer on the sofa, she tells her about her first love, whom she last saw in 1939.

Mihail, brother of her friend Ana. He had the most beautiful eyes! But it was not until she was sixteen, she tells Sable, that he finally took notice of her. It happened at a dance. There were weekend dances back then, everyone would go. A favorite song had started up, and out of a sense of duty—it seemed—Mihail asked her to join him. Moving together, their bodies warm and full of life, she glimpsed a change in his face, some new softness, or perhaps simply attention. He was, she realized, seeing her anew. After that, he was always walking her home, loping along beside her, carrying her books, and, in the dark of the cinema, warming her hands in his, trembling when he dared lean in to kiss her.

When the war came, the grandmother and her family fled to the countryside, while Mihail and Ana and their parents hid in town. It did not matter; in the end, all of them were sent to the camps—but the grandmother escaped!

On the run, hiding in safe houses, in abandoned homes, miserable places she has blocked from memory. Entire weeks, months, erased from mental record.

Even when she gave her testimony to the Institute, she found she could not account for great swaths of time. That troubled her. It made it seem those painful stretches never existed.

She tells Sable some of what she remembers—far away, now, perhaps, from what she meant to explain. There was a courtyard where she found herself alone, a searing hunger in her stomach, no strength left. No last surge of energy to move forward, to make a decision, to save her own life by shoving one raw inflamed foot in front of the other.

Looking at the rusted gate to the courtyard, thinking that if she looked long enough, her father would appear and tell her what to do.

The hunger, she tells Sable, is what she has never forgotten. That was something she tried to convey during her testimony—how even after many decades, the hunger has never gone away.

◊

. . . *causing physiological mutations, including increased chances of stress disorders such as anxiety, anorexia, and addiction. In this manner, the epigenetic effects of history are passed inter-generationally through the body . . . .*

◊

In the kitchen, the two ducks are roasting, grease dripping into the pan. The salad has been assembled but not dressed. The potatoes await mashing, and the asparagus still needs to be sautéed. For Sable there is also a lentil burger slowly shriveling in the toaster oven.

Lea adds a ladle of broth to a small saucepot of simmering water. Next comes a dusting of her mother's signature ingredient, which the grandmother considers a spice though really it is MSG. Lea cracks an egg into a bowl, shakes some salt at it, and briskly scrambles the egg with a fork. She sifts a tablespoon of farina into the bowl and stirs. Too runny. She adds more farina, stirs again. The trick is not to add too much, or the dumplings won't hold together.

When the mixture looks about right—a sticky yellow paste— Lea lightly drags the tines of the fork across the top. The indented lines remain briefly visible, then start to fill in.

That's how you know it's the right consistency, her mother taught her many years ago, in this very same kitchen, when Lea was a little girl. Guiding her hand, dragging the fork.

The motion of another hand, of another girl, in a drafty kitchen in Brașov. Young Ana, sister of Mihail, showing her friend

190

how to test the *gǎluşcǎ*: "Just pull the fork through, until it leaves a mark, like this."

◊

"Like this," Brynn tells the young dancer. She lowers herself into a wide plié—slowly, careful with her knee—while her arms push above her head, palms flat and wide, as if trying to push away the sky. Fascia stretching, ligaments tightening. "Muscle memory"— though for Brynn the emotions, too, return, how it felt to be young, knowing her choreographer was in love with her, and that she did not need to love him back, that it was enough to dance for him, to be beautiful and follow his direction with her body.

No matter that she had not yet lost a loved one, had not, yet, known what it meant to be bereft. Her body seemed to know, and carried her to those bleak places.

That is why there are no recordings of the dance. No one seems to remember this—that the choreographer forbade it. To Brynn this lapse is just one more reminder that what once seemed to matter greatly can be so quickly forgotten. The very point of the piece, the choreographer told her, was its brief flicker amid the indifference of war. Like the brevity of life, Brynn always thought. Ephemeral. Lost.

Now, though, its loss seems a mistake. She is here to bring it back.

◊

We could not risk looking as if we were going on a journey, the survivor says on the videotape from 1996. *That is why I have no photographs or family keepsakes. We had to leave everything behind.*

For the Institute, that same survivor left behind a buccal swab of her DNA. Which is how, nearly two decades later, subject 1207B—the "girl"—came to be asked to participate in the study here at the university, and why she has stopped by this air-conditioned room, missing her morning tae kwon do class, to answer a detailed questionnaire and open her healthy, strong-jawed mouth wide for the research associate, who leans forward and rubs a sterile swab inside the girl's cheek.

◊

"So you see, I have no pictures of him," the grandmother explains to Sable, nudging herself toward the edge of the sofa to pose for her photo. "But to this day, I have never met anyone with such beautiful eyes."

She leans forward, toward the coffee table, bringing her face closer to the flowers—the bouquet sent by her granddaughter. Sable is leaning back, cellphone raised. "Say cheese!"

When Sable shows her the image, the grandmother nods approval. And with another push of a button, the picture flies off to a cellphone in California.

"That is the reason," the grandmother tells Sable, "they bring me these flowers. These ones here, they are the exact color of his eyes."

◊

Brynn tries to be exact. To describe precisely, for the young dancer, the movements her own body can no longer enact.

While there are various dance notation techniques, the GoFundMe page states, *few choreographers or dance historians know these "languages" (Labanotation, Benesh Movement Notation, Eshkol-Wachman Notation, Dancewriting) sufficiently to record or translate. There is no substitute for* **seeing** *movements in their full combination, expressed by the body as originally intended. This is why funding these archives is so important.*

They have come to the most difficult section. Down on her knees, then leaping to the sky. Spinning and spinning and spinning, into the indifferent, expanding universe.

"Lead with the hip first, yes, but, no. . . ." Frustrating, these failed attempts to describe things her body can no longer oblige. Shapes she can no longer make, compromised gestures carving the air. What she wants to explain is beyond language.

192

So she stops, just briefly, to think. She is deciding what to do. Then she begins, again, to move.

◊

In Palo Alto, the first of the day's subjects has been set free. If she hurries she might make the next tae kwon do class. Or maybe she should skip class and study for her Latin exam.

As soon as she has left the lab, she checks her cellphone, where she finds a text from her sister-in-law. With a photograph.

i love this! she taps back. Just seeing it makes her smile. With a quick push of a button, she displays it on her Instagram account. *My bunica,* she types, *91 years old today!*

By evening, two hundred and ninety people will have seen the photograph of her grandmother with the periwinkle bouquet. Ninety-seven of them will have "liked" the exact color of Mihail's eyes.

◊

Knee popped, Brynn writes to the fans on her blog. She is typing on her iPad in her casual, pokey way, sitting in a firm-cushioned chair in her doctor's waiting room, her bad leg fully, painfully, outstretched. The flight home was tricky, with her leg sticking out into the aisle, annoying everyone. Not to mention the long awkward car ride home, and the depressing drive here today, propped like an invalid in the back seat of her friend's sedan, and then having to use the cane again, like some old lady.

She thinks for a moment, then resumes her typing. *And yes my dears, it was worth it.*

Linda Dittmar

Tantura

> Once located on a spur off the coastal road between Tel Aviv and
> Haifa, Tantura was a fishing and agricultural village counting
> 1,490 residents. Attacked on May 22-23, 1948, the village fell
> after a brief battle; claims of a massacre are still debated. Some
> twelve hundred residents were expelled to nearby al-Fureidis and
> then expelled from Israeli-held territory altogether. Some two
> hundred, mostly women and children with male relations in
> Israeli detention, remained in al-Fureidis, sleeping in the open.
> Nothing further is mentioned about their fate. *

Summers are not the time to go to the beach in Israel. The deceptive
coolness of dawn turns into a sticky humidity at the Israeli
seashore, where the lukewarm water of the eastern Mediterranean
offers little relief from the salty film that clings to one's skin, hair,
and food. Yet that was what I suggested to Deborah one oppressively
hot evening.

"How about going to Tantura?" I said, using the old Arab
name for this fishing village, the name etched in my memory from
childhood. "It's a beautiful beach, the prettiest in Israel."

By then, in the fall of 2006, Deborah was no longer simply
a tourist. An American landscape photographer, she joined me, an
Israeli-American, on a special project: we were combing the country
for Palestinian villages destroyed during the war of 1948—the "War of

---

* Based on research by Walid Khalidi

Independence" for us Israelis, but the "Nakba" for the Palestinians, the "Catastrophe."

Though Deborah was new to Israel, she was not new to this work. By the time she joined me there she had already completed an acclaimed series about historic battlefield panoramas as well as other historic sites that got recast over time: the Plymouth Rock, for example, chipped over time by souvenir collectors and now protected by a spiked iron fence; a defunct atomic reactor hidden in the woods outside Chicago; or the old mills of Lowell, Massachusetts, preserved as a tourist attraction. Documenting lingering signs of the Nakba, now assimilated into the vibrant young Israel, was, for her, an extension of that forensic interest. For me, however, it was a different matter. I was to be Deborah's companion and guide, the insider who speaks the language and is intimately familiar with Israel's geography, but I was also an Israeli deeply implicated in the painful history we were documenting—a history about which we, Israelis, had been silent for years.

Finding what little can still be seen of such villages (four hundred or more in total) is arduous at all times, but especially as the summer advances. With the villages erased from current maps and memory, one needs to learn to see this scarred land with new eyes. It is a decoding that comes with experience. Sometimes one finds clear markers: a tomb or a minaret that still stands, a building where the masonry is recognizably Palestinian, or even just the remnant of an archway still attached to a crumbling wall. All are telltale signs. Often the decoding is harder, as Deborah and I discovered. We learned to "read" the land by trial and error: to register that a clump of cactus bushes may actually be the remnant of a hedge, that certain rock striations are the remains of agricultural terracing, that a lone fig tree may have once shaded a house, or that a pile of rocks may be hiding a well. One can only know by walking towards such signs, stepping through thorns and clambering over rocks to see what may be found nearby.

Inevitably, this was a melancholy task, especially for me. After all, it is my own history—my family's and my people's—that remained in question. Deborah and I each needed some relief from our Nakba work and Tantura suggested that. The beach I remembered

195

seeing shortly after the war, in 1949 or 1950, was pristine and safe from undertow, its sparkling cool waters encircled by flat rocks and protected by small offshore islands.

"There are cabins to rent there." I said to Deborah. "No Nakba. We could stop overnight."

I should have known better.

◊

You will not find "Tantura" on current road maps, only the old Canaanite name of "Dor," now reclaimed for Israeli use. There is no simple way to get there either. The access road requires a detour from the new coastal highway through the old coast road, and then a badly marked turnoff that leads, after several kilometers, into a parking lot where drifts of sand half cover the dead grasses peeking through creviced asphalt. This access road, which brought Deborah and me to Tantura in 2006, was the same one my family took for beach outings almost five decades earlier. It is also the road Tantura's refugees trudged along in the opposite direction, eastward, in May of 1948, when they were expelled from their homes by the Alexandroni Brigade. There is no sign of their exodus now, but there are records, some of them tangible, as Deborah and I discovered during our research, and as we were about to discover yet again.

Today, if you drive to Dor's beach, you'd hardly guess that the desiccated land you are crossing was once a village. All that's left are dun weedy mounds that turn green during the short rainy season—seemingly natural land formations. But the memory of a blurry black and white home movie shot with my father's ancient 8mm camera still haunts me. It showed the barely recognizable human form that was me, filmed in Tantura during the early 1950s. Taken at a distance and transposed onto video many years later, the image was rendered almost indecipherable, though you could still see my skinny shape silhouetted against a murky gray sky. There are smudgy chunks at the lower part of the frame where a tiny figure seems to be clambering. The terrain is obviously uneven. Sometimes the girl bends to hold onto an invisible support, and sometimes she's upright, her arms extended for balance.

DITTMAR

Those chunks, I could see even then, were the remains of Palestinian homes. What's left of them now became covered with sandy earth and dry weeds. But when my father filmed me edging my way across them, I already knew that I was walking over ruins, or at least half knew. Some masonry was still exposed, peeking through the thin layer of soil and sand that was already settling over the ruins.

This layer of soil had thickened by the time Deborah and I arrived at Tantura during that pleasant afternoon in 2006. The calm bays of my childhood were still there, encircled by the same rocks, but the beach itself had been fenced off for paid use. The entrance gateway was stained with salty humidity, and the rusting turnstile coughed and grated as it struggled to let us in. A lone ice cream vendor heaved his dented icebox over the turnstile as his last customer approached the exit—a tired-looking woman shepherding three irritable children. Behind them we could see that the beach litter had not been picked up for some time.

Still, something of the old beauty lingered over the beach in the late afternoon light. It was that magical hour "between the suns," as it's called in poetic Hebrew, when the light in these parts turns limpid, leaving everything awash in a golden pink glow that edges into mauves and blues. People are gone, the birds settle in for the night, and the trash recedes from sight as the shadows deepen. Peace, it seemed, settled over the land.

That illusion did not last. Walking down the beach, Deborah, who was walking just ahead of me, suddenly paused, staring. A minute later I stopped in my tracks too. A strangely futuristic colony of white-domed cabins came into view, each shaped like a concrete igloo whose size and shape were faintly reminiscent of Palestine's Moslem shrines.

"What's that?" she said.

"Well, I suppose these are the cabins. One of these must be ours. What's our number?"

Deborah looked at the hefty key she was holding but did not answer.

"Look at that," she added instead, pointing toward the small terracotta fawns—identical, orange-colored Bambis—that stood splay-legged along the sandy paths.

197

Though I still chuckle at this incongruous scene, I felt betrayed: this was not the beach I loved, *my* beach, as it seemed to me, pristine and safe. Still, at least for a few hours, as darkness descended and the lulling whisper of the waves took over, reality receded. The iridescent cabins and the fawns melted into the darkness, as did the mounds on which I had walked half a century earlier.

Of course, this place was never mine. Some fifteen hundred Palestinians lived here till their expulsion in 1948. They fished and farmed and had two schools and more than two hundred houses. What I remembered as a pristine beach was actually a village, leveled beyond recognition.

In a rare archival photograph that has since become iconic of the Nakba, you can see a long row of women and children leaving the village, carrying bundles and babies that will soon be too heavy to carry. The image is slightly overexposed in the unforgiving sunlight. Taken by Benno Rothenberg, it is one of the few Nakba photographs in public circulation.

What this photograph doesn't tell us is that Tantura suffered a massive attack and that, except for this one narrow road, all escape routes had been blocked. Though women and children are pictured walking, the photograph does not record the fate of the men who were separated from their families. It does not tell us that scores died during the attack and many more were wounded. Hundreds were imprisoned, and all ended up in exile.

Though as a child, heading for the beach with my family, I did not realize it, the destitute Arabs I saw shortly after the war, penned behind barbed wire near the Palestinian village of *al-Fureidis*, were Tantura's refugees. Among them were girls my age and younger that, for a few seconds, returned my gaze. I remember my horror at the desolation that was there in full view, my fascinated recoil. *That's what Arabs are like?* I wondered. What did they think of us, neat and well fed, as we sped by what I now realize was their detention camp?

I remember this scene in monochrome—in muddy browns and grays—an expanse of grimy tents and listless people meandering aimlessly on hard dusty ground, a scene of utter abjection. Every so often, another image invades my resisting memory: the flies creeping near the runny eyes, nostrils, and mouths of children standing by a

198

barbed wire fence, staring at us, impassive, not bothering to shoo the flies away.

In her memoir, *In Search of Fatima: a Palestinian Story*, Ghada Karmi describes her parents shielding her from the facts of war, much as mine did. A Palestinian my age—we were both about ten in 1948—she also writes about recoiling from the refugees who arrived in her family's hometown of Tulkarm. Like me, she too is distressed now, as an adult, at that recoil. It is hard, and sometimes terrifying, to see the suffering of others.

And yet that's where any parallel between us ends. For Karmi, the destitution she saw could have become, in an instant, her own. Her family escaped it only by a slight turn of fate. My family was swept along in the euphoria of nation-building that caused that suffering. As the desperate mood of post-Holocaust days dictated, we, Jews, *had* to survive—to survive at all costs. Karmi knew the refugee girls as classmates. I glimpsed them only in passing, on my way to a beach where the ruins of their homes were my playground.

◊

I was not thinking of any of this when I suggested to Deborah that beach outing. When we arrived there that evening, I was amused and put off by the domed cabins and tacky fawns, but I still thought of this visit as a reprieve from the Nakba. Not for long, though. As we were soon to discover, even at this holiday beach traces of the Nakba emerged from behind the scrim: Palestine's Tantura refused to be naturalized into the Israeli modernity of Dor's cabin complex.

The next morning it all came back, both the present and the past. Walking toward the beach, our eyes were drawn to a large building perched near the water's edge: excellent masonry, massive proportions, grand vaulted arches open both to the sea and inland, and yet no windows and no other buildings nearby. A large sign warned, DANGER DO NOT ENTER. Some fishing tackle was visible under its vast arches, apparently for use along with two small dinghies beached nearby.

Once again, as it happened so often during our travels, we found ourselves debating the purpose of this strangely solitary building, so odd at the edge of this shallow bay.

"What's that?" Deborah said.

"How should I know?" I shrugged, frustrated by my failure to be the good guide I was supposed to be. "It's too close to the water. See the watermarks? The water can reach it in storms. It doesn't look like anybody lived here."

"OK, but what does the Arabic inscription mean?" she said, pointing to the elaborately carved Arabic keystone, high above the main arch.

The early morning sun put that inscription into high relief. Deborah removed the lens cap from her camera and adjusted some dials.

"The light is excellent," she said as she aimed her camera at this wall.

Though I knew Arabic, I could not make it out. The carved arabesque bas-relief, both beautiful and elaborate, crowded the stone's surface to the point where letters and ornament melded together. Clearly there was something official about the place—the size, the workmanship, the calligraphy served something other than a family—but what?

I did not yet know that this had been an important seaport: Canaanite, Phoenician, Crusader, Ottoman, and Arab. It had also been a garrison port for Napoleon and, as it got silted, the fishing village of Tantura, and now the tiny Israeli settlement of Dor. The information is readily available, except that Deborah and I did not anticipate needing it. Standing in front of an ancient building that we couldn't quite place, we found ourselves in a familiar conversation—redolent with questions, skimpy on answers, impatient with guesses. But the building was clearly ancient, its masonry excellent, the curve of its arches probably Crusader, and its keystone Arab, perhaps Ottoman.

That much we could guess, though not much more. According to Walid Khalidi's research on the Nakba, the keystone inscription named this building as the al-Yahya family home, dated 1882, but to me it looked like the remnant of a fort, not a home. The

200

construction was too massive, the windowless walls too solid, and the arches too tall and wide for a residence. The ancient port became silted and at some point the al-Yahya family moved in.

As Deborah and I turned back toward our cabin, still wondering about that mysterious structure poised at the water's edge, another strange sight awaited us: a *makam*—a Sheikh's shrine—standing among the cabins, its domed roof repeated in each cabin. This, I later read, was Sheikh al-Majrani's shrine, now incorporated as yet another ornament in the beach colony's grounds. Legend has it that this Moslem tomb survived the Nakba when the bulldozer's blades broke, refusing to demolish it.

"Were Dor's domed cabins designed to copy this shrine or to disguise it?" Deborah wondered.

I shrugged.

She was walking around the building, her camera ready, looking for a good angle on it, with me tagging along. She sounded irritated. The light was no longer good for photography.

"Do vacationers even notice this shrine as the holy Moslem tomb it used to be?" she asked.

It probably recedes behind the fog of inattention, I thought. Should I tell her about our own inattention, I wondered, way back when we went swimming here? Yes, after all, Moslem shrines and minarets still dot the Israeli landscape, protected by law but often allowed to crumble. This one may be so protected because of its location, I thought. For visitors, like my family and me at the time, the choice remains: to see or not to see? Later, I thought, after dinner, I'll tell Deborah about my Dad's filming me climbing over the ruins.

◊

When Deborah and I returned to that beach later that year, hoping for better light for her photography, the air thrummed with gentle drumming and pastel banners waved in the breeze. Young people streamed in through the creaky turnstiles carrying food, sleeping bags, and musical instruments. There was an abundance of sun-bleached dreadlocks and tie-dye in view as people set up pup tents and settled down to smoke weed and make music.

"They are here for the Purple Festival," the woman at the ticket booth told us with a shrug. She didn't seem curious. Selling tickets was routine.

Deborah rolled her eyes in irritation, adjusted the heavy camera bag on her shoulder, and turned back towards our car. On the way to the weedy parking lot I thought about the young people gathering on the beach, Israelis seeking respite from a war that is taking over their lives. A gentle crowd, this one, yet they will all serve in the military or already had. How, I wondered, do they reconcile this festival with the military's treatment of Palestinians? Do they know anything at all about the Nakba that occurred right here in Tantura?

Thinking of these young people lounging near Sheikh al-Majrani's shrine, I found myself humming an old Israeli song from the 1948 war—Ha'pgisha, "The Reunion." Its lyrics describe a group of soldiers meeting and reminiscing about the war they were still fighting, as if it were already past: *"How goes it? . . . Haven't seen you in ages!"* the refrain goes. Mostly it is a song about the comradeship of men at arms, except that two Arabic words stand out among the Hebrew lyrics. *"Yahrab Beitak,"* the men say in greeting.

To me as a child this was gibberish, nonsense syllables, fun. Now I know better. Repeated in the refrain with percussive emphasis, the words translate as "May your house be destroyed," or perhaps as "Your house *will* be destroyed."

DANIELLE JONES-PRUETT

Elegy for Bodies Bending

The man runs across the water. He tries
to outrun his shadow. His shadow

keeps up, skitters across the water.
They run toward a group of bodies,

bodies kneeling in prayer. Not prayer,
protection, bodies bending to shield

other bodies. They are under a shelter
that looks like a plane. Wing of a plane.

A toy plane. Our kids are in planes,
our kids play war. They push a button—

No, not water, blood, the man runs across,
the shadow shimmers, surpasses the man

because the man has fallen. Bodies
bending over bodies have no protection,

no time for prayers. If I knew the names
of all those who died, I would write them here.

There would never be enough time, enough space,
to write them all. If I knew the names

of those who killed—what? What would I say?
Unsure, I call them soldiers. I call them

country. I almost forgot to tell you
about the goat slaughtered on the hillside.

How the brightness of its skin
belied its stillness. I had almost forgotten,

how soft the word slaughter sounds.
How often it's mistaken for prayer.

JONES-PRUETT

LYNN MARIE HOUSTON

The Base Burns Every Night in Your Dreams

In front of the fire, you confide in me
that you used to love hunting before you
deployed, but after shooting other humans,
you can't stomach the sport anymore.

As the embers die and darkness closes in on us,
you tell me that, as a captain, you plan to protect
your men better than the commanding officers who
sent you to fight in Afghanistan, the outpost untenable
at valley's bottom, surrounded by mountains
of well-armed insurgents, a land too hostile for either
man or machine—the eight brothers you lost,
the Humvees that rolled off the too-small roads,
and the Chinooks that exploded when trying to land
in precarious spaces between branches and crags.

That night, your sleep is animal—hunted.
I place a hand on your chest to calm your
twitches and jerks, grasp the trigger finger
firing on top of the sheets. With my palm
against the too-rapid working of your heart,
I whisper, *You're home now. You're safe.*
In the morning, your skin still smells of smoke
when you wake and roll away from me.

ELISABETH LEWIS CORLEY

Five O'Clock

A slight breeze on the veranda.
The maid and the men in uniform.
The drinks tray, the colonial air. *Run*

the air whispers to the young, *run*.
The war is everywhere except on the veranda.
The Frenchman spreads his uniform

courtesy like tapenade on toast, uniform
slices, perfectly prepared. A run
to Saigon every Saturday for drinks on the veranda.

To hell with the veranda, the maid in uniform, *run*.

JENNIFER CONLON

On Receiving War Stories From My Brother

Did you think I'd had enough
and so you hid each one, a noose-trinket,
into pockets, empty tins of dip,
the nape of your bedsheets.

You don't know how to console your family anymore.
We live in various states
of different-than-you. You who suffer invisibly.

We wait for you by gas-fire
and dog-haired blankets. You miss dinner.

I imagine you
imagining us building a coal mine from your body.
Do you see us—
mom measuring the seams,
dad with a headlamp wandering the room of you.

I am flicking matches into air,
hoping for an explosion, a fire to make you clean of us.

VALERIE MINER

Iconoclast

There went in two and two unto Noah into the ark, the
male and the female, as God had commanded Noah.
Genesis 7:9. *King James Bible*

Üçhisar, Cappadocia. A crisp March morning. Our twentieth
anniversary. We really are here.

I slide gently from bed as sun begins to pink the sky. At the
window, I watch the rosy horizon relinquishing to a pale spring blue.
Then. Balloons! Stripped and polka dotted. Red, fuchsia, chartreuse
and golden hot air balloons. Shimmering plump jewels ascending
and floating over the Gaudi-like formations of porous rock.

Gratitude is all I feel: for Layla; for twenty years of love; for
finally spending our honeymoon in this mythical land we used to call
Asia Minor. Home to Noah's family and his ark of creatures. World
of the Bosphorus Straight, the Mediterranean, Aegean, Marmara and
Black Seas. Birthplace of Layla's Kurdish grandparents who met in a
Detroit Laundromat.

She's always dreamed of ancestral voices and people with
familiar faces walking down the street. Light brown eyes; dark, wavy
hair; long, elegant noses.

For my part, I dreamt of Noah and eggplant—or aubergine
as they call it on the English menus here. Ah, this is the land of a
thousand aubergine dishes.

"Hey, hey, where'd you go?" Layla sits up sleepily, the white
sheet over one shoulder exposing a sweet brown breast.

"Stunning morning," I say. "Balloons!"

She pats the bed. "It's what? Dawn?" She's groggy. "And
we're supposed to be on vacation. Please Beth, come back to bed."

I kiss her forehead and, tempted as I am by her dark, alert aureole and the warmth between those sheets, I decline. "Sorry, sweetheart. I'm wide awake. Think I'll stroll into town, get coffee and meet you back here—when—eight o'clock—breakfast?

"Deserted on my honeymoon," she moans, already halfway back to sleep. "Better make it nine."

I slip on my down jacket, perfect for spring at this high altitude.

Then, as if from a coma, her voice rises, "Be careful! Remember that American photographer who was kidnapped."

"Yes, sure," I answer softly, hoping she'll drift back to sleep. I don't remind her that the American was taken way out east of Gaziantep, hundreds of miles from here. "Your grandmother told you too many stories, darling. Sweet dreams."

The air is crisp and I'm glad I brought a shawl. Silk and cashmere according to the hobbled old merchant in Istanbul's Grand Bazar. Who knows? Whatever the fabric, it's warm and deep purple. A lush, aubergine shade.

The scruffy little coffee shop is surprisingly crowded.

Of course I'm the only woman. Bald men leaning on small tables, chatting softly in Turkish. In the background, they're playing an intricate Persian oud piece. I sniff the coffee in my miniature cup. Yes, enough to propel me right into the day. The first sip is sublime. Thick, black, Turkish sludge. Edges of the room suddenly sharpen. I smell musky tobacco, sweet honey and fresh yogurt. Heaven.

"Pardon, you look like a visitor here." He's tall, thin, red-haired. Midwestern accent. Wisconsin or Minnesota. His tweed jacket and horn-rimmed glasses are the perfect costume.

I do not want to chat. I want to continue sipping *kahve* and marveling that I am in Turkey. Fertile womb of civilizations. Ancient land of the Hittites, Assyrians, Jews, Romans, Byzantines, Kurds, Alevis, Sunnis, Shias, Orthodox Greeks, Armenians. . . Home to Holy Mary and the Apostle John.

"*Parlez-vous français?*"

Yep his accent is quintessential Milwaukee.

He smiles earnestly, waiting.

209

No point in being petulant. "Yes, I'm visiting for a few weeks."

"American, hey," he sighs. "Great. Do you know the way to Göreme?"

I look through the intruder, willing him to disappear.

He tries again. "The UNESCO World Heritage Open Air Museum?"

He says this slowly as if recalling a page straight out of *The Lonely Planet*. And I do mean straight.

Thing is, my entire life is about caring for people—the kids I counsel, their parents and lots of burned-out teachers in Philadelphia. Here I'm on vacation.

"They say walk through Pigeon Valley," I allow, "but. . ."

"Hmm." He frowns. His eyes look watery—watery sad or watery sick, I can't tell—and his hand trembles as he lifts the tiny cup. "I tried that way yesterday and got lost. This is my first trip to Cappadocia, a world apart from the rest of Turkey. From the rest of the cosmos, hey."

"You can walk along the road. Not as picturesque, but direct. That's what Layla and I are going to do."

"Ah," he says, expectantly.

It takes all my willpower not to invite him. The hazardous helping reflex. I swallow the rest of the coffee too fast and grab my purse. So much for savoring village color.

He nods good-bye. "Nice to meet you."

◊

Our hotel serves breakfast in a charming brick room with a roaring fire, evoking the famous local underground caves. Eight tables are discreetly set apart in the windowless, lamp-lit chamber.

The first to arrive, we take the corner spot.

Layla selects a fragrant lemon poppy seed muffin from the inviting basket. "Glad you made it back alive." She winks.

"Good sleep?"

"Delicious. Just missing one thing. The warm body next to me." She takes my hand.

I squeeze her long fingers. "This isn't Philly," I whisper. "You have to tamp down the PDA."

A waiter pads up silently and places two steaming omelets on our little table.

"*Teşekkür ederim*," I say in my best Turkish. My only Turkish so far.

"You're welcome." He grins.

◊

We've fantasized about visiting Turkey since we met. Layla ached to see her grandparents' land. She adores the rugs. Yes, I was hooked on the food, but I also felt a childhood tug from my church days, to see where Noah landed. Although access to Eastern Turkey—where our dreams reside—is prohibited, Cappadocia strangely feels close enough.

Both of us shed religion in college. Mine was evangelical Christianity. Layla was Kurdish Muslim on her Mom's side and Nation of Islam on her dad's. Her brother Mika is still in the Nation. We both, in our separate ways, always felt we belonged here.

◊

Mr. Lonely Planet ambles into the dining room, laden with maps, two newspapers, a paperback guide and a library book.

I concentrate on the delicious omelet. "Perfect," I coo to Layla, "golden on the outside and gooey on the inside."

"Like someone I know."

I blush. "Really now, cut that out. Save it for home—or for our fall trip to San Francisco."

"Hello again," calls the ginger-haired tourist. "I didn't know you were staying here."

Layla looks him over with practiced journalist eyes.

"Oh," he explains uneasily to her. "We met this morning in the coffee shop. Well, we didn't introduce ourselves." He extends his hand, dropping books and papers. "My name is Richard Maxwell." He's distracted by Layla's beautiful face. A lot of people stare; some ask what ethnic mix created this woman with cherry wood skin, haunting pale eyes and softly curling hair.

I don't draw much curiosity since my blond locks and blue eyes bespeak a pretty common English-German partnership.

In spite of myself, I reach down and hand him his copy of *For Whom the Bell Tolls*.

Layla continues studying him. All she has to do is look and people yield, not knowing to what. "Where're you from?"

"Wisconsin. I teach history at Beloit."

"Beth Langley from Philadelphia. And this is my partner, Layla Waters."

He pulls up a chair, then places his books and papers on the floor. "Mind if I join you?"

Layla is quick. "Plenty of tables, Rick, if you want to spread out your library—over there or there." She points to the farthest table.

"Richard, actually. And I wouldn't mind company. My wife stayed behind in Istanbul—for the museums. And of course, the shopping. I could hardly pry her away from that damn covered bazaar."

Layla smiles thinly, unwilling to admit her fellow feeling.

The waiter appears with an extra place setting and more muffins.

"So you must be on spring break." Cordiality is my professional reflex and liability. "When do you go back?" I'm hoping he'll say tomorrow.

"In fact, I'm on sabbatical. So I have all the time in the world, until late August."

Layla asks, "How do you like the novel?" Somehow, this seems a more polite question.

"Oh, Hemingway, one great writer. A classic. I've read everything he's written."

Layla digs into her eggs, handing the conversation back to me. I can just imagine what she'll say on the walk to Göreme.

I learned to read her expressions in college. Douglass completely transformed our lives. As a hyper Christian freshman, I was phobic about near occasions of sin. I graduated as a lesbian socialist with a full fellowship to grad school and a most unlikely lover.

President of the Black Caucus and two years older than I, stunning, brilliant Layla was thoroughly intimidating. Like everyone else, I admired her from afar. Late one evening, we found ourselves walking in tandem back from the library. In the chilly darkness my shyness lifted. The following week we went out for pizza. Then a couple of movies. One three-day weekend, we checked in at the Starry Night budget hotel and we've been together ever since. I chose a graduate program in Philadelphia, because Layla had been recruited by *The Inquirer*. A fast, and as I would have said in the past, a "blessed" two decades.

Eventually, Layla quit *The Inquirer* to do investigative work. For the last two years she's commuted to DC as the go-to freelancer on the DIA, DHS, NSA, CIA. I'm still learning about the Bureau of Counter Terrorism and the National Reconnaissance Office and—hundreds—thousands—of other intelligence programs. Her articles are weighty, edgy and a little scary. I'm a worrier, so she spares me some background. Anyway, we both love our jobs and do pretty useful work. We have a comfortable condo and a wacky dog.

Each December, I send a donation to Douglass and a Christmas card to the Starry Night Hotel.

◊

Naturally, Richard tags along on our walk to the museum.

"Terrible sense of direction," he explains.

"I bet." Layla says archly.

"Hope you don't mind the company." He's speeding, looking better after a big breakfast and four cups of *kahwe*. "I always find it more interesting to *share* an expedition."

"Especially on one's honeymoon," Layla mutters not quite under her breath.

"Oh, my, congratulations," he declares. "When did you get married? Can you *do* that in Pennsylvania? I know you can in Iowa and Massachusetts."

Layla pretends to clean a spot from her sunglasses.

"We've been together twenty years." I don't bother to express our queer disdain for bourgeois matrimony.

"Ah," he fills the silence. "Aren't we lucky with the weather?"

Neither of us responds.

"I mean, because it's an open air museum."

"Unh hunh," Layla allows.

Her resistance winds him up. "They have the best Byzantine art in Cappadocia. Frescoes and paintings dating from the tenth century."

"You've done your homework. Or do you teach *Turkish art* history?" I ask in spite of myself.

"Well the art, it's all part of studying a culture."

"Perhaps you can show us a thing or two," says Layla, making the most of our abduction.

"I'll try. Hey, thanks for letting me join you."

"It's nothing." Layla shrugs, then glares at me.

Our trek takes us through a greening valley. It's longer than we expected—four miles—and we arrive at the same time as four coaches.

"Let's start at the end," Richard says. "That way, we'll avoid crowding into those little churches with the organized tours."

"Good idea." Layla nods, almost warming up.

Richard, of course, knows all about the Byzantine bishops and saints and icons. He's full of information, but not pedantic. Probably a good teacher.

The Dark Church is supposed to be a highlight, but the Chinese arrive first. Trailing close behind are the French.

"It's worth waiting for." He snaps his fingers nervously.

Richard is right. Under protective dim candle light, the ceiling murals are astonishing, yet nothing compared to the almost living scene of the crucifixion above the altar. The iconoclasts missed

214

this church in their rampage, beheading and defacing Christian images.

Four hours pass and we're starving.

◊

Our companion knows a café in the Cave Hotel and greets the owner Mehmet by name.

"Richard, you are back! And with beautiful women. Come, come to my best table, here against the wall."

Richard ushers us in as if he's the local pasha. "What would you like to eat, Layla and Beth?"

"I don't care as long as it's aubergine," I proclaim.

Layla cracks, "I'll have a bacon cheeseburger." Registering Mehmet's troubled eyes, she quickly adds. "Joke. I like all the food in this country. What do you recommend?"

Two hours later we are sated.

Throughout the lavish lunch, something nags at me. "Richard, this morning you said you didn't know the way to Göreme."

He takes a sip of the dark purple wine. "Yes."

"But you've been to this restaurant." I'm getting nervous. "You know Mehmet."

The men exchange cursory glances.

Richard starts laughing.

Mehmet blanches, retreats to the kitchen.

"You know my terrible sense of direction," Richard falters, staring absently at Mehmet's empty chair. "Yesterday I got off the bus here, I mean, uh, outside Göreme, instead of in Uçhisar at our hotel."

"That's right," Mehmet confirms, carrying a tray of coffee and sweets. "At lunchtime. So Richard ate. And since it was early in the season and he was my only customer, I drove him to Uçhisar."

I cock my head waiting for Layla's response. She's blissed out by the dessert.

"Rose petals, sugar, almonds. Perfect," she purrs deliriously.

"You know?" Mehmet throws up his hands in surprise. "You know this dish?"

215

"My grandmother made this for birthdays."

"A Kurdish dessert," observes Richard.

"Yes," she grins.

"Of course. Layla is a Kurdish name," Mehmet muses.

She smiles, takes another bite. "Yes, my grandparents were born east of here."

"Really," remarks Richard. Then adds for some reason, "I have a lot of Kurdish friends."

Why does he make me so nervous? He's just an awkward nerdy guy, right?

By late afternoon, we manage a successful escape. Richard does not follow us into the *hammam*.

Quiet. Yet another place where we are the only customers. Layla was right about traveling off season.

First: the facials. A small young woman wearing a turquoise hijab paints our foreheads, noses, cheeks and chins in a grainy substance with a rude odor. Then she leads us to the sauna. It's pretty much like our YWCA sauna except for the presence of a majestically large woman in a black bra and lace-trimmed black panties.

Layla raises her killer eyebrows.

The woman ignores us. She exits every five minutes and returns quickly with wet hair. Finally, she leaves for good.

We hear a rap on the sauna door.

It's our midnight negligee lady. She takes my hand and whispers, "*Seni seviyorum.*"

I smile, completely lost, but this is just a bath house, nothing to worry about.

She tightens her grip on my fingers. "That means, 'I love you,' in Turkish."

"*Teşekkür ederim,*" I murmur.

"My name is Aydan, meaning 'moonlight.'"

"Nice to meet you. I don't reveal the meaning of my name—"house of figs"—to her or anyone else. "I'm Beth."

"This I know."

Aydan scrubs me as if I were a muddy five year old—between my toes, behind my ears—then orders me to lie on the marble slab. Across the room, Layla is getting similar treatment. All of a sudden,

I'm pummeled by a huge plastic bag of sudsy water. Again. And again. And again.

Aydan sits me on another marble surface, pours clean water over my head and torso as I watch the soap gurgle down a large drain in the stone floor.

◊

Layla is already stretched out on the massage table on the other side of a latticed room divider.

"You OK?" she asks.

"Clean," I say. "And apparently well-loved."

"What?"

Our masseuses swish in. Khushi, from Krgyzstan, diagnoses my back as "a catastrophe." After twenty minutes, she says, "I think you need another half-hour."

◊

I admit, Derinkuyu is my idea. I've always loved hidden things. And this ancient city is ten stories underground.

We've rented a car for the expedition and as we drive through the emerald countryside we find snow clustered around tree trunks and in crevasses in this season between winter and spring. A few purple and blue wildflowers grow low to the ground.

"OK," Layla looks at me pointedly from the driver's seat; I want her to focus on the twisting road. "I'll visit this ancient town for you because you agreed to have dinner at the Museum Hotel for me. But I'm not looking forward to it."

Although I fret about prices at the posh hotel, I've agreed. You learn compromise during twenty years.

"At least we have privacy today." She shakes her head. "I really thought Richard was going to trail us into the *hammam*."

I laugh at the image of him pummeled with soapsuds by those sturdy women. "He's just a lonely guy." I'm following Khushi's advice to lighten up.

"I don't know." Her eyes grow serious. "There is *something* weird about him."

◊

Along with the entrance ticket, we each accept a plastic wrapped hand sanitizer. I've collected five of these wipes at different tourist sights. Are they meant to protect us or the museums? We pass through a metal detector and enter the cool, dark cave, where the last vestiges of a traditional museum disappear.

"Can't see a fucking thing," groans Layla.

"*Voila!*" I switch on a halogen flashlight.

"I've always said my girl was brilliant."

"And practical," declares a man behind us.

My stomach flips.

"Professor Maxwell, I presume?" Layla doesn't bother to turn around.

"From your voices, I'd guess Bethany Langley and Layla Waters."

Lightheaded, I wonder how he knows my birth name. Everyone assumes it's Elizabeth and I never reveal my tribe of raging born-again sibs: Constance, Beulah, Caleb, Gideon and Zachariah.

"Clever to bring a flashlight." He fills the silence. "If you don't mind sharing your illumination, I'll share some of mine about this astonishing site."

"You're an expert on underground cities?" Layla assesses him.

He's wearing a striped sweater over his checked shirt and I'm grateful I can't make out the colors in this dim light. He seems even taller and wraith-like in this spooky atmosphere.

"I've read up on the place, but I'm no expert."

Resigned, Layla concedes, "Lead on."

"The site goes back to 2,000 BC. The Hittites built here first, digging into the porous rock to make winter shelter for themselves and their animals. They settled the top two floors."

One by one, we slither down narrow, low-ceilinged passages toward the floors and civilizations below.

MINER

One long chamber, he explains, was a classroom. Early Christians hid down on this level from the Romans. Throughout the rooms and passageways, we find air holes reaching to the sky, to admit light, to release smoke.

He takes our photo in front of the baptismal font. He says he wants to send it to his wife, to show her what she's missing.

So much in this country happens *underground*. The *hammam* yesterday. Derinkuyu today. Although the mysteries of Turkey always attracted me, the hiding, the secrecy is unnerving.

"They have everything: bedrooms, kitchens, wine presses, animal stalls. The Byzantine Christians were the ones who dug the very bottom floor, hiding from the Muslims, who—depending on your politics—were conquerors or invaders."

"And yours would be?" Why am I so testy?

"Pardon?" He snaps his fingers nervously.

"Your politics?"

He steps back. "Oh, I'm a registered independent. But I suppose I'm a wishy-washy liberal like most of us."

Us. I wonder.

Layla is moaning.

I rush over. I've been so preoccupied with Richard that I just now notice that she's sweaty and trembling.

"Oh, god." She slips to the floor.

"Are you OK?" He bends down to take her hand.

"It's just," she wheezes, "that I'm having trouble breath . . . breathing."

"Are you claustrophobic?" He's acting like Dr. *Médecin sans Frontières*.

"No!" she snaps as if he inquired about an STD.

"Some people react."

She takes a long breath. "This place is kind of freaky. Imagining twenty thousand people burrowed together down here."

"Take my arm," he says, all bedside manner. "We'll walk slowly. You'll be in the fresh air before you know it."

Outside, the late morning light is blinding.

"Breathe deeply," he instructs, "slowly."

Color returns to her cheeks and focus to her eyes.

219

"Gee, thanks," Layla rubs her temples. "I knew I didn't like heights but this is my first–and last–underground city." She continues hectically, "I guess I'm basically a functional person; there isn't much call to climb ten stories down into the earth."

I wonder how deep missile silos are.

"This happens to many people." His hand is still on her shoulder, the red curly hairs creeping from the cuff of his green checked shirt down to his manicured nails.

We stand silent and awkward for a moment.

"Really, thanks Richard." Layla says with renewed confidence. "Nice to see you. We're off to Soğanlı for lunch and some above-ground churches. Enjoy your adventures."

◊

As I open the door to our rental car, he calls to us.

"If I'm not intruding. . ."

I get in the car, pretending not to hear.

"Yes, Richard, what is it?" Suddenly, she's solicitous.

"Well, I have an old bus schedule and it turns out I'll be waiting another two hours. I was going to those churches–some of my favorites–9ᵗʰ to 13ᵗʰ century–too." He looks pointedly at the empty back seat.

"Hop in," she says, as if he were an old friend.

He buckles the seat belt and leans forward. "I know a café where we can get great lentil soup and *Patlicanli Pilav*, oozing with onion and eggplant."

"I bet you do," I say, almost *sotto voce*.

◊

Despite my big attitude, I enjoy lunch.

He's as curious as ever, asking about life in Philadelphia. Our work. Again, he knows just the right wine to order and Layla, still ascending from Derinkuyu, enjoys several glasses.

"I admire good reporting." He's leaning a little too close to her. "It's like being an historian, only in real time. I guess you always

220

have to be 'on;' anyone could be a source."

"Not really. Here, for instance, Beth and I are just on holiday."

"Oh." He's momentarily disconcerted. Then: "Tell me more about your family. Where in Turkey were they from?"

"Grandfather was born in Hani. Grandmother left the Dersim region in the 1930s."

"Ah, the famous Dersim Rebellion. Was your grandmother a hero for the cause?"

I fiddle with the pepper mill, untwisting the bottom to find the hidden microphone.

"No, but she was proud of her father's involvement. Quite a fiery guy, apparently."

I've never heard of this relative, her great-grandfather, let alone of the famous rebellion. The wine—and the relief of escaping Derkinkuyu—are having strange effects on Layla, who is cryptic at best with strange men.

"Those were hard times in Turkey," Richard nods. "But now the country is so open."

◊

Naturally Richard knows all about the churches. He explains which frescoes were defaced by Muslim iconoclasts and which by more recent vandals. Still much of the ancient paint—deep blues as well as the bloody reds—survive.

At a higher elevation now, we're bundled in coats and scarves. The photos Richard takes make us look like Siberian refugees. I doubt his wife will feel she's missed much.

◊

Driving back to Uçhisar, past snow-covered fields, I gaze at the late sun blazing in the golden grasses.

"Thanks for letting me tag along," he says.

"No problem," says Layla. "Our luck to find a whiz in Turkish history."

"Hardly a whiz."

"But you're a professor at Beloit," I declare. I feel prickly, perhaps it's the red wine headache. "Speaking of the college, doesn't Nick Adams teach literature there? He'd be an old man now. But it's a small campus, right?"

"Now that you mention it, I think I met him at a reception." He drums his fingers on the door handle. "So many of these social functions, you know."

Layla is grinning, looking like her old self. "Richard, as thanks for guiding us around, not to mention for rescuing me from Derinkuyu, let us take you out to dinner tonight."

"Why I'd love. . ."

I interrupt. "Layla, don't you remember we got the last reservation at the Museum Hotel."

She stares at me. "We could go somewhere else."

"You promised the Museum Hotel. Don't you remember, for my birthday?" I'm frightened now by all the coincidences and inconsistencies. And determined to dodge Richard—or whatever his real name is—as long as possible.

"Oh, riiight," she finally tunes into my urgency. "How did I forget? Sorry, Richard. But thanks for everything."

"My pleasure," he says in that forlorn Mr. Lonely Planet voice.

◊

This last evening, I try to concentrate on the beautiful village. I listen to the percussion of our heels on the cobblestones as we walk from dinner to our room. A sliver of moon shines along with Jupiter and Venus, and I recall the logo of the Starry Night Hotel.

Layla is softly humming "If I Ain't Got You."

I can't help myself, and soon Layla and I are arguing about Richard again.

"You know, I'm usually the suspicious one with my journalistic trigger," she shakes her head. "But he seems harmless. So there are a few discrepancies. So you think he's what—CIA? MIA? MIT?" She laughs.

222

"A *few* discrepancies?"

"He was pretty useful in that goddamn cave."

I keep my voice low. "He's a helpless stranger on Monday morning and then gives us a complete tour of Göreme. He stalks us to Derinkuyu."

"*Stalks?* Come on. It's a small place. You run into people."

"How about 'Bethany?' No one's ever guessed my given name. You wouldn't even *believe* it at first."

"So maybe his family is fundamentalist, too."

"The guy who's read all of Hemingway, cops to maybe meeting one of his fictional characters at a *Beloit Faculty Reception?*"

"Adams is a common name."

"Wake up, Layla. He was super curious about your NSA articles. Mika's work for the Nation, your Kurdish grandparents."

She takes my hand. "Darling, you were interested in those things when we met."

"Any of them could get you arrested here."

She laughs, "Calm down, Beth. Remember Khushi's hard work on your rhomboids. Besides, Turkey is a democracy, a NATO member, an American ally."

"And he's probably wondering if our Layla is an American ally."

"Enough," she tickles my palm. "This is our last night. We'll be in Philly tomorrow. Let's enjoy these beautiful mountains under the stars."

I gaze at the bright sky and remember the first Cappadocian dawn of dazzling balloons. I try to be grateful that we truly are here, in the land of our dreams.

◊

Damn. The flight from Kayseri lands late, so we have to sprint across the Istanbul airport. Sprint as fast as we can, lugging big suitcases stuffed with rugs, woven pillow cases and ceramics.

Check-in goes smoothly.

And the security line isn't long.

"We'll make it easily," Layla says. "Time for a latte and one more baklava."

"Maybe." I'm sweating despite the aggressive air conditioning. Pulling out the hand sanitizer from Derinkuyu, I wipe my forehead. "You still have your passport? Your boarding pass?"

"Of course! What's going on with you, Beth? We're taking a simple, non-stop flight to New York. We've got good seats at the front of economy. We'll be fine."

Obviously, she's right. Security is a breeze. Now we have seventy minutes before the flight. Plenty of time for coffee and to browse the duty free chocolate for our dog-sitter. Right on schedule.

"Sorry, don't know what got into me."

"You've stopped fantasizing about J. Edgar Jr?"

"Yeah, yeah." I rub my tired eyes.

"Coffee?" she offers.

"No, I'll watch the carry-ons. I don't want to get too wired before the flight."

As she walks away, I hear a child giggling. I turn to find a woman waving a yellow balloon animal at her toddler.

A sports team—young boys in green uniforms—are laughing and jiving outside the electronics store.

Beyond them, in a corner, I notice a uniformed man listening closely to a tall, thin guy in a baseball cap with his back to me. I try not to stare. Try not to watch the skinny guy snapping his fingers.

Suddenly, the world turns red and silent.

The men are both running toward the coffee bar.

Layla looks up, startled.

The click of handcuffs echoes across the duty free zone. Some travelers stare. Others turn away quickly.

I run toward them, dragging the briefcases and backpacks, shouting, "No, no, no!"

Out of the blue, a round woman uncannily resembling Aydan from the *hammam* takes my elbow. "Relax. They will just ask her a few questions. But your friend may miss the flight." She checks the baggage tags and hands Layla's carry-ons to another woman. "I will escort you to the gate." There's a compact black pistol at her waist.

MINER

"Layla, Layla," I scream.

She turns, tugging away from the man in uniform. Richard has disappeared. "Call Uncle Daras," she shouts. "As soon as you land. And Mika."

I try to pull away, but the guard's grip is too tight. "Yes, yes." Tears stream down my cheeks. I can't leave her. But Aydan's sister gives me no choice. "Oh, Layla, Layla."

"Come!" the woman demands, yanking me toward the gate.

I stand firm, turning back, but Layla is nowhere in sight.

Willa Elizabeth Schmidt

How I Lost You

> *I hope you died quick and I hope you died clean*
> *Or, Willie McBride, was it slow and obscene?*
> —Eric Bogle, "No Man's Land (Green
> Fields of France)"

In 1965 I see Vienna for the first time, and while I'm there, Poldi Tante takes me to Ybbs on the Danube, your hometown, and that of our mother. We walk along a winding medieval street to the main square and Saint Laurentius church, with its gothic steeple towering over the landscape. Poldi shows me the school where our mother, and later you, once warmed wooden benches, and we gaze at the river flowing full and broad, if not exactly blue. A marker of floods over centuries and into the present day bears witness to the water's powerful presence.

She leads me to a stone monument with names of the town's war dead, and among those of World War II, we find your name. You are remembered there, immortalized, young warrior for a misguided land. My mother's firstborn, my only sibling, the half-brother I've never known.

What else? A few old pictures, stories from Poldi, this aunt who wanted to be your mother. A small book bound in scuffed leather, found on you when you died in Russia, soldier for the country that was no longer Austria, during the battle at Wosty on a steaming August day.

Nothing more. Precious little, but it's all I've had to work with. No one else can tell your story.

◊

Hot, hot along the marshy Zhizdra, summer in Russia choked as a Florida swamp. Hitler in his headquarters in the nearby Ukraine, fires every general who offers sensible advice. Does it happen there, at that sun-drenched river, or in some nearby contested wood? Or afterwards, as they carry you off on a stretcher, or when they try to staunch the bleeding in the field *lazarett*? You died miserably, Poldi Tante tells me, that's what she'd heard. Heard from whom and how did they know?

Nineteen years old, too young to die miserably. Too young to die.

◊

In the first photograph you are perhaps fourteen. You lean over a workbench, not yet soldiering but soldering, fresh-faced and totally absorbed. Your left hand holds the solder wire while the right directs the iron; the object worked on is lost in a glare of heat. I cannot see your eyes. Goggles protect them, metal cups with holes for ventilation. Your mouth opens slightly in concentration. Your hands grasp the tools delicately but firmly, as a musician handles a fine instrument. Your hair is dark, trimmed short in back but richly waved on top, the sort of hair a mother might run her hands through.

Are you at school? At work? The image is without explanation. How have you learned this task? Not from your father; he is gone. Do you even know who he is? Your mother you remember, but she is gone too. She is in America, newly married.

The next photo shows you athletic, with a taste for adventure. You climb a cliff over a river, most likely the Danube, in bulky sweater and hiking shorts. One foot is perched on a narrow pinnacle while the rest of your body clings to a wall of sheer stone that you will scale successfully, though it looks impossible. You stare at the camera without fear. You are still a boy and the world is not yet finished with you.

Now you are taller. You stand in deep snow on the slope of a mountain with your legs apart, skis and poles planted jauntily at your side. You wear a smart beret, but your face is unreadable; you are too far away. Is this at the Semmering pass, or somewhere in Tyrol? Again, no place or date. Someone, Poldi Tante?, has written "Bernhard" on the back, nothing more.

How little I know, even about these few tangible bits.

Finally I can place you in time. A year is provided, 1939: you are sixteen, wearing a uniform. You stand at the base of a gentle slope, a backdrop of waving grass. Two old women, grandmother and great-grandmother, stand beside you in ankle-length skirts. *Großmam* is full-figured in a plain dress and sports a little straw hat, while *Urgroßmam* wears a white babushka tied under her chin. She leans on a cane and stares into the distance, seemingly lost in thought. You and our grandmother—for she is mine too—look at the camera. Your uniform is odd: dish-like hat, woolen jacket with wide lapels, and what looks like a dark blue or black skirt, knee length in kilt fashion. I translate what *Großmam* has written on the back: "This is when he had to go to the Voluntary Work Service, in the Hitler time. Bernhard, Great-grandma, and Yours Truly. Ybbs, August 15, 1939."

Mußte. Had to. *Freiwillig.* Voluntary.

Perhaps you have a clue, tall and knob-kneed on that day of lush green summer, your cheekbones gaunt and eyes so darkly solemn—perhaps you have a suspicion of what lies ahead.

◊

I have a picture of our mother as a young woman, an old studio photograph pasted on heavy cardboard embossed with a gold flower and the words "Viktoria-Portrait." She wears a striped blouse with wide collar and long sleeves. Her hair is short and dark, with those thick waves you inherited. She has the full, soft cheeks of youth but her eyes are skeptical, almost sullen; the words *Sommer 1923* are scrawled below her face. She sends this picture to her best friend, who has gone with her family to America. You, my brother, are not quite one year old. She has, as they say, been around the block. Where is your father, the man who impregnated her?

You are not with her, Bernhard. You are in Ybbs, with Great-grandmother, who raised you and our mother too because our mother

SCHMIDT

too was a father-gone child. And her mother, our grandmother, was busy with the others, the children who came after her marriage. What a complicated story! So many questions! So much is hidden in the blur of years . . .

Then she leaves for good, your restless mother, following her friend to Chicago and leaving you behind. You are six years old—how do you feel? Do you cry your tender heart out? Do you begin to hate her, as she hated her own mother?

Years later, in that new world, she becomes *my* mother. And I love her and lose her when I am also still a child and do not know of you, her other child.

Now I live with the mysteries, making of them what I can.

◊

The next photograph gives the best view of you, the closest and clearest. It is 1940 or 1941; you are a soldier. Your face is in half-profile: dark eyes, strong nose, our mother's soft mouth. Those sticking-out ears are from the mystery man, not from her. Your fine black hair is covered by an army cap with a visor and thick headband, adorned on top by an eagle insignia with a little circle underneath that is indiscernible but surely holds a swastika. The *Anschluss* is three years old and you are a soldier in Hitler's army. The insignia indicates your rank and status as *Panzer Pionier*, tank infantryman or combat engineer. You are serious but still boyish, handsome in a heavy woolen coat with brass buttons. You stand in formation; behind you are other soldiers in the same uniform and hints of faces: an ear, an Adam's apple, a chin. A fresh-baked batch of young men marching off to battle on the Eastern Front. You are eighteen years old.

Poldi Tante is our mother's half-sister. She has the same silvery hair our mother developed in middle age, worn in the same wreathed coils, but her eyes are blue instead of brown. She is petite and my mother was tall; nevertheless one sees a resemblance, especially around the face. She keeps in touch, writing letters to Chicago. She and Pepsch Onkel have no children. They would have adopted you, she tells me; you could have lived with them in Vienna after the war as their son. Unless, of course, you chose to go to America, where

229

your mother had her new life and was eager to see you.

When you come home on leave though, you already know. "Pepsch Onkel will be back," you tell her—Poldi's husband is on the Western Front—"but I won't. You'll see." "Don't say that, Bernhard," she scolds, "you mustn't say that."
You are right. Right on both counts.

◊

The last photograph . . . No. I need to talk about the book, that worn leather notebook found on you when you died. It is sent to our aunt's apartment, where you were staying before going off to war. "You should have it," Poldi says, when I visit Vienna. She is over sixty, her hair is white; you've been dead more than twenty years. Our mother—yours and mine—is gone too, and who is left to care?

I care, though for a while I stop thinking about you. I tuck the photographs and notebook away and go back to my old life, not knowing that one day I will try to write your story. I return to the States and enter graduate school and for a while, the present takes precedence over the past.

In 1969, I return to Vienna on a Fulbright Grant to do dissertation research. For months I am busy in libraries, taking notes on a turn-of-the-century Viennese playwright. I am not thinking about you. I visit my aunt and other relatives, but you are more or less forgotten. When I return to my university in the Midwest, I spend months writing and finally finish the dissertation, earning the PhD and vowing never to break my head over footnotes again.

Eventually, as academia falls away, the past and its revelations gain renewed importance. I decide to write about the people, the history of that dark time, the lives that have shocked and shaped me. I want to write about *you*, my lost brother, to assemble the bits and pieces. I turn to the photographs, and at last to the notebook: the only record you left.

Its yellowed pages hold the notes of a soldier-engineer trained to build systems, set traps for the enemy, scope terrain for troops

230

coming after. *Pioniere* were "jack-of-all-trades," the army's point men, who suffered very high casualties.

You record a wealth of practical information: how to build a fire, anchor a tent, dig a trench, tie complicated knots. There are chemistry tables, weights and melting points of metals, contents of chloroform, firebombs, Cyankalium (KCN or potassium cyanide). Much of it I don't understand. What strikes me is your fastidious lettering, the intricate drawings accompanying these notations. Terrain symbols that go on for pages, Morse code alphabet and messages, animal tracks and the above-mentioned knots, all drawn in bold black ink with careful shading and minuscule printed labels. Random instructions, always with illustrations, on setting up communications using sirens and flags, or preserving pencil drawings by coating them with fresh milk. Night blindness is mentioned, with a list of vegetables to counter it, and a rare prose paragraph that advises, "Questions must always be asked in such a way that the man cannot answer with yes or no. They should therefore begin with 'why, for what purpose, where, how, which, when, etc."

From her, your talent for drawing. Our mother left paintings, delicate work, of people and flowers. She was musical too, could sit down at our old upright and tear off Viennese waltzes by ear. Who was *her* father? Another unknown. I have the music a bit, not the hand for drawing. That gift is yours.

When the book is turned upside-down and around, one finds addresses, from your hometown of Ybbs, including that of *Urgroßmam* Anna. Poldi and Pepsch are listed on Vienna's Eduardstrasse, as well as army friends, and photography studios and workshops. Could the mystery man be here somewhere too, or has he disappeared forever? I find our mother with my father on Wrightwood Avenue in Chicago, and a line underneath that stops my breath. My birth date, and *Wila Elisabeth*. Misspelled, but there.

You knew of my existence, long before I learned of yours. What did you think, or did it matter at all? Your knowledge was severed at the start, while mine, belated, lingers on.

A few things remain. A photo of a boy your age in crewneck sweater, school friend? Another of soldiers, one of higher rank standing in a field while others are heads poking out of the ground— some sort of maneuver. A well-preserved one-pfennig stamp shows the profiled head of General von Hindenburg, white against a black background. Finally, a small section titled *Lieder!* with three sets of lyrics. The first is a Tyrolean folk song proclaiming love for the mountains. The second is a *Luftwaffe* song: "My dearest *Mädel*, give me your hand / We're flying off to Engeland / And if we don't return, / We did our duty, don't forget us." Finally, you've copied verses of the "Edelweiss" march composed in 1941 for the troops, about a young man climbing treacherous heights to secure the flower found only there for his dearest, most beautiful sweetheart. The lyrics are saccharine, but the music is martial; no wistful Rogers and Hammerstein here.

I wonder if you had a *Mädel*, a sweetheart. If you knew that kind of love. If you even had time to learn.

On the spring day in 1938 when Hitler makes his triumphant entry into Austria, welcomed by women and children tossing flowers, where are you? A schoolboy, not yet sixteen. Are you aware of the greater world and its sinister machinations? Knowing what lies ahead, some choose suicide, but hundreds of thousands of others cheer wildly on Vienna's Heldenplatz when their new *Führer* greets them, fulfilling his dream of bringing the land of his birth home to the Reich. I assume that you, like the very young everywhere, are caught up in your own life, parroting the opinions of family and friends if you think about it at all. Provincial, Catholic, patriotic: exuberant at this union with a powerful, annoyingly strident but German-speaking neighbor, more like you than the alien east with its Slavs and Soviets, Communist disruptors of order.

Never mind that this *Anschluss*, this annexation, means that your beloved Austria would be the *Ostmark* now, no longer a land of its own but Nazi Germany's eastern flank. Never mind that Jewish citizens are being humiliated, forced to scrub sidewalks and barracks— do them good, they'd milked the economy, hadn't they, with so many unemployed and wanting? Never mind that soon you will put on your first uniform and report to the *Freiwilliger Arbeitsdienst*, whose youthful members built roads and bridges but will now be dedicated to military support. Your friends and schoolmates are in it as well, for jobs are few, and the FAD pays a minimum wage. Could you have refused?

Six months FAD, now turned RAD—*Reichsarbeitsdienst*—with low pay, long hours, barracks life. Camaraderie too; young men together, all being prepared. Readied for Russia, the Eastern Front. For Stalingrad some, death in the mind-numbing cold. For you the Zhizdra River on a sweltering August day.

This is Hitler's folly, coveting Baku's rich oilfields and industrial Stalingrad, disregarding generals, splitting up his forces: in time he would pay, but never so dearly as you.

◊

At Klosterneuburg for training, then off to the east. I picture you in a tent, some makeshift barracks, inking entries in your book, that small bit of evidence you've left of your thoughts. Are you with the troops pushing toward Moscow in late 1941, whose tanks got mired in mud and snow? News still reaches you from home, from family, for how else could my name have made its way into those pages?

The temperature on December fourth drops to minus 31 Fahrenheit. The Soviet counteroffensive is unexpectedly effective, the Wehrmacht forced to withdraw. Moscow isn't taken and for some months afterward the Eastern Front is quiet. Perhaps that is when you make it back to Vienna on leave, find your way back with a chunk of war behind you, to make your dire prophesy.

A fateful month, December 1941. Pearl Harbor is attacked on the seventh, bringing in the US. On the eleventh, Germany and Italy declare in support of their ally, Japan. Now it is truly World War and Hitler has a more powerful enemy.

233

In the Reich, meanwhile, relocating the Jews has proved problematic and the Final Solution—gas chambers, extermination—is about to take on its horrendous shape.

◊

I suspect your diagrams, your fastidious drawings, stem from your training days, before you were a soldier in the field. Whereas the addresses, our mother's and the others, are scrawled hastily, perhaps during lulls in disruption and chaos. My September birthday is the only date in the book. By late 1941 there is no more communication, no news from a mother far off in the enemy's world.

How much can you have known of the events that would spell your fate? Your job is to man a tank, build communications, set traps for the enemy. Your job is not to question but to support the heroic cause. You are a *Panzer Pionier* with the 86th Battalion, and the army has work for you.

◊

Oil and greed and conquest: 1942. Forget Moscow. On to Baku and the Black Sea; the Wehrmacht needs fuel! On to Stalingrad and the strategic Volga! Too much, the generals insist. Hitler orders them dismissed.

My brother, you and your group are moving south. You are held up at the Zhizdra, keeping the Russians engaged. The heat is oppressive, the air sulphuric with exploded ordnance. Your unit is undermanned; the Soviets fight back fiercely. On August 24th Colonel General Franz Halder, one of Hitler's savviest advisors, suggests withdrawal. The *Führer* shouts him down. Withdrawal is a sign of weakness! Withdrawal is *verboten*!

August 24th is the day that you die.

◊

The final photograph shows a cross, fashioned from raw wood. A shorter plank nailed perpendicularly to a longer, stamped at

234

the top with the German symbol of bravery in battle, the black Iron Cross. The perpendicular gives your name: Pion. Bernhard Größ. Under that, on the vertical, your rank and dates of birth and death:

2.Pz.Pi.86
4.11.22
24.8.42

Farther down one finds simply the number 58—your place in another formation, the long rows of the battle's dead. In the background one sees an entryway, to a church or barracks maybe, a heavy stone building with stairway and light slanting through arched windows. It frames your graveyard, hastily dug.

Such a temporary fixture, this cross—how long will it have stood? One reads of cemeteries in France where graves of American soldiers are cared for, preserved. But they were the rescuers, welcomed and honored. Enemy soldiers in Russia—how long before they are ploughed under, turned back into the endless Russian soil?

◊

A last memento: your death notice, rimmed in black. This too from Poldi, who kept your memory as I do now. A card of commemoration, with photograph of the deceased. I translate its lines.

In blessed memory of
Bernhard Größ
Pionier,
who, on Aug. 24, 1942, in the
battle at Wosty in Russia, died
a hero's death.

Ich weiß, ihr werdet bitter weinen,
Daß ich so ferne sank in's Grab,
Wo nur die stillen Sterne scheinen

235

In meine dunkle Gruft hinab;
Doch einmal kommt der Tod zu allen
Und brichtder Liebe zartes Band;
Wo wäre ich herrlicher gefallen
Als kämpfend treu für Gott und Vaterland.
Süßes Herz Mariä, sei meine Rettung!

I know that you'll shed bitter tears
That I was lost so far away,
Where only silent stars look down
Upon my grave, so cold and gray.
But death must find us all one day
To break love's sweet and tender band,
And how could I have better died
Than here, for God and Fatherland.
Sweet Heart of Mary, be my salvation!

On the reverse is a portrait of Mary holding a cross, with children at her sides and the words "Faith, Hope and Love will bring you peace."

A Catholic tribute. When annexing Austria, Hitler is warned not to threaten the Catholic Church, as he did in Germany. He agrees, knowing his birthplace well enough to understand the church would present no obstacle to perfecting his plan.

In this last small likeness on the commemoration card, you are a boy again. Your jacket, with its oak leaf lapels and cloth of heavy wool, is from your *Arbeitsdienst* time, when you were not yet a soldier. You stare at me with doubtful eyes, those sticking-out ears, your full lips unsmiling. Your hair is dark as our mother's once, though in my time she was already gray.

Yours never had a chance to turn.

SHANNON KAFKA

Kintsugi

for the Veterans of Warrior Writers

Nails, with clay horizons
  dig deep, throw a mound
  on spinning wheels, silted
  fingers shape

Oh, Makishi,
  with your earthen hands
  mold a body made for use

Fingers drag
  like fish nets cast
  in slow moving streams
  comb soft white bands
  sculpted, encircling

A generous round mouth
  pulled open, awaiting
  the cycle of use: full
    & thirst

A vessel set on loamy seas
    with wind & storm
  & choppy body
        cracks
    they gather
like stories over time

And the acci-
   dental frac-
            tures, rup-
ture—violent shat-
ters, a jag-
            ged
fate.

Oh, Makishi,
make gentle hands dance
restore your sun-
                  dered

Find surrogates
   where they
fit,
     as if
   they were made for
this

Ground bones, mix sap
   & gold, brush resined life
   with horsehair tips, line
   he lips of lacquer edges
         & hold

When gleaming seams dry
gold webs of repair rise
to firm a veiny resilience

A history illuminated
rather than disguised

*Kintsugi or Kintsukuroi is the Japanese art of fixing broken pottery with a
gold lacquered resin, making it more valuable than before.*

238

KAFKA

BARBARA MUJICA

The Chaplain

On the afternoon Captain Guthrie appeared on my doorstep, I was wearing a bathing suit and a beach wrap. It was embarrassing. After all, I'm not a young woman and I don't have the figure of a teenager.

It was a sultry afternoon in July, one of those muggy summer days that make your clothes stick to your body like a membrane. The men were all out, so I'd slipped into my grungy old swimsuit and had been down on all fours scrubbing the kitchen floor when the bell rang.

"I wasn't expecting you so early," I said, rag in hand. "Sorry I'm such a mess."

Captain Guthrie smiled. "Don't worry about it."

I'd been taking in veterans since my son Ignacio left for Ramadi in 2005. To supplement my income, I told myself. After all, bank cashiers don't make much. The truth is, though, that it was to help me cope. I was crazy with the kind of fear a mother feels when her child is in a war zone—a soul-numbing fear that made me feel as though I were suffocating. The sleepless nights. The panic at the sound of loud noises. Having around young men about Ignacio's age forced me to focus on other things. With boarders to care for, I couldn't allow myself to be paralyzed by anxiety. I had to go to the market and then make dinner. I had to chop onions and grate cheese. I couldn't dwell on ambushes and firefights because I had to think about the guys: Had John paid his rent? Did Corey need cough medicine? Did we have enough toilet paper?

One veteran brought in another, and soon I'd rented every possible space in the house. When summer evenings were cool, we sometimes barbecued in the backyard, but most of the time, I'd get busy in the kitchen right after work, and soon the spicy fragrance of freshly baked empanadas and *pastel de choclo* or hearty beef stew filled the house. I began to look forward to dinnertime. I'd set the table with flowered dishes and colored tumblers. I'd decorate with gourds in the fall and poinsettias at Christmastime. I wanted to make it nice for them.

The men sat around the table and ate with gusto. They'd had their fill of MREs and welcomed a home-cooked meal. I loved hearing their fierce opinions about football and politics, but also the chitchat, the laughing, and the teasing. I had a "no-swearing within earshot of Mrs. Montez" rule, which most of them respected most of the time. They never talked about war at the table, but sometimes, one of them would wander into the kitchen late at night and tell me stories over a cup of coffee—decaffeinated for me, high octane for them. Having vets around made life more bearable.

Captain Guthrie was a different kind of boarder. Identified only as M. L. Guthrie on the application, all I knew was that the candidate was an Army chaplain with a master's degree in Religious Studies and plans to pursue a degree in counseling at the local university. I imagined a hefty Irishman with a sour demeanor who would snap every time a vet said "shit." The person who appeared on my doorstep was a pert young woman in her late thirties with an easy smile and eyes that reminded me of pools of chocolate. She was dark-complected and small-framed, but muscular. She looked like she could hold her own in a fight. On her left cheek, she had a burn scar the shape and size of a maple leaf, burgundy-colored and shiny, like polished leather, with a spider web of blood-red capillaries running through the center of it.

"Bet you were expecting a big Irish sourpuss," she said by way of greeting.

I burst out laughing. "What are you, a mind reader? You must be Captain Guthrie, the Army chaplain."

"And you must be Mrs. Montez, the Marine mom who rents out rooms to vets."

"Jacqueline Montez," I said, holding out my hand.

"Margarita Luisa Guthrie. People are always surprised when they meet me. You can call me Meg, but not Maggie, please. What should I call you?"

"I prefer Mrs. Montez," I said, tugging at the wrap to cover more of me. "Now that you've seen all my bulges and bruises, I have to assert my authority somehow!"

She grinned. "Montez sounds Spanish."

"So does Margarita Luisa."

"My mother is Mexican. My father was a lay instructor at the Jesuit college in Guadalajara. I grew up there. *¿Habla español?*"

"Not very well. I was born in Chile, but my family left when I was about twelve."

"I'm rusty, too. I haven't spoken Spanish in years. We spoke mostly English at home, and I moved back to the States when I was a teenager. Before they meet me, people always assume I'm a ruddy blonde. Afterwards, they don't know what to think. I always have a lot of explaining to do. But to tell the truth, you don't look like my idea of a Montez. I mean, you're so blonde and fair . . . "

"People make all sorts of assumptions about Latin Americans, but Chile is largely European. I'm a Sephardic Jew. Montez is my husband's name—he passed away five years ago. My family name is Jaén, but here they pronounce it 'Jane' instead of 'Ha-en' so I use Montez. It's easier."

"Wow, jumping to conclusions like that . . . I should know better."

I laughed. "Happens all the time, Meg," I said. "You never really know what the other guy's story is. Here, let me show you your room."

Meg was my first female boarder, and I felt an instant connection with her. I loved my male boarders, but Meg was special. When I got home from work, she'd have set the table. Often we'd spend hours in the kitchen comparing recipes. She fried empanadas— those succulent meat pieces ubiquitous in Latin America—and I baked them. She used *jaldepeños*, I used coriander and chives. She made *carne guisada* (stew) with meat, chili and cumin. I made *cazuela* with beef and chicken.

I had a gas range, and I noticed she was squeamish about fire. She'd stick things in the oven, but when it came to placing pots on the burner, she'd hang back a moment to see if I'd take care of it. If I didn't, she'd take a breath and approach the flame, but I could tell she felt uncomfortable, so I tried to deal with the stove myself. On the nights we barbecued, she'd stay in the kitchen making a salad until one of the guys—usually Corey or John—got a flame going. I figured it might have something to do with her scar, but I never asked. I'd learned early on that when dealing with vets, it was better not to ask questions. You never knew what ugly memories you might conjure up.

When I made *a bistec a lo pobre* or a *palta reina*, I'd sometimes become melancholy.

"This is one of Ignacio's favorite dishes," I whispered one evening, blinking back tears.

"God is watching over him, Mrs. Montez. Would it help if we prayed together?"

"I don't pray. I just want my son to come back safe and whole from this damned war."

She placed her hand on my wrist and squeezed gently.

After dinner, we'd sometimes watch a movie together or sit in the kitchen drinking tea.

"You know," she said one evening when we were relaxing on the porch, "prayer really can be helpful—even if you don't exactly believe . . . well . . . completely. Whenever we had a risky mission ahead of us, the guys would form a circle and just observe a few moments of silence. I'm sure some of them prayed, but not all of them. A sergeant named Alan told me he was an atheist, but even so, those circles helped calm his nerves. He was the sweetest kid, so kind to everyone, even the Al-Qaida we dragged in. He adopted a couple of stray dogs, and we all helped him hide them from the commanding officer. 'I don't know,' he told me, 'I just don't believe in God.' 'It doesn't matter,' I said. 'God believes in you.'"

I smiled. I imagined Ignacio saying something like that and then smirking when he heard her answer. "Sometimes, when I was a child, I'd hear my father chanting," I told her. "*Sh'ma Yis-ra-eil, A-do-nai E-lo-hei-nu, A-do-nai E-chad.* It was beautiful." I paused and remembered my father, his prayer shawl wrapped over his shoulders, chanting and swaying back and forth rhythmically. "We belonged to a Sephardic synagogue in Valparaíso," I went on, "but here, I pretty much lost contact with the community. And now, with the boarders, I do what I can to make them feel at home—bacon and eggs, Christmas decorations—that sort of thing."

"My mother taught me the rosary. *Dios te salve, María. Llena eres de gracia: El Señor es contigo. Bendita tú eres entre todas las mujeres. Y bendito es el fruto de tu vientre: Jesús.* I had to serve soldiers of all faiths, so I only said it when someone asked, but I repeated it to myself over and over whenever I felt afraid."

"And were you afraid often?"

"I had every reason to be. IEDs were everywhere. Once one of our conveys rolled over a bump in the road outside of Nasiriya. Boom! The flames were so high and so intense, you felt as though your body were melting off your bones." Instinctively, she brought her hand to her cheek.

"Is that where . . . ?"

"The first two trucks were in flames. We lost four men. The medics had set up a large tent about two clicks from there. They arrived almost immediately and started pulling guys out of the fire. They were applying first aid even before they got the wounded into the helicopter. I ran in and helped drag men to safety. *Líbranos del mal*, I prayed. *Deliver us from evil.* "Yes," she said softly, "that's where I got this burn. Before I knew it, I was being evacuated myself, and you know what I was thinking, Mrs. Montez? I thought, boy, am I useless. The medics were trying to save lives, and me, all I could do was pray!"

"But you were also helping to get the men out of danger."

"You should have seen how those medics worked—applying tourniquets, compresses, salves. Bandaging up limbs." Her eyelids were moist. "And then they were attending to me, to *me*, when they should have been taking care of the wounded fighters." She fell silent. "I thought, these men don't need God and they don't need me. They need painkillers." She was dabbing her eyes on her sleeve. "It wasn't until the next day, when I was bandaged up and back on the job, that I realized that I did have a role, that prayer was what a lot of them needed after all." She went silent. I sat with her a moment longer, but she was lost in her thoughts, so I got up and went into another room.

◊

Our routine changed when classes began in September. Meg was planning to become a rehabilitation counselor. She was studying on the G.I. Bill, and had a limited time to complete her degree, so she had taken a full load—The Psychology of Trauma, Medical Ethics, and Pacifism, a course taught in the Philosophy Department by Dr. Donald Thurston. Meg Googled him. "He's a smart guy," she told me. "A renowned anti-war activist. I'm sure we'll have a lot to talk about. I'm psyched!"

But when Meg returned from her first class, she was less certain.

"He began with a question," she said. "'What do Albert Einstein, John Lennon, and Mahatma Gandhi have in common?' Of course, there's always some guy who knows all the answers. 'They're all pacifists?' the bright-eyed kid sitting next to me piped up. I must have smirked or scowled or something because Professor Thurston turned to me and frowned. I didn't think it was a big deal, though, because a few seconds later, he went on with his lecture." Meg stopped and looked at me before continuing.

"At first, he droned on and on about the meaning of pacifism: the absolute opposition to violence in all its forms. 'A real pacifist refuses to pay taxes, since the state is the perpetrator of war,' he proclaimed. 'Of course, I do pay taxes. It avoids hassles with the government.' A couple of students chuckled and Thurston looked pleased with himself. But the more he talked, the more agitated he got," explained Meg. "He was turning the color of a persimmon. He evoked everyone from Uchimura Kanzō to Joan Baez. By the end of the class, drops of sweat fell from his brow to his desk. For a pacifist, he seemed strangely fierce," remarked Meg.

"I raised my hand and asked, 'What if a nation is attacked? What if a tyrant as evil as Saddam or Hitler begins torturing citizens? Doesn't the world have a duty to intervene?' But he just shrugged. 'That's a sophomoric question,' he said. 'The same question kids like

244

you always ask. Violence begets violence. Even if in the short run you save a few thousand lives, in the long run, you lose many more.' He hurried out of the room without giving me time to respond."

"Sounds like a bully," I said. "And what's this business about 'kids like you'? Damned patronizing!"

But Meg just shrugged and changed the subject. "I feel like cooking," she said. "What about if I make a *pastel de tres leches* for dessert?"

◊

Fall was settling in. A misty drizzle coated the leaves. Clusters of red, orange, magenta and yellow gave the trees in my front yard a festive look. Soon I would be getting up early on Saturday mornings to rake and clear, but for now, I was enjoying the hues of the season. And the scents—pine needles, chrysanthemums, pumpkin pie spice, cornbread, sweaty socks left on the floor after football practice.

I slipped on my rain jacket and went out to the porch to wait for Meg, who usually came back from the university around four.

"I caught Professor Thurston before class today," she called as she strode up the steps. "I wanted to have a conversation with him. 'I hate war as much as you do,' I began. 'I've seen it first-hand. I was a captain in the Army.'"

"That must have taken him by surprise."

"He glared at me. 'I doubt you hate war as much as I do,' he said. 'In an all-volunteer army, people are there only because they want to fight.' I looked him straight in the eye and said, 'I've never met a man or woman who's actually experienced war who wants to fight. It's because I've seen war that I want peace. That's why I'm taking this course.'"

"That should have calmed him down. Maybe you'll develop a real friendship with Thurston."

"I doubt it. He just stood there glaring at me. 'How many innocent children did you kill?' he said suddenly. 'I didn't kill anyone,' I whispered. 'I was a chaplain.' I admit I was shaken. He burst out laughing. 'I suppose you told all those little morons that their cause was destined for victory because God was on their side.'

I couldn't believe it, Mrs. Montez. Why such venom? I was trying to have a conversation, not an argument."

We went indoors. I'd bought some avocados a few days ago, and they were beginning to turn mushy. Meg spied them.

"I'm going to make guacamole," she said. "I feel like mashing something."

"Good idea." I paused a moment and then started quartering limes. "But listen, Meg, you have to get through the course, so it might be more expedient to grin and bear it than to try to have a meaningful conversation with Thurston."

A few days later, she told me he'd confronted her again after class. "What does an Army chaplain do anyway," he'd growled. "These kids can pray all they want. It's not going to prevent their heads from getting blown off."

"God doesn't prevent bad things from happening," Meg told him, "but faith gives us the strength to deal with evil when it occurs. God doesn't create wickedness. People do, or sometimes harmful situations occur because of natural phenomena. Earthquakes, that sort of thing. Know what he said? He said, 'Bullshit!'"

I squeezed some limes into the mashed avocado. Meg stared at a pair of onions with an intensity I had never seen in her eyes before. Then she started chopping—*chop chop chop.*

"He started class with a glower," she told me the next day. "He began, 'The word *ahimsa*, to do no harm, is the core of pacifistic Buddhism and Hinduism. So you see, a healer must be a pacifist. One cannot be both a soldier and a doctor or a nurse or a chaplain. The concepts are diametrically opposed.' He was staring right at me. 'With all due respect, sir,' I said, 'soldiers do not declare war; governments do. And when a nation sends its military men and women into battle, some will be wounded. Doctors must care for them, and chaplains must comfort them and tend to their spiritual needs.'"

"Boy, what self-control you have!" I interjected. "If it'd been me, I'd have told him to go to hell!"

Meg continued. "'Don't call me sir,' he snapped. 'This isn't an Army base! And no guy has spiritual needs when he thinks his balls have just been blown off. You think you're a spiritual guide?

You're part of the problem! You're a gear in this military machine. You justify your part in the war by injecting religion into this whole rotten mess! You think you're so damned virtuous because you convince young men that killing is not a sin as long as they do it for God and country? Well, guess what? Al-Qaida fighters have been sold that same bill of goods. They think it's okay to kill Americans because they're doing it for Allah!' Mrs. Montez, the mole on his nose was trembling like a beetle in the rain. 'You never had any doubts about what you were doing in the military, did you, Captain Guthrie?' he said. He spat out the word *Captain* as though it tasted like dung. 'Many, many doubts,' I answered. He turned away from me and started talking about Buddhist pacifists. The other students were getting jittery. Some of them eyed me with curiosity, and some with irritation.

"But I was pissed. 'You know,' I said, 'most of the kids in this class have never been to war. I have. In a battle, you don't demoralize soldiers by talking about sin. You try to help them find spiritual strength in times of danger. I know what stress can do to a soldier. One time . . .' 'We're not interested in your war stories!' thundered Professor Thurston. 'How dare you interrupt my lecture!' But then one of the students blurted out, 'I am! I'm interested in her stories!' 'Yeah,' said someone else. 'Let her talk!'"

"I admire your gutsiness," I told her. "Did he let you go on?"

"That only enraged him more," she said. He walked over to my desk and stood right in front of me. 'You think you're the only one here who's been in a war zone?' He was screaming now. 'You think you're the only one who's seen death? I lost my . . .' He caught his breath. Everyone was staring at him. 'Please be quiet,' he said. He turned and stared at me. I recognized that look. I'd seen that pain in the eyes of too many soldiers. I pursed my lips and stared at my book."

I hardly saw Meg for the next couple of days. She was studying hard, staying in the library until late at night. She had to pass every course in order to keep her G.I. Bill funding, and for that to happen, she had to avoid irritating Thurston.

247

One evening, we were sitting in front of the TV, sipping wine and not really watching. "How's it going with the Pacifism course?" I asked cautiously.

"That guy's got a head full of rotting fish. The worst thing anyone could wish on him would be to be himself. I'm trying to make him happy, but I'm convinced it's a lost cause. I've got an essay due next week. The topic is Peace and War."

"That should be fairly easy for you," I said.

"Except that he wants me out of the program. No matter what I write, he's going to fail me."

"Write a really good argument, Meg. You'll see. He'll change his mind. Do you really think that deep in his heart he doesn't appreciate what you've done to help our soldiers?"

I knew Meg thought about her essay for a long time. She read about everyone from the Chinese activist Liu Xiaobo to the Berrigan brothers. In the end, she wrote about the IED incident she'd told me about. She showed it to me before she handed it in: "We were in the medical tent a couple of clicks from Nasiriya. It was a huge tent, latest equipment, even air conditioning. They'd sent in about fifteen doctors and a bunch of Black Hawks, but still, IEDs always catch you by surprise. It was horrible. There was nothing I could do but pull men out of the rubble."

He's not going to like this, I thought as I read through the paper. It's all about war, nothing about peace. But I didn't say anything. I read on:

"I felt useless. At a time like that, you don't think about politics. You don't think about morality. You think about the parents of these kids, what they're going to feel like when they find out they've lost a child. You think about the survivors, how they're going to get through this psychologically. They've lost limbs. Worse yet, they've lost buddies. To be honest, I really didn't know what to do. Finally, I met with each one of them individually—each one who wanted to talk to me—and we prayed together and we cried. They needed a safe space, a space to cry. Yes, I talked to them about God, about the Cross if they were Christian, about how injustice and suffering are part of life. But this wasn't about Christianity or any other religion. It was about helping them find some sort of inner peace in the midst of the horror of war. I wasn't their commanding officer. With me, they didn't have to be strong, stoic soldiers. They could just let go. They could weep. That was my role as chaplain: to give permission to weep."

I could feel the passion in Meg's words. She hadn't even mentioned her own injuries. That's what he's afraid of, I thought. Her passion. Her commitment, not to an ideology, but to other human beings.

She described the ensuing confrontation with Thurston to me, and I replayed it over and over in my head:

"That wasn't the topic!" he barked at her in front of the whole class.

"Finding peace in your heart amid the savagery, Sir . . ."

"Thou shalt not kill, Chaplain. It's the sixth commandment. You should know that."

"A time to love, and a time to hate; a time for war, and a time for peace. Ecclesiastes 3:8. That's what I know."

I was proud of her. She'd stood up to him. She'd fought him with his own weapon: words from Scripture. But I was worried. Men like Thurston didn't like to lose, and she'd embarrassed him. "What do you think he'll do now?" I asked her. But she shook her head and said nothing.

A few weeks went by without Meg mentioning Thurston. She rarely helped me in the kitchen now. I served dinner to the boarders every night at seven o'clock, but she seldom joined us, preferring to grab a sandwich after her last class and head directly to the library. When she returned after midnight, I was usually in bed. After a while, it occurred to me that she might be avoiding me. Maybe I was asking too many questions, I thought. Maybe she didn't want to talk about the Army, about classes, about Thurston.

But one Saturday evening, when the other boarders were out on dates or drinking at some bar with their buddies, she suggested we go out to a movie. We checked the newspapers but couldn't find a film that interested us, so we finally decided to stay home and watch *The Hurt Locker* on Netflix.

I watched the roadside bombs go off, producing mile-high explosions, and grimaced.

"It wasn't like that at all," she grumbled when the movie was over.

"You mean the guys who get an adrenaline high dismantling bombs?"

"In my experience, all the bomb squad wants to do is deactivate the thing and get the hell out of there. They don't get a big thrill out of risking their lives every day by pulling apart explosives." She paused and thought about it a minute. "When guys are injured, you know what the first thing they ask is?"

"Whether you notified their mothers?"

She burst out laughing. "No! They ask whether they've still got their balls! They don't care whether they've lost a leg or an eye, as long as their manhood is intact."

"I can understand that," I said, thinking about my own son and praying to God that he'd come home from Iraq uninjured. "You know," I murmured, "I just realized that I've been praying. I've been praying all along and didn't even know it."

She squeezed my wrist in the darkness. "I'm not surprised," she whispered.

◊

Before I knew it, the semester was winding down. Most of my boarders were making plans for Christmas. Some were going home. A few were looking at brochures for ski resorts. I'd already begun pulling out the boxes of ornaments and tinsel. I was looking forward to the scent of pine needles and eggnog, bayberry and cinnamon.

A few days later, I eyed Meg sitting in a corner looking dejected. "What's the matter?" I asked.

"Professor Thurston made it pretty clear that he wasn't going to let me pass."

"Meg, you have to go see the dean." I felt as though I had a wad of cobwebs in my throat. "You've worked so hard. Listen, Meg, if Dr. Thurston wants to be a pacifist, that's his business. He has a constitutional right to his opinions. But he has no right to impose those opinions on his students, and he certainly has no right to humiliate you in public—or in private, for that matter!"

"I just don't want . . . problems." Suddenly tears flooded her cheeks.

How can this be? I thought. How has this monster brought a strong, beautiful, principled young woman to tears? I handed her a Kleenex, then took her hand in mine. "Do you feel like praying?" I asked. My own words surprised me.

"Not really," she whispered.

"Go see him in his office," I coaxed. "Up in front of the class, he has to play the tough, uncompromising idealist. After all, he has a reputation to uphold. But sometimes even a brute will soften when you talk to him one-on-one. You don't have to be confrontational. Just explain that you're an idealist, too. You want to help wounded veterans transition to a new life. You want to help people, just as he does. That's why you're studying to become a rehabilitation counselor. Does he even know what your career goals are?" I gave her another tissue.

She shook her head. "It won't do any good," she hiccupped. "He won't listen."

Nevertheless, a few days later, she pulled her jacket hood over her ears and pushed out into the icy, razor-sharp wind toward the building where Thurston had his office. It was one of those days that turn your lips and nose brittle, and you feel like you have hoarfrost in your throat. But she had to do *something*, she told me. The situation had deteriorated. Thurston was ignoring her in class, not recognizing her when she raised her hand, not answering her questions.

When she arrived, she didn't ask for permission. She just walked in and sat down. "He looked smaller up close than in the classroom," she said. "His face was white as milk stone, as chiseled as a statue. A prim, starched little man," was how she described him. The mole on his nose had taken on a reddish hue, and it reminded her of a ladybug that wanted to take off on its own. She had prepared a speech about her desire to become a rehabilitation counselor, but instead of delivering it, she sat there in silence, her eyes darting around the room.

The books on the shelves were predictable, she explained: *The Power of Non-Violence*, *Pacifism through the Ages*, *Christian Pacifism and Just War Theory*. She noticed a rather large section on Vietnam.

A First-Hand Account of the Vietnam War, *A Bright Shining Lie*, *The Things They Carried*, and four or five rows of volumes on the My Lai massacre, in which US Army officers killed some five-hundred unarmed Vietnamese civilians, including women, children, and babies, in 1968.

Meg noticed a photograph on one of the shelves—a young man, perhaps twenty-five or twenty-eight, seated on a rock. He wore shorts and a t-shirt. His feet were bare. His lips were pulled back in an easy grin. He bore a definite resemblance to Thurston, she told me, but he was better looking and seemed more relaxed.

"Your son?" she finally asked Thurston, even though she knew it wasn't his son. The photo was old, a Polaroid from decades ago.

"My brother Robbie," Thurston replied.

Meg felt as though she should say something about Robbie— how attractive he was or how much he looked like Thurston, or she might ask where or when the picture was taken. She didn't, though, because she was anxious to get to the subject of the final exam and her grade in Thurston's course. She had questions, she wanted to tell him, and he was refusing to let her ask them. The way he treated her in class was unacceptable, she'd planned to say. She struggled to organize her thoughts. She opened her mouth to speak.

"He's dead," said Thurston abruptly.

"What?" Meg caught her breath.

"Robbie is dead. My Lai."

"Thurston looked as though his milk-stone veneer was going to shatter," whispered Meg. I imagined how devastated she must have felt at that moment. He peered at her with unblinking eyes as if to make sure she had understood. She peered back to let him know she had. Then suddenly, Meg's thoughts began to spin like windmills. It was a lie, she said to herself. The old bastard was trying to manipulate her. Robbie couldn't have died at My Lai.

"I thought all the casualties were Vietnamese," she said coolly.

Professor Thurston stared at her as if she were a dolt.

"In a war," he said glacially, "there are different kinds of casualties."

Meg cocked her head.

"Suicide," he said, and Meg realized his voice was quivering. "Some of them just couldn't live with it."

That's all she told me about her visit with Professor Thurston, but I had the impression that nothing had been resolved.

"What are you going to do?" I asked.

She shook her head. "I honestly don't know. For now, I'm going help you get dinner. What are you making?"

"*Enchiladas mexicanas*, especially for you." She smiled weakly.

"But there's no rush, Meg. Take your time. Go freshen up."

She disappeared into her room. A few minutes later I heard her murmuring: "*Salve María. Llena eres de gracia . . .*"

I remembered my own father chanting the *Sh'ma Yis-ra-eil*, and felt calmer.

Book Review

SUSAN MCCALLUM SMITH

Song of a Captive Bird by Jasmin Darznik
Ballantine Books, February 2018

> *Remember the flight, for the bird is mortal.*
> —Forugh Farrokhzad

> *The Shah did not understand that even if you can destroy
> a man, destroying him doesn't mean he ceases to exist. The
> scythe swings, and at once the grass starts to grow back.*
> —Ryszard Kapuściński, *Shah of Shahs*

In February 1967, the Iranian poet and filmmaker Forugh
Farrokhzad died in a car crash in Tehran at the age of thirty-two.
A tremendous outpouring of grief followed both overseas and in
Iran, where hundreds of people lined the streets on the day of her
funeral. Every year since, thousands more make the pilgrimage to the
Zahirodo'allah Cemetery on the anniversary of her death.

Due to a combination of linguistic brilliance and physical
beauty (not to mention that prerequisite for myth—the early death),
Farrokhzad is often carelessly labeled the Persian Sylvia Plath, but
this grossly underestimates her status. Unlike Plath, the impact of
Farrokhzad's work transcended notions of personal, familial, and
gender politics, and was ultimately perceived as a direct threat to the
body politic. Despite spending much of her short life being slandered
and scorned by her family, her country's political elite, and its press—
and a not inconsiderable number of its citizens—her passing, and
public reaction to it, illuminates something profound about the role
of the poet in Persian culture.

In an interview with the Institute for Policy Studies the contemporary Iranian writer Farideh Hassanzadeh explained that, with the exception of the Quran, the books of the great poets like Hafez, Rumi, Sa'adi, Khayyam, and Ferdousi, enjoy the largest circulation in Iran. "This means," said Hassanzadeh, "poets after prophets rule the hearts and minds of my people." Mehdi Jami, the Iranian journalist and commentator, went further in an interview with *The Guardian* (February 12, 2017) suggesting Farrokhzad fulfilled both roles. "In every culture you have icons, like Shakespeare in Britain. Farrokhzad was like that for contemporary Iran," he believed. "She was the last prophet of truth-telling that our country has seen."

It takes guts to fictionalize the life of an icon, but Jasmin Darznik pulls it off. The accomplishments of *Song of a Captive Bird* are twofold: it not only beguiles with a gripping history of an extraordinary artist, but plants seeds, quickening the reader's curiosity about its subject, directing us beyond the confines of its pages into the poetry and films of Farrokhzad. Born in Iran and raised in the United States, Darznik currently teaches at the California College of Arts. *Song of a Captive Bird* is her first novel, and her second book, following her best-selling memoir *The Good Daughter: My Mother's Hidden Life*, in 2011.

Darznik dramatizes Forugh Farrokhzad's life over three acts: "I Feel Sorry for the Garden," "The Rebellion," and "A New Birth," and each follows quite faithfully—with the exception of a few fictionalized scenes or name changes here and there—her true, brief but blazing flight. It opens with a disturbing event when Forugh is a teenager, but it is another character that soon grabs the reader's attention: the country itself. "Vast deserts of salt and sand extend from east to west, and on any day of the year all four seasons take place within Iran's borders," she writes. "Here under a continuing shifting surface of wildflowers, sand, rock, and snow, black veins of oil plunge to the heart of the earth." Iran is personified as a diseased paradise; a Garden of Eden infested with a cancer that, time and again, spouts symptoms of power and greed. At the time of Forugh's birth, Tehran "was still an old-fashioned city of dirt roads, narrow passageways, and flat-roofed family compounds," but by her death it had been erased, westernized by the Shah's attempt to drag his reluctant country into the twentieth century. Yet in her memory, and in her poetry, Forugh's beloved Tehran remained perfumed with "black tea steeped with rose petals and cardamom pods, coriander and cumin," where, "even in summer the air carried the scent of snow."

Forugh is born in 1935. Her mother, Turan, had married her father, Colonel Farrokhzad, when she was fifteen and he was thirty-two. "Unveiled, corseted, and lipsticked though she was, my mother's life would always be a prayer rug spread at the altar of fear," within "a house whose women believed the very walls listened for signs of sin." To Turan marriage is "an act of faith" but her selfless devotion proves to be an altar built on sand. In both his professional and domestic realms Forugh's father applies the king Reza Shah's dictate of "strike first, show no mercy, trust no one." Under this tyrannical, but not atypical, rule, the Colonel kicks Forugh and her six siblings awake every morning to perform exercises accompanied by a phonograph. When Reza Shah is deposed following the Anglo-Soviet invasion in 1941, in favor of his son Mohammed Reza, the Colonel, despite some misgivings, transfers his loyalty wholesale. "Bound in service until his death," he expects his family to do the same.

Turan raises her daughters with a benign neglect until they are mature enough to enter the marriage market. The girls complete their education by ninth grade. Confined to the family compound, which they are forbidden to leave unaccompanied, they watch their brothers playing in the street, watch them leave for college overseas. From the start Forugh proves too feisty for her mother, who, believing her spirited daughter haunted by a wayward *jinn*, instructs a servant to drop sedatives in her food. Intelligent, curious, and bored, Forugh spends as much time as she can in her father's well-stocked library, where he keeps, like all cultured Iranians, the great works of Persian literature. When her father's friends gather to socialize, she spies on their poetry recitations, smitten by the music of Farsi, "a language that can sometimes sound like susurrations of a lover and sometimes like the reed's plaintive song." At age eleven, she scrawls her first poem down the margin of a scavenged newspaper. "The more I read, the more I longed to let loose the words inside me."

McCALLUM SMITH

Tentatively she begins to share her verses with her father—although she fears him she longs to please him—and her precociousness stokes the Colonel's vanity. He listens "as if assessing not the poem's value, but mine." Thus, begins a pattern of yearning for male approval and patronage that repeats over her lifetime, fueling her creativity, provoking her public undoing: she is incapable of keeping her heart off the page. Soon enough, her fledgling artistry receives a severe clipping, and she orchestrates an exit through the only door open to her, exchanging the imprisonment of being a daughter to that of being a wife.

By sixteen Forugh is married (unhappily) and living under the eye and control of her mother-in-law, in a rural outpost over five hundred miles from Tehran, "a scrubby land, without hills or meadows, a country of stones and stunted blooms." The Shah's modernization efforts, including outlawing the veil and ridding his land of "camels, donkeys, beggars, and dervishes," win patchy support within Iran's cities, and almost none beyond their borders. In this predominantly rural nation, religious conservatism holds its ground. "Unveiled women would be showered with insults and, in some neighborhoods of the city, with fistfuls of stones. It wasn't only the mullahs who'd protest the shah's new law; thousands of women refused to set foot outside their homes once the veil was banned." Forugh scandalizes her husband's village with her uncovered head and modern clothes—and with each rebuke, the skirts get shorter and the heels get higher. She refuses to pray five times a day and fails to learn to cook. Her mother-in-law scolds her to "Shhhhhh" and submit to *besooz o besaaz*, the Iranian code of wifely conduct meaning to "turn inwardly and accommodate." Listless and ravenous for intellectual life, Forugh devours the books in her husband's library and begins to write again. She invents an excuse to take the twenty-four hour train journey to Tehran where she meets an editor who calls her "not a poet, but a mere poetess," a derogatory term with almost onomatopoeic qualities—you can practically hear him patting her on the head—and tells her to go home to her husband. She does, but not before a much more consequential encounter.

"I'd expected motherhood to temper my desire to write, but the less time I had to devote to it, the more the idea of writing consumed me." The birth of a son fails to distinguish her ambitions, and she resumes her scandalous trips, unaccompanied, to Tehran. When she is nineteen years old, an Iranian literary journal publishes her controversial poem "Sin" and she catapults from obscurity to notoriety, overnight becoming exhibit A against the emancipation of women, and symbolic of Iran's cultural decay. "Woe to the daughters of Eve who spurn God's will and take up their pens to write," screams the press, reflecting the cultural belief that a woman has no business creating art, let alone art of such sensuality. "I sinned a sin full of pleasure," her poem runs, "next to a shaking, stupefied form, / o, God, who knows what I did / In that dark and quiet seclusion."

"Who did my days belong to?" she asks herself, after a query from a lover. She concludes that not only should her days now belong to her, but furthermore, "it's shame, not sin, that's unholy." After reaching these momentous personal (and politically reckless) conclusions about the ownership of her body and her intellect, Forugh spends the remainder of her life fighting to secure them. Her lover commits a despicable betrayal, compounding the scandal caused by her poetry. Later, she will reflect, dryly, over the innocence of that nineteen-year-old girl who had thrown herself, "headlong into the future . . . thinking I might escape without consequences or regrets," because the consequences of her "taking what I wanted from life" are, predictably, swift and brutal, and orchestrated with the collusion of her family.

During her darkest days, Forugh meets a woman in the surreal surroundings of a Tehran clinic lit by Parisian streetlamps, who had been forced to undergo a lobotomy while awake. The doctors had told the woman to keep singing during the procedure, and "when she stopped singing, they knew it was done." This physical muting parallels Forugh's cultural suppression. "Because I was a woman they wanted to silence the screams on my lips and stifle the breath in my lungs. But I couldn't stay quiet . . . we too, have the right to breathe, to cry out, to sing."

Divorced, ostracized, severed from her son, nevertheless she persists. "When I left my father and then my husband, I lost my name and I was no one. But there was freedom in this." In 1955 she publishes *The Captive*, her first volume of verse, and over the following decade she publishes four more, "poems about the feeble threads of faith and justice, the law's black kerchief, fountains of blood, my country's youth cloaked in a funeral shroud." She secures a powerful female ally, and in 1957 meets a documentary filmmaker, Darius Golshiri, who plays a consequential role in her development as a film editor. When news leaks out about their affair, once again she is seen as a whore. The press and the political elite, frustrated by her failure to stop writing while reluctantly awed by its quality, insinuate that it is Golshiri's hand behind the pen.

During the late 1950s and early 1960s different strands of revolutionary forces, including communists, nationalists, and the Islamists—led by the fiery cleric Ayatollah Khomeini—threaten to destabilize the Shah, whose autocratic rule is propped up by the Americans and bankrolled by a conglomeration of foreign oil companies. SAVAK, the brutal secret police, begin a bloody crackdown. "Every death was telling some part of our story, which was Iran's story." The Shah's oppression encompassed literary censorship and the rounding up and exile of clerics and mullahs. Golshiri warns Forugh to be careful of her allies, careful of her words—"If we say what we want, in the way we want, who do you think will be left to make art in this godforsaken country?" She fails to heed his advice. Although forewarned of a tragedy, I still found it appalling. Even though there were times I wished I could give its heroine a good shake and an earful—get a grip, woman, he's a plonker!—I confess that by the end of Darznik's lyrical novel I had fallen a little in love with Forugh.

> No one wants to believe the garden is dying,
> that the garden's heart has swollen
> under the sun,
> that the garden's mind is slowly
> being drained of its memories of green.
>   ("I Feel Sorry for the Garden")

Darznik's allusions to nature, gardens, and corruption, rooted in those early pages of her personification of Iran, eventually spread and entwine *Song of a Captive Bird*, binding the life of Farrokhzad to that of her country, like a living allegory. Her mother's joy had been her garden. The bearer would bring water to their house, with which Turan tended her "roses, nasturtium and honeysuckle," and her "quince, pomegranate and pear," and where, in the honeyed dusks, the Colonial entertained his guests over samovar and sweets on carpets spread under the loggia. But when Reza Shah was deposed in 1941, the rush to modernity was accelerated by his successor, Muhammad Reza Shah. "The whole country is diseased, contracted over decades of imperialism," Forugh overhears one man say at a party, "And it's called Westoxification." The old values, as espoused in Omar Khayyam's *Rubiayat*, of scorning wealth in favor of the simple pleasures of bread, grape, and discourses on love, are perceived as uncomfortably anti-capitalist:

> I need a jug of a wine, and a book of poetry,
> Half a loaf for a bite to eat,
> Then you and I, seated in a desert spot,
> Will have more wealth than a Sultan's realm.

Colonel Farrokhzad's first act after the new Shah's ascendancy is to destroy Turan's garden. After bulldozing, it's replaced by a car park rimmed with plastic plants, both byproducts, ironically, of the cancerous oil. "We couldn't yet imagine what we had lost would be lost again and again." In 1958, Forugh accompanies Golshiri to the Iran border to make a documentary about a refinery fire. "Every conversation, no matter the subject, circles back to oil," she says, of her country, and "BP built everything here. All those shanties, but also the country club and the tennis courts. The Iranians weren't allowed over there, not even to use the drinking fountains." It took over ninety days for the refinery fire to be contained after the intervention of a Texas engineer. The foreign companies had contrived to ensure that none of the local Iranians would gain either the expertise or the authority to exploit and manage their own resources. In the non-fiction classic, *Shah of Shahs*, Ryszard Kapuściński coined the term "petro-bourgeoise," to describe the new social strata created by Iran's most valuable asset. "Oil is a resource that anesthetizes thought, blurs vision, corrupts," he wrote. It was "a fairy tale and like every fairy

McCALLUM SMITH

tail, a bit of a lie." While making documentaries during the last years before her death, Forugh witnessed her country's struggle to shake off the greedy shackles of stubborn colonialism. "The lottery was our faith and greed our fortune. Our intellectuals were sniffing cocaine and delivering lectures in the back rooms of dark cafes. We bought plastic roses and decorated our lawns and courtyards with plastic swans. We had pizza shops, supermarkets, and bowling alleys. We had traffic jams, skyscrapers, and air thick with noise and pollution. We had illiterate villagers [but] still our oil wasn't our own, our country wasn't our own."

The novel's gender politics and social theory converge in the black gold: "Mine was a country where they said a woman's nature is riddled with sin, where they claimed that women's voices had the power to drive men to lust and distract them from matters of heaven and earth." Women, like oil, it was presumed, have the power to corrupt. But in the end, as Kapuściński argued, it was the Shah's staggering corruption, bolstered and milked by the petro-bourgeoisie, which forced the Iranian people in 1979 to choose between SAVAK and the mullahs.

For many women, regardless of whether they lived in the cities or the countryside, this was a choice between a rock and a hard place, between one form of patriarchy or another. The Shah's modernity was cosmetic; it didn't look beyond loose hair and lipstick to gender equality or democracy, and this was exactly the approach preferred by the British and American empires. Growing up, Forugh never addressed her father by anything other than Colonel or *ghorban*, "you to whom I sacrifice myself," and after she died, ownership of her body returned to him.

Courted, invaded, oppressed, silenced, and plundered—I could be describing either Forugh or Iran—nevertheless during Forugh's short flight between cradle and grave she refused to play the victim, she took what she wanted and transformed gender relations through her poetry by swapping the pronoun 'she' with 'I'. Under the traditional mores of Persian literature the woman's role was always that of the object, *never* the subject; a woman could incite desire, but never before had she been portrayed as expressing it.

261

While on the subject of pronouns, Darznik's decision to narrate *Song of a Captive Bird* in first person rather than third raised particular craft challenges. Although the first person narration provided intimacy, Darznik couldn't resist the siren's call of the epilogue therefore Forugh 'tells' her story from beyond the grave. (Prologues and epilogues—like impulse buys—are often a mistake.) When a writer decides her protagonist will narrate an ambitious political novel, she must find a way to impart enough information about the setting. Some readers in the United States may be unfamiliar with the questionable roles Germany, Russia, the United States, and the United Kingdom have played in Iran's turbulent history—which is unfortunate given its continuing importance in our present foreign policy and its influence on the wider Middle East—but, overall, Darznik navigates this precarious path with considerable skill. Only now and then do Forugh's deviations into wider events seem out of character or expository.

Darznik's Forugh is sensual and deeply engaging, yet sometimes the writing feels more tentative than in her earlier memoir, the pacing a little too careful, as though Darznik's admiration for her subject made her wary of trusting her instincts and allowing herself full fictive reign. We learn what the character Forugh thought about the oppression of women, about desire, about love, but she gives little away about her wider geopolitical or spiritual beliefs, though it can be found in Farrokhzad's poetry. With sensitivity toward Farrokhzad's surviving family, Darznik chose not to include certain events within the novel, and changed the name of a key player. Earlier this year, the filmmaker Ebrahim Golsetan, who is the inspiration behind Darius Golshiri, gave an interview to *The Guardian* (February 12, 2017), in which he admitted to his relationship with Farrokhzad after decades of silence out of respect for his late wife. Golestan denied he had any impact on Farrokhzad's art. "She was influenced by her own efforts," he said. "I never saw her in a state of not being productive . . . I rue all the years she isn't here."

Let me, at this late stage, confess—sheepishly—that I'd never heard of Farrokhzad prior to reading *Song of a Captive Bird*, and I'm so grateful that Darznik introduced me to this enigmatic artist. Several clips from Farrokhzad's documentaries are available on the Internet,

McCALLUM SMITH

including *The House is Black*, her celebrated short film about an Iranian leprosy colony. Narrations on these clips allow us to hear her beautiful speaking voice.

> I plant my hand in the garden soil—
> I will sprout,
>> I know, I know, I know.
> And in the hollows of my ink-stained palms
> Swallows will make their nest.
>
> ("Reborn")

Autocracies and theocracies the world over never seem to learn that the most effective way of turning a dead literary irritant into a martyr is to ban her books. Art can survive, as Forugh contends, "far worse fates than fire." In the decade following the 1979 Islamic revolution, Farrokhzad's poetry was prohibited in Iran, the Ayatollah failing to heed wisdom attributed to Omar Khayyam:

> The Moving Finger writes, and, having writ,
> Moves on
> nor all thy Piety nor Wit
> Shall lure it back to cancel half a Line
> Nor all thy Tears wash out a Word of it.

One might be tempted to feel sorry for all those men—all those daft, deluded, frightened sods—for their failure to make this woman shush, turn inwardly and accommodate. But I don't. It seems so timely that in our present overdue reckoning with the patriarchy, Forugh Farrokhzad—through Darznik's remarkable first novel—rises again like an exquisite phoenix weeping healing tears.

263

Book Review

DANIELLE JONES-PRUETT

Watch Us Reap What We Sow

Reaper by Jill McDonough
Alice James Books, 2017

Anyone familiar with Jill McDonough's two previous collections of poetry is aware of their differences. *Habeas Corpus* (2008) is a carefully constructed machine: fifty sonnets, each one marking (memorializing) an execution that took place in America from 1608 to 2005. The collection is an example of form as function, each sonnet using source material to create an intimate portrayal of the executed (and, at times, the executioner), each word necessary—connective tissue bringing back the dead, their lost lives rising up before us on the page: William Fly, "[a] boatswain on an English slaver, he threw / his masters overboard"; Susanna Martin, executed for "just and sufficient proofs" of witchcraft; Willie Francis, the "fifteen-year-old colored boy" who was executed a second time when, "like Daniel in the lion's den" he survived the first electrocution.

Where You Live (2012) is, seemingly, its opposite. The poems scrawl across the page, unselfconscious, conversational, playful, profane. But here, too, McDonough is telling the story of how bodies move through the world and, more importantly, why: life, one big party, "OMG" and "LOL," "the yellow light / [in] your own kitchen," "the snooze's seven minutes," the beloved Josey—her wool socks, her fabulous arms, her grin—martinis and breasts, both "overflowing, reeking of juniper, spilling all over the bar." We walk through the world with McDonough meet the people she meets, hear their voices. Many of the poems are about teaching in prison, and it's clear that the sound of the cell door closing has taught her to pay attention to the delights of life, to "each day fresh with the gift of it."

I expected *Reaper*, with its grim title and heavy subject matter, to be more like *Habeas Corpus*—precise, restrained, technical language chiseled into traditional forms. Instead it moves between the two worlds, embodying both the public and personal.

In "Offices," a health scare becomes a chance to count "ways to love more the world." The speaker's acknowledgment that "[o]ne of these days / the news won't be good" swings into a love poem:

> . . . I'm always wanting more of you, even
> in the doctor's office, the Breast Center waiting room.
> I always want your neck within reach of my mouth.
> More of your pulse, more smell of your hair. Let's spend
> more hours in offices, wanting to hedge more bets.

With the next poem, "World's First," we pivot from this intentional living and loving to " . . . shifts of schoolgirls in school yards, sumo / halls" across Japan, mindlessly—laughingly—"pasting sheet after sheet of *washi*," making balloons which will carry bombs across the ocean. "They sent ten thousand off blind and made it / to Echo, Oregon and American Falls. To Walla Walla, / to Kadoka, South Dakota." Here, the poet could turn her focus to the pregnant mother and five children killed in Oregon when they happened on a Fu-Go bomb during a family picnic. Or, after signaling danger, she could have returned to the girls—doing what they're told, unaware of the consequences. Instead, she drifts with the balloon-bomb into Hanford, Washington, where one "broke power lines" and "shut the reactor / down but not for long; we still filled Fat Man for Nagasaki, / still tested The Gadget." McDonough chooses to explore our own culpability, our own mindless complicity. On either side of the Pacific Ocean, humans are drifting through their days, cogs in machines, not noticing the violence underlying their actions—a slow violence which reverberates through time, spans generations. The poem ends in the voice of a woman conceived while her mother worked at the nuclear plant: "I don't think anyone really knows if Hanford's radiation / will affect future generations. But I can't help but worry." How can we? In McDonough's poem, all the people are innocent and guilty, victims and assailants, and the violence drifts between us—delicate and deadly—a balloon we all keep afloat in our turn.

These dreamy, meandering balloons shape-shift, morph into something more sinister in "Lofty View," where "our young people fly our drones surrounded by high-tech TVs." In this poem, McDonough lists the killing machines: the infrared, "killer robot planes," a dog "trained to take out your throat." We can "set / a Hellfire missile and forget it," easy as a Crock-Pot, or a DVR. ("Crap," our poet has already warned us, that "doesn't work for long.") In modern warfare, we watch "our victims on screens," but in McDonough's poem the victims slowly morph from foreign to familiar, from public enemy to hero: "we killed / a guy who was tall like bin Laden, John / Sifton, Abe Lincoln, my father." Suddenly the stakes have been raised, and then it's revealed that "Daraz Khan, / a farmer, was tall, so now he's dead." By telescoping down to the personal, McDonough resists the lofty—detached—view that allows us to "think we see the bad guys / and hit a wedding, a funeral, two kids on a bike."

Reaper was written during the war in Afghanistan, our country's longest war. It's a war that is ubiquitous, yet oddly absent from our everyday lives. The paradox of modern warfare is that while a full generation of Americans has never known a country not actively engaged in war, an all-volunteer, professional military means we lack the shared experience and sacrifice of this reality. We lack the *reality* of this reality.

And yet, a country perpetually at war cannot separate itself from systemic violence. McDonough brings some of the horror of war home to us in "Try." The entire poem consists of a single tercet, and yet it is one of the biggest poems in the book:

> *You just try to hand them some hot chocolate,*
> said EMTs at the scene, of the unscathed
> milling in shock, after someone opened fire.

The poem presents a scene that is both (hopefully) personally unfamiliar to us, and entirely imaginable as we grapple with the reality that there are more mass shootings in the United States than

JONES-PRUETT

in any other country in the world. In these few lines, McDonough raises a multitude of questions for the reader, creating a sense of unease, confusion. Are we in a war zone? The Mall of America? At an elementary school? If the scene we're witnessing is "the unscathed," where are the wounded? The dead? McDonough leaves us a lot of white space to wonder why, and when will I, or my beloved, be one of "them"? But the poem preceding it, "I Dream We Try Gun [Manufacturers]," has already provided us with an answer for "who": "And we know who the terrorists are."

It's no accident that McDonough uses the universal "we" throughout the collection. If we are not participants, we are spectators. "We, We, We." To be complacent is to be complicit, and it is her resistance to complicity that will have her turn to the makers, the soldiers, to "go to the park and see the robots rise." She wants to know. She won't look away.

But there is something to be said for the way she looks—the rise and fall of it—how she shifts between the importance of paying attention to everyday life, to the god in the details, and panning out to see the bigger picture, like standing back from a pointillist painting.

McDonough encourages us to resist the mindless drifting that would turn us into robots ourselves, to hear the "[chalk] on a chalkboard, / a bell at noon." To notice the "neighbor's fresh clapboards," the "drag queens / [speaking] Spanish," the "laughing baby on the T." She wants us to take an extra minute on "the hug goodbye." She's asking us to look away from the "robot overlords" that have already come for us: "bimbots," "chatbots," "iCal," "iPhones," "E-cigarettes [glowing] red / and blue in bars." This paying attention is a protest, an active resistance to daily detachment and distraction. "We're not there. / Not really here, either. All of us always everywhere: / work, home, faces lit by our phones." It is this detachment which leads to "war with computers," "our young people" flying drones ". . . like rich villains in James Bond movies." It is the same surrendering to technology that allows us to "kill innocents, or citizens" from "five thousand feet."

At the center of the book is a triptych of poems examining our normalization and randomization of violence through the tight, obsessive form of the villanelle. The most haunting of the series is "Twelve-Hour Shifts," where the form is used less as a mode of propelling movement forward, more for its humdrum rhythm and mind-numbing repetition. We watch as the drone pilot, for "[another] day / another dollar," sits in "[a] small room, a pilot's chair, the mic and headphones / [crowding] his mind, [taking] him somewhere else." "Smell of burned coffee in the lounge, the shifting kill zone." This is the kind of routine shift Americans are all too familiar with, whether on the factory floor, in a hospital, or at war. "Hover and shift, twelve hours over strangers' homes."

It is not the love of the machine that disturbs Jill McDonough, but the dehumanization that accompanies it—the industrialization of our relationships. In the tradition of Whitman singing America, McDonough croons people out of the crowd: she's introduced us to Angela, the "cute waitress at the Alembic," who is also a vet with PTSD; the homophobic cab driver from Somalia, "poor man," who "sort of wants [her and her wife] dead;" the meter maid "hiding" in the ladies' room at the Boston Athenaeum to get off her feet for a bit; Monica at DBs's Golden Banana, "her eyes . . . doves / unseen," "her layers of pink labia, / tiny powdered asshole." Whether she's writing an ode to a stripper, sonnets to remember the executed, or memorializing the beloved in her "Husky Boys' Dickies," all of McDonough's poems are, at their core, love poems. If it matters enough to draw her gaze, she's falling in love.

McDonough cares who we are with each other; how we look at one another. Nowhere is this more evident than in "The Beautiful Woman," where the poet turns her gaze to the "beautiful woman" sitting across from her on the bus who is "laughing and fat." It's an ode, listing all the details deserving of praise: "her braided hair," "her ring, her laughing / mouth," "her spill of thigh-fat freed from that rise of grey knit skirt." The speaker "[loves] her so much [she] takes her picture." "I think she knows I'm taking her picture. I think she doesn't care." But here the poem shifts a bit. Or, at this point, we know too much. "Ravens, Predators, Reapers." The speaker is looking with love, but this small intrusion reminds us of the surreptitious photos we've all seen posted to social media, mocking the fat body, or some other unsuspecting "fool," for easy laughs and "likes." But the

JONES-PRUETT

power remains with the "beautiful woman" who "doesn't care we're trying not to stare." "It's always like this for her: she moves through a world that's wilting / with love." And perhaps, in the end this is the only power any of us have—to walk through the world wrapped in love. To love each other, ourselves, to love our country, not with a blind eye, detached—lofty view—but fully aware, paying attention. Celebrating the best, naming the worst, believing in and fighting for better. "Watch us reap what we sow."

2017 Consequence Prize in Fiction

Selected by Siobhan Fallon

Awarded to

Ruth Edgett

How is it that our agony has been rendered so gracefully? asks the narrator in "Hill 145" as he gazes up at a war memorial. And isn't this both the question, and the answer, to all art about conflict? The experiences of those who have survived war take a violent, ugly thing and try to translate it into something the rest of us can comprehend. Art becomes a way to channel epiphany and empathy into those who are lucky enough to remain unscathed.

"Hill 145" brings us to 1936, to Canadian World War I veterans returning, nineteen years later, to the battleground in France that cost them 3,598 lives. The story is amazingly sophisticated, novelistic in scope and detail, yet intimately probes the guilt of a soldier who outlives all of the friends he swore to protect. On the surface, "Hill 145" paints a rosy picture, with green fields, grazing horses, and poppies in the distance, but the reader, with awful hindsight, knows that in a few short years the evils of the First World War will not only be repeated, but grossly intensified. Ruth Edgett's "Hill 145" strikes a delicate balance of nostalgia and impending doom, brilliantly illuminating how Vets are "well-practiced at moving between worlds" when reconciling their soldiering pasts and civilian presents.

—Siobahn Fallon

RUTH EDGETT

Hill 145

L affy in his ear for the ten-thousandth time: "If we're gonna die,
we might as well die tryin'—Right, Georgie?" And, for the ten-
thousandth time the clock strikes o-five-thirty, they clamber over top
of the trench and Laffy flies to pieces beside him.

He knows it's a dream, but he keeps on wading through the
sleet and the mud anyway, because there's no time to lose beneath
this thundering barrage. Once Laffy and his bloody crater are well
behind in the chaos, he frees a hand from his rifle and slaps at his
face and chest to clear away all that's left of his friend. It's a movement
he can't stop, even nineteen years later, and the only thing that can
bring him fully awake—always in a sweat and always gasping.

Even so, it takes more than a dozen galloping heartbeats to
push himself upright in his deck chair and remind himself this is not
April 9, 1917, but July 25, 1936; and he, along with several hundred
of his fellow pilgrims, is aboard the SS *Duchess of Bedford* at Le Havre,
France, waiting under a clear summer sky to disembark.

He pulls a handkerchief from his inside jacket pocket and
drags it across his face, just as Elizabeth rounds the corner.

"Two other ships are already docked alongside!" she calls,
breathless, before she's even reached him. "Everyone's still talking
about the harbor escort with all the lights and hubbub last night."

The last time George came ashore here, it was on the quiet
and under cover of darkness.

◊

He's well-practiced at moving between worlds, so he settles
back beneath the warming sun, stows his handkerchief and takes the

271

time, now, to admire his wife: Wisps of honey-colored hair framing her flushed cheeks, her keen hazel eyes, the curving lines of the navy travelling suit she sewed to match his jacket with the Royal Canadian Legion crest on the pocket. A man would never know she turned thirty-eight in June and left six children ages eighteen months to fourteen years back home on their lighthouse island in the care of their Aunt Annie and Uncle Aubrey.

George, on the other hand, shows every year of his thirty-eight; feels another thirty-eight after that and, perhaps even, a hundred more. Sometimes he wonders if he's living an extra, parallel life with his buddies who never made it home. There's a weight to them sometimes, like he carries them with him.

Elizabeth leans over the rail toward sounds on the dock below. Aside from this voyage, her only sailing experience has been shuttling a row boat the half mile between the landing of Pomquet Island and the government wharf on the Nova Scotia mainland.

"I met a nice man from the Legion," she says over her shoulder. "He told me they've hired scores of train cars, plus a whole bus line and then some to get us around." She straightens and turns. "He seemed very calm, but I can't imagine how they're going to keep six or seven thousand pilgrims from five ships organized through Vimy Ridge tomorrow, let alone for the next three and a half weeks."

George slides forward in his chair and raises his hands—one behind, one in front—to straighten his khaki beret. "You'd be surprised," he says, "what military minds can do."

◊

He knows this pilgrimage is Elizabeth's trip-of-a-lifetime. He will have memories to reconcile, of course, but he plans to keep most to himself and let her enjoy the spectacle. Still, he needs her to know some things. She already knows that every one of the 78th Battalion was a good soldier: a fighter, a digger, a builder—or whatever he was called upon to do.

If we're gonna die, we might as well die tryin'—Right Georgie?

He hasn't told her about this kind of thing, though; or how he still wonders which took more courage: marching into the fire thinking it was his day to die, or hanging onto life battle after battle in an endless war going nowhere. She's asked, of course, what memory it is that has, for years, catapulted them both from sleep with no rhyme or regularity, but some things a man doesn't talk about.

He's happy to talk about the 78th, though. He's proud of them—all eight hundred who sprang into battle that day, even if only a third of them walked away—even if only eight of them are making the return trip—even if he's the only one of . . .

So, he will put up with being fêted and toured and made much of with the rest of the Canadians if it means being allowed tomorrow to salute the unveiling of the great monument that sits on the very piece of Vimy Ridge that the 78th helped capture. It's the least he can do.

◊

Elizabeth is keeping a diary of the pilgrimage. This pleases George because he can know her thoughts without having to talk about them. A couple of hours into their train ride, he picks up her notes: *Such wonderful country we are passing through! George says I've been so busy looking that I barely take time to sit and I guess that's just about right.*

He can't help but smile.

What impresses me most is the trees. There are acres and acres of them set in precise rows, each one with its face washed and hair combed, is what I think, they look so neat . . .

The fields were not like this when he was last through this country, helping to rip and tear and blow them apart, struggling through the slick and sucking mud, toppling sometimes into mine craters and praying to God that, if he were going to die, it would not be in their turgid water alongside the others who'd already drowned there. He saw no trees then—or what could rightly be called trees. There were only the dark bones of trees against an iron-gray sky, or torn stumps with not even enough remaining to take cover behind.

Everywhere we see patches of poppies, and sometimes a large field of them in the distance looks just like a field of blood.

He closes the book and passes it back.

◊

This is only the first day, and it's a long one, journeying north by train and bus. There are many old battlefields to visit, speeches to stand for, and memories that make him tired. Finally, after much touring and congratulation, the pilgrims board buses that take them south and west toward Arras, the French town that lent its name to the larger battle for which Vimy was meant as the opening skirmish.

Settled into his seat, George closes his eyes, hoping for a sleep of the weary that will not be disturbed by the parallel sleep of the dead. Elizabeth bends to her journal as the chatter gradually dies down. He must be in a pleasant doze when she starts prattling on beside him.

"Look, George!" She shakes his arm. "They're lining the street!

It's growing dusk, and George cranes over his wife's shoulder to see what she's talking about. On a street corner, where an old stone barn meets the curb is a sign. "Souchez," it says. George knows this place.

"See that woman in the upstairs window!"

He takes an elbow to the shoulder as Elizabeth stands and twists around to get a better look.

"She's waving some—George, she's waving her knitting!"

Other passengers begin manhandling the windows open so they can wave back. Through the openings comes a chant, scattered at first, then stronger as more people come into the street: "Vive le Canada! Vive le Canada!"

Elizabeth is thanking the man in the seat behind for helping to push her window open, and now she's leaning out and calling along with the other pilgrims, "Vive la France!"

Perhaps the dead can hear, so George squeezes in next to her and joins in the roaring. She stands back, so he can lean out to get a look at the long line of buses in front and behind, and he sees in the fading light the navy gabardine arms of the men and the multi-colored arms of their women, all waving. Some are hanging out as far as their shoulders, brandishing their berets and hailing.

"Vive la France!"

274

Cars and pony carts have pulled onto the sidewalks. Shopkeepers and customers have rushed out of doors, still making change and bagging their merchandise. Dogs are running alongside the pilgrims' convoy, adding their voices to the din.

"Vive le Canada!"

Gradually, as the buses move into the countryside, the sounds die away. No one expected that. Many of the men are blowing dust from their noses, or wiping it from their eyes after hanging out the windows, so George doesn't feel out of place doing the same.

"Wasn't that something?" says Elizabeth, looking so proud beside him, tears brimming behind her lashes.

George pats her knee, leans back and closes his eyes. "Maybe now we'll have some quiet," he says.

◊

Next morning in their Arras hotel room, Elizabeth is dressed, hair already rolled up at the back when George awakens. How could he have slept so long? At home, he rises before dawn and climbs the tower to extinguish the light before she even opens her eyes. But sounds of their boisterous countrymen in the tavern below kept them up last night until well after twelve.

The sun is leaking around the drapes, and as soon as Elizabeth sees he's awake, she flings them wide so that he must shield his eyes. "Let's not miss breakfast," she says. "It's going to be a long day."

By the time they reach Vimy Ridge, thousands have already gathered. George is sent to the base of the monument with the khaki berets while Elizabeth is kept back with the blues. They've been told to expect speeches and fly-pasts, cavalry formations and displays of great military precision. The sky is clear, the sunshine is brilliant, and the monument fairly glows in the attention.

Up close, staring at the colossal human figures that begin at his level and climb to the very heavens, George wonders: *How is it that our agony has been rendered so gracefully?* The glare of sun on new white limestone hurts his eyes, and he must blink often and cast his gaze downward. On his chest is a Victory Medal, the surviving soldiers' consolation for staying alive, but he has never been particularly proud of his. Certainly, not today; not when he stands atop this earth while Laffy and the others lie beneath it.

There comes the instant in King Edward's speech when a great, draping Union Jack is pulled back to reveal the gigantic female figure of "Canada Bereft." As George gazes upward, he feels the weight of grief in this stone woman's face, in the stoop of her giant shoulders and the droop of the laurels she dangles from her hand. She is grieving for her country, for his friends. For him.

For some time after the ceremony, he lingers to watch her, letting the crowds of pilgrims flow past as they search for the names of loved ones carved into the stone that surrounds and supports her. When he's ready to leave her, he sees it will take a bit of roaming and dodging to find Elizabeth. She's around the other side making animated conversation inside a knot of other blue-beret women when he locates her. He hangs back but she spots him, excuses herself and hurries over.

"Oh, George!" she calls, eyes wide, as she swims through the throngs.

He manages a tight smile and waits. "Something, isn't it?" he says, once she's reached him.

"They said we're a hundred thousand," says Elizabeth, spinning in the sea of people, clasping her notebook to her chest. "There's so much to write. I need to get it down while it's fresh."

"Follow me," he says, and leads her away from the crowds, past a memorial to the Moroccans and down a narrow dirt path where the sounds of celebration begin to fade. Remnants of the battle are all around them: old shell holes, smashed concrete from captured German gun emplacements, grass-covered craters large enough to fit a house into. They are silent for some time.

Finally, Elizabeth says, "After those beautiful words from King Edward and President Lebrun, I can see how the battlefield is healing. Perhaps I'll begin with that," and she heads toward the lush bowl of a small crater. "I can sit here in the sunshine and write while you—"

Quick as a shot, George grabs her arm and wrenches her back to the path, sending her book skidding to the ground.

"What in . . . ?" says Elizabeth, catching her balance, glaring at him as she brushes her sleeve where he pulled her. "What do y—"

"Never!" says George, chest heaving. "Ever!" is all he can get out over his image of Laffy exploding, and it must be his panic that drives her backward a step.

"Ever what?" she says, still rubbing her wrist.

Perhaps he should have been easier with her, but there was no time. "It was one of the first announcements today," he says, still panting. "Didn't you hear it?"

She looks back toward the crater, and he sees it dawning on her: "You mean . . . ?"

"I mean you could go up just like that," he says, realizing he's trembling. "Mines," he says. "Old shells. Just because they didn't go off then doesn't mean they won't now."

"Oh," says Elizabeth. "I didn't . . ."

"No," says George, stooping to pick up her notebook, dusting it on his pant leg and handing it to her. "I guess you didn't."

His knees are wobbly, but he keeps leading her farther into the quiet until they come upon a tall concrete cross of the style that marks all the Canadian cemeteries. *Givenchy-en-Gohelle*, says the plaque. This burial place is tiny compared to the others they've visited. It is partly sheltered by a small cathedral of trees, surrounded by a low stone wall and, beyond that, horse pasture on three sides. George wanders the perimeter as Elizabeth takes a seat on a bench in a patch of sun. He stops at the wall opposite her, facing outward. Near a place where two horses graze nose to nose, he spies a zig-zag of old trench snaking up the slope, its chalky edges now rounded and overgrown.

"I remember that," he says, pointing in the direction of the horses. They stop eating and cock their ears toward him. "Had more than one detail out there."

He contemplates the scene for a while before swinging around and lifting his gaze over Elizabeth's head toward the pasture behind her. He can see she's still writing, but begins anyway: "Not far from here," he says, "back a bit more the way we came, is the tunnel the 78th used. Won't find 'em now, but those subways were how we made it to the trenches without being spotted."

277

Elizabeth lays her book aside and draws her knees up under her chin, watching.

He gestures to his right, where the monument is still visible above the tree tops. "Hill 145: That was our objective," he says. "Drilled into every man in the Twelfth Division, every day for five months."

Laffy in his ear: *If we're gonna die, we might as well die tryin'—right, Georgie?*

"We waited all night. Quiet as the dead. Then: O-five-thirty and over the top we went," he says, even now spurting ahead a few steps before springing a hand to his face, knocking his beret to the ground and swatting at the gore that is no longer there. As if that cap were Laffy, he whispers to it, "I had no choice but to keep going."

He waits a few breaths to collect himself, sees she's listening and carries on:

"The 78th was one of the battalions that made up the Twelfth. It'll all be over in a few hours, they told us, but they didn't factor in the snipers. That's when everything went to pieces. Four days they pinned us down. Us waiting for relief, wondering who'd be picked off next, all the time praying they weren't mining beneath us."

On the ground where he's scuffing his foot, George can see again the furor and confusion of that fight, feel the soldier's mad hope that he'd come out of it—and the grim acceptance that he wouldn't. When he lifts his gaze toward Elizabeth and she's not there, he spins, heart thundering.

There she is, just a stride or two away now, diary open in her hand. "See what I've written," she says.

Looking at those craters I can't help but wonder: How, when they blew such holes as that in the earth, did anyone ever come out of it alive? He squeezes his eyes shut and tries to level his breathing. *I am beginning to realize, as we explore parts of the Ridge, how it must have taken every ounce of courage and strength . . .* She's not finished the thought, and neither can he.

When he tilts the book closed, she's reading headstones. "Look," she says, running her finger along the close-set tops of a dozen or so. "These are all 78th Battalion and they all died on April 9, 1917."

278

George stays quiet.

"Come see the names," she says. When he doesn't move, Elizabeth stops her tracery and stares. "Don't you want to see whose names you know?"

He turns away and back toward the horses. "I know them all," he says.

◊

This diary he's holding reminds him of Elizabeth's letters; and of how they have belonged to each other since the day he showed up, motherless, in her Nova Scotia schoolyard. In Elizabeth he found, not pity, just kindness and a knowing that he needed a friend—even while he needed also to be hard. They were both twelve-years old.

A couple of years later, family still asunder, George hopped aboard the Harvest Excursion Train bound for the wheat fields out west and didn't even say goodbye. But in 1915, after he'd answered the greater call in Winnipeg and signed his pay over to the keeping of baby sister Annie, he took a chance. He sent Elizabeth his only photo as a fresh recruit and wrote, "From one who cannot and will not forget you."

She wrote back. And for four terrible years, while he fought through this hell, she sent him letters. As he began to wonder if the world back there was something he might only have dreamed of, she made it possible for him to believe it was not a dream. All these years later, she still has no idea how much he has needed her.

He wants this, today, to explain him a little better; for he knows he can be unexplainable, that it is hard on the children, that they wish for a father not quite so stern—one who might put an arm around them, or show them he is proud, or that he loves them. Because he does. He does with all his heart, though he can never say.

◊

When he feels like speaking again, he still has his back to Elizabeth. "Not far from that crossroad down there is where we went in," he says, pointing to a place where the plain meets the first rise of the scarp. He swings around. "Over there: That was No Man's Land, where we burst out," and his voice goes thin. "Laffy must have stepped on something," he says.

Elizabeth stops her wandering among the stones and turns to regard him.

"A few minutes after that, Harry Logan went down with a sniper shot to the leg. He told me, Keep going, Georgie. Go, go, go! And I did. Then, Louie Reddy fell in front of me and I jumped over him, thinking, I can stop here and die with him or keep going and die trying."

He turns again to the pasture, and it might be a few minutes or a lifetime that he's lost inside this memory before he feels Elizabeth beside him, pressing the rolled-up beret into his hand.

Her voice is soft. "I'm glad those horses are there," she says.

But he's coming back from a long way and has trouble comprehending.

"There's something good about those gentle creatures grazing near our men who've fallen, don't you think?"

He watches her watching the animals.

"This is how I would want to lie if I were one of your friends," she says. "Next door to horses: strong beasts who do what they're told when they have to, but who really want nothing more than peace and a good patch of grass." She smiles up at him. "If it were me, I would take comfort in that."

George clears his throat and carries on: "We knew we wouldn't all make it home," he says. "Four greenhorns at the Somme. We swore to watch out for each other . . ." And, for this next, he can't look anywhere but down or do anything but mumble: "But I couldn't—"

And it doesn't matter what he says from here on, or whether he says anything at all, because Elizabeth has placed herself in front of him, eyes on his, showing she's received every memory; that, from here on, she will keep each one safe so he doesn't have to hold onto them by himself anymore.

"Here I still am," he says, surprised even now.

Elizabeth eases the diary out of his hand. "I'm glad of that," she whispers, tracing a fingertip along the side of his nose, making him realize there is a trail of tears there. "Your children are, too," she says; and, coming from her, George can almost believe that is true.

◊

Back at the hotel that night, the carousing has been only half-hearted, so it's much earlier when the last of the revelers spill up the stairs and muffle themselves behind closed doors. As their final sounds gradually fall off, George watches Elizabeth from the bed. She's wearing the soft pink nightgown she made for this trip and is working her long, honey hair into a thick braid over one shoulder. She smooths a hand over it one last time before switching off the light, lifting the covers and climbing in beside him. With a grace borne of long practice, he raises his near arm up and away so she can slide over and rest her cheek on his chest.

"Maybe now we'll have some quiet," she says, warm breath grazing his skin.

"Maybe," says George, lowering his arm and drawing her snug against him. "Maybe so."

◊

It is midnight by the time George and Elizabeth pull the dory up at the Pomquet Island landing after nearly a month away. The light tower is sending its steady red beam far out over St. George's Bay, and the ruby color dances on distant waves. They unload their suitcases and leave them for the children to fetch in the morning. As they approach the house, they see that someone's left a lamp burning on the dining room table, an extravagance of kerosene that George would never countenance. At the door to the summer kitchen, he's ready to burst straight through and put out that lamp, but the door won't open.

"Why would they lock the door?" says George. "What kind of burglar do they think is going to paddle half a mile to a lighthouse and half a mile back!"

"Annie and Aubrey live in town," says Elizabeth. "It was automatic, I suppose."

"Stupid more like it," says George. "I could have told her she was marrying an idiot!"

"Oh, how quickly our dream evaporates and real life comes crashing back in," says Elizabeth as George stamps around the house to the front parlor window. "Quiet," she says. "We don't want them to think the Huns are invading."

"This is the only one that doesn't stick," he whispers as he presses carefully on the sash and works it upward. "Go wait at the kitchen. I'll come let you in."

He must wriggle and scrape, but after a few minutes of small struggle George lands hands-first on the oil cloth floor and brings his knees down behind him. As he comes stiffly upright, he touches something yielding: A head of thick, wiry hair like his own. He doesn't need the moonlight to tell him this is Grace, their first; the one who showed him that he truly was done with ending lives—that he was now in the business of beginning them. One hand goes to her shoulder and, before he can stop it, the other pulls her to him.

At first she is stiff in his arms. But, then, George feels about his waist the light and tentative pressure of a returned embrace. At his chest, there is warm breath where his ribs meet just below his heart, and he hears a muffle that sounds like, "I was dreaming and thought I heard you say, Wait and I'll come . . ."

From the ends of the earth I would come, he wants to say. *Or die trying.*

". . . but I didn't want to wait," says Grace, into her father's shirtfront.

George lowers his head until he can feel the tickle of her short-cropped hair against the end of his nose. He would like to tip up her face and kiss it, but if he does she will feel his tears. So, hoping the dark will hide the wet on his cheeks, he pushes his daughter from him.

"Your mother's waiting at the kitchen," he says to her. "You'd better go open the door."

2017 Cosequence Prize in Poetry

Selected by

Danielle Legros Georges

Awarded to

Esther Ra

For her poem

[...---...]

The poem's wordless title signals a grappling with the very language that makes war known to us; the language with which we attempt to make sense of the seemingly senseless rifts delivered to our countries, homes, and selves. The speaker's—and author's—vulnerability and implication in the questions of voice and verity made this poem for me a keen and reverberating thing.

—Danielle Legros Georges

ESTHER RA

[...---...]

Fingers of barbed wire
Dragged across our country
And North Korea's mouth
Slammed shut.

~~~ + ~~~ + ~~~ + ~~~ + ~~~

In the blank that came after,
I groped at anything
To understand—

Songs whispered through
The underground churches,
Fragments
Cleaving like glass
From the lips of refugees.

I washed my coins together
And flung them into the darkness,
A wishing well
Where bodies lay buried
At the bottom.

In my ignorance
I crushed hope between my teeth,
A bitter and blistering lollipop
That grew smaller over the years.

In North Korea, government-hired writers
Hamstring poetry

In praise of Dear Leader,
And people are stoned
With bandaged mouths.
No prayers released by the rubble-filled dead,
No martyr to stand for the living.

In the south, our teeth clench around coins
Like corpses, too busy being chased by life
To remember death.
I am their tongue, faulty and soft,
Trembling when I taste
Where the wind blows.

Every night, as sleep falls over our country,
Our radios hum awake.

Brother,
Are you still there?
Broadcasts wash over the border in waves.
Barbed wire cannot keep out our tears.
To our dearly beloveds, we say,
We have not forgotten you.
Tonight we will read aloud
Matthew, Chapter One...

And pages tremble open
As pens scratch down
Each shining verse,
To bring a forbidden Bible
To life.

O speech untamed,
Be careful what you wish for.
A single word can river
A glacier to water,
A tongue spear generations
To silence.

CONSEQUENCE

Marjorie Agosín is the author of numerous works of poetry, fiction, and literary criticism including *The Angel of Memory* (2001), *The Alphabet in My Hands: A Writing Life* (2000), *Always from Somewhere Else: A Memoir of my Chilean Jewish Father* (1998), *An Absence of Shadows* (1998), *Melodious Women* (1997), *Starry Night: Poems* (1996), and *A Cross and a Star: Memoirs of a Jewish Girl in Chile* (1995). She is a recipient of the Jeanette Rankin Award in Human Rights and a United Nations Leadership Award for Human Rights. Agosín is the Luella LaMer Slaner Professor in Latin American studies and a professor of Spanish at Wellesley College.

Jennifer Barber is the author of three poetry collections: *Works on Paper* (2015 Tenth Gate Prize, The Word Works), and *Given Away and Rigging the Wind*, both with Kore Press. She has recently been the recipient of a MacDowell Fellowship. She teaches literature and creative writing at Suffolk University, where she also edits the literary journal *Salamander*.

Lily Bowen's poems have been published in Clemson University's *The Chronicle, Best American Poetry Blog*, and are forthcoming in the anthology *Inheriting the War: Poetry & Prose by Descendants of Vietnam Veterans and Refugees*. She is an MFA poetry candidate at The New School. She received a BA in English with a minor in poetry from Clemson University in South Carolina.

Martha Collins has published nine books of poetry, most recently *Night Unto Night* (Milkweed, 2018) and *Admit One: An American Scrapbook* (Pittsburgh, 2016), as well as four volumes of co-translated Vietnamese poetry. Founder of the creative writing program at the University of Massachusetts Boston, she served for ten years as Pauline Delaney Professor of Creative Writing at Oberlin College and is currently editor-at-large for *FIELD* magazine.

Jennifer Conlon holds an MFA from Arizona State University and a BFA from the University of North Carolina at Greensboro. She was awarded the 2017 Katherine C. Turner prize from the Academy of American Poets, the 2015-2016 Aleida Rodriguez Memorial Award in Creative Writing, and a 2016 fellowship from The Virginia G. Piper Center for Creative Writing. Her poems have been published by, or are forthcoming in, *Four Chambers Press, Blue Earth Review, Meridian, Bennington Review,* and elsewhere.

Elisabeth Lewis Corley's poems have been published in *Southern Poetry Review, Hyperion, Carolina Quarterly, Feminist Studies, BigCityLit, New Haven Review,* and are forthcoming in *Cold Mountain Review.* She holds an MFA in poetry from the Warren Wilson Program for Writers and a BA with Highest Honors in Poetry from the University of North Carolina at Chapel Hill where she sometimes teaches poetry in performance and screenwriting. Her short film, "About Time," directed by Joseph Megel and produced by Harland's Creek Productions made the festival rounds in 2013.

Linda Dittmar grew up in Israel (1939-1960). She served in the Israeli military, including the Suez Campaign (1956). A PhD from Stanford University, she taught literature and film studies at the University of Massachusetts Boston for forty years. Her publications include *From Hanoi to Hollywood, The Vietnam War in American Film,* and *Multiple Voices in Feminist Film Criticism.* Now Professor Emerita, she is writing a memoir about Israel/Palestine and the war of 1948.

Malina Douglas is inspired by encounters, small beautiful details, and the unfamiliar. She has published in *Metamorphose V2, Indigo: A Western Australian Journal of Writing, Every Second Sunday: A Seoul Writers' Anthology,* and in the Jungle Age, a website for writers. Her poem "Red Fading" was published in *Fusions,* a collection of paintings and corresponding poems. She is currently based in Chiang Rai, Thailand, where she teaches English at a Montessori school.

Virginia Dwan is a former gallerist and owner of the Dwan Gallery, Los Angeles (1959–1967) and Dwan Gallery, New York (1965–1971), a contemporary art gallery closely identified with the American movements of Minimalism, Conceptual Art, and Land Art. Beginning

287

in 2014 she dedicated three and a half years to documenting soldiers' graves across the United States, and in 2016 published *Flowers* (Radius Books), a photographic work of military cemeteries that convey the enormous consequences of war.

Ruth Edgett is author of *A Watch in the Night* (Nimbus, 2007), the story of her mother's family and their light-keeping life on a tiny island off the north shore of Nova Scotia, Canada. "Hill 145" is inspired by her grandmother Ruth's diary of the 1936 Royal Canadian Legion Pilgrimage to Vimy Ridge, France, site of a major Canadian victory in World War I. Originally from Prince Edward Island, Ruth lives and writes in Southern Ontario.

Christine Evans is an internationally produced playwright. Her plays include *Trojan Barbie* (Jane Chambers Award, American Repertory Theater premiere), *Slow Falling Bird* (Rella Lossy Award), and many others. Her plays are published by Samuel French, NoPassport Press, and excerpted in Smith & Kraus' "Best Monologues" series. She is a MacDowell Fellow, an Australian Fulbright alumna, and an Associate Professor in Georgetown University's Department of Performing Arts. Her first novel, *Cloudless*, was published in 2015. www.christineevanswriter.com

Siobhan Fallon is the author of *The Confusion of Languages* (June 2017), and *You Know When the Men Are Gone*, which won the 2012 Pen Center USA Literary Award in Fiction, the Indies Choice Honor Award, and the Texas Institute of Letters Award for First Fiction. Theatrical productions of her stories have been staged in California, Colorado, Texas, and France. Her essays and fiction have appeared in *Prairie Schooner*, *Guernica*, *New Letters*, *Huffington Post*, *Washington Post Magazine*, and *Military Spouse Magazine*. She and her family moved to Jordan in 2011 and they currently live in Abu Dhabi, United Arab Emirates.

Ida Faubert (1882–1969) was a Haitian writer born in Port-au-Prince and reared in Paris. Faubert was a complex literary figure: bicultural, biracial, and privileged. She neither easily fit socially-prescribed categories for women of color in France or Haiti, nor conformed to them—living and burning through France's *Belle Époque*, world wars, and Haiti's *Indigenist* revolt in art. She supported writers of and participated in the Haitian and French artistic and literary movements of her day. While her work has received little critical attention until recently, she is now beginning to be considered one of Haiti's great women poets.

Ru Freeman is the author of the novels *A Disobedient Girl* (2009) and *On Sal Mal Lane* (2013), a *New York Times* Editor's Choice Book. She is the editor of the groundbreaking anthology, *Extraordinary Rendition: American Writers on Palestine* (2015). Her work has appeared in *The Guardian*, the *New York Times*, and the *Boston Globe*. She blogs for the *Huffington Post* on literature and politics, is a contributing editorial board member of the *Asian American Literary Review*, and is the recipient of many fellowships including from the Bread Loaf Writers' Conference, Yaddo, Hedgebrook, and the Lannan Foundation. She is the 2014 winner of the Sister Mariella Gable Award for Fiction, and the Janet Heidinger Kafka Prize for Fiction. She teaches creative writing at Columbia University.

Danielle Legros Georges is a writer, poet, editor, and translator. She is the author of two books of poetry, *Maroon* (Northwestern University Press, 2001) and *The Dear Remote Nearness of You* (Barrow Street Press, 2016), and the chapbook *Letters from Congo* (Central Square Press, 2017). She is the editor of *City of Notions: An Anthology of Contemporary Boston Poems* (Boston Mayor's Office of Arts and Culture, 2017). In 2014, she was appointed Boston's Poet Laureate.

(Corinne) Renny Golden was a Pushcart nominee in 2016. Her book, *Blood Desert: Witnesses 1820-1880*, won the WILLA Literary Award for poetry 2011, was named a Southwest Notable Book of the Year 2012, and a Finalist for the New Mexico Book Award. *The Old Woman and the River* will be published in 2019 by University of New Mexico Press. Her work has appeared in *Water-Stone, International Quarterly, Literary Review, Dogwood, Main Street Rag, Windhover, Able Muse, Borderlands:*

Texas Poetry Review, Split This Rock, Nagatuck River Review, Crosswinds, and elsewhere.

Erica Goss served as Poet Laureate of Los Gatos, CA from 2013-2016. She is the author of *Night Court* (2017), winner of the 2016 Lyrebird Award, and *Wild Place and Vibrant Words: Ideas and Inspirations for Poets.* She is co-founder of Media Poetry Studio, a poetry-and-film camp for teen girls: www.mediapoetrystudio.com. Her poems, reviews and articles appear widely. www.ericagoss.com.

Melissa Green is the author of three books of poetry, *The Squanicook Eclogues, Fifty-Two* and *Magpiety*, and two memoirs, *Color Is the Suffering of Light* and *The Linen Way*. She is currently working on a book of anti-war poems that address the ways women bear witness to the consequences of war.

Noor Hashem holds an MFA in Fiction and PhD in English Literature from Cornell University. Her research focuses on Muslim fiction, critical theory, and cultural studies. From 2014-2016, she was a Mellon Postdoctoral Fellow at Johns Hopkins and taught creative writing to Syrian refugees in the south of Turkey. She has fiction and essays published in *New Letters* and *Mizna*. "Recounting Syria" is an excerpt from a longer essay.

Jen Hinst-White holds an MFA from the Bennington Writing Seminars. Her stories and essays have been published in *The Missouri Review, The Southampton Review, The Common, Big Fiction, Image Journal, Cactus Heart, Print Oriented Bastards*, and elsewhere.

Lynn Marie Houston's poetry has appeared in over thirty-five literary journals and in her book-length collections: *The Clever Dream of Man* (Aldrich Press, 2015), *Chatterbox* (Word Poetry Books, 2017), *Unguarded* (Heartland Review Press, 2017), and *The Mauled Keeper* (Main Street Rag, 2018). The editor-in-chief of Five Oaks Press, she holds a PhD from Arizona State University and an MFA from Southern Connecticut State University. www.lynnmhouston.com.

Danielle Jones-Pruett holds an MFA from the University of Massachusetts Boston, and is assistant director of the Writers House at Merrimack College. Her work has appeared in *Beloit Poetry Journal, Memorious, Southern Poetry Review,* and elsewhere. She is the recipient of a 2014 Rona Jaffe Writer's Award.

Shannon Kafka is a poet, visual artist, and an MFA candidate at the University of Massachusetts Boston. Born in the Cayman Islands to military parents, she lived in many places before calling Massachusetts her home. She currently resides in Boston with her partner, Adam. She's an active member of Warrior Writers, a non-profit, veteran-focused organization devoted to the arts, stories, and healing of veterans and other survivors of war.

Daphne Kalotay's books include the bestselling novels *Sight Reading* and *Russian Winter* (Harper), and the fiction collection *Calamity and Other Stories* (Doubleday), shortlisted for the Story Prize. Her work has received fellowships from the Christopher Isherwood Foundation, the MacDowell Colony, and Yaddo, among others. Her interviews with Mavis Gallant can be read in the *Paris Review's* Writers-At-Work series. She is currently teaching at Princeton University's Program in Creative Writing.

Judy Labensohn is a multi-cultural writer and teacher, raised in Cleveland, Ohio, living and writing in Israel since 1967. Her fiction and nonfiction have appeared in *Lilith, Brain Child, Michigan Quarterly Review, Ilanot Review, Kenyon Review, Creative Nonfiction, Hadassah Magazine,* and *Southwest Review,* as well as in college writing textbooks. In 2013 she was a Pushcart nominee. Currently, she lives in Tel Aviv where she grandmothers and teaches writing. www.writeinisrael.com.

Laura Laing's work has appeared in *The Rumpus* and *Full Grown People,* and many other national, regional, and local consumer and trade publications. She is currently an MFA student in Goucher College's creative non-fiction program. The author of three books, she is currently writing a nontraditional memoir.

Kristie Betts Letter's work has been recognized in *Best American Short Fictions 2016*, and pieces have appeared in *The Massachusetts Review*, *The North Dakota Quarterly*, *Washington Square*, *Passages North*, *Pangolin Papers*, *The Southern Humanities Review*, and elsewhere. Her poetry collection *Under-Worldly* was published by Editorial L'Aleph.

Susan McCallum Smith writes fiction, essays, and reviews. Her work has appeared in the *Los Angeles Review of Books*, the *Scottish Review of Books*, the *Dublin Review of Books*, *Agni*, *The Southern Review*, and *The Gettysburg Review*. She has received a Pushcart Prize, a fellowship from the NEA, the Walter Sullivan Prize, and recognition by *Best American Essays*. Her literary memoir, *The Watermark*, is forthcoming from Viking. She recently returned to live in her native Scotland.

Jill McDonough's books of poems include *Habeas Corpus* (Salt, 2008), *Where You Live* (Salt, 2012), and *Reaper* (Alice James, 2017). The recipient of three Pushcart prizes and fellowships from the Lannan Foundation, NEA, NYPL, FAWC, and Stanford, her work appears in *The Threepenny Review* and *Best American Poetry*. She teaches in the MFA program at the University of Massachusetts Boston and directs 24PearlStreet, the Fine Arts Work Center online. Her fifth poetry collection, *Here All Night*, is forthcoming from Alice James Books.

Valerie Miner is the award-winning author of fourteen books. Her work has appeared in such journals as *Salmagundi*, *Ploughshares*, *Triquarterly*, *The Georgia Review*, *New Letters*, *Prairie Schooner*, and *Gettysburg Review*. She has won awards from The Rockefeller Foundation, Fulbright Commission, the Jerome Foundation, Fundación Valparaiso, Bogliasco Foundation, MacDowell, Yaddo and other sources. Her work has been translated into eight languages and has been broadcast on BBC Radio. She is a professor and artist in residence at Stanford University. www.valerieminer.com.

Barbara Mujica is a novelist, essayist, and short story writer. Her novel *Frida* was a bestseller and appeared in seventeen languages. *Sister Teresa* was adapted for the stage at the Actors Studio in Los Angeles. A Spanish edition will appear later this year. *I Am Venus* and

Lola in Paradise were winners of the Maryland Writers' Association novel competition in 2012 and 2016, respectively. The mother of a Marine, Mujica is the Faculty Adviser of the Georgetown University Student Veterans Association.

Ruth Mukwana is a fiction writer from Uganda. She is currently working for the United Nations on humanitarian affairs in Sudan. She has an MFA from the Bennington Writing Seminars, and a Bachelors degree in Law from Makerere University. Her short story, "The Smell," has been published by Solstice Magazine, and her short story, "Taboo," was runner up for the *Black Warrior Review* 2017 Fiction Contest.

Joyce Peseroff's five books of poems are *The Hardness Scale, A Dog in the Lifeboat, Mortal Education, Eastern Mountain Time,* and most recently *Know Thyself* (Carnegie Mellon, 2015). Her poems and reviews have appeared in the *Atlantic Monthly, Agni, Ploughshares, Southern Review, New York Times Book Review, The Women's Review of Books,* and *Slate.* She has been coordinating editor, managing editor, and associate poetry editor of *Ploughshares,* and edited *The Ploughshares Poetry Reader, Robert Bly: When Sleepers Awake,* and *Simply Lasting: Writers on Jane Kenyon.* She directed the MFA Program at the University of Massachusetts Boston during its first four years.

Esther Ra lives in Seoul, South Korea, and Walla Walla, Washington where she is currently the editor-in-chief of *Freedom Songs Magazine,* a literary magazine exploring themes of racial justice. Her work has been published in *blue moon,* and her upcoming novel, *Tadpole Pond,* appears on the publishing platform Radish Fiction.

Alison Ridley teaches Spanish at Hollins University in Roanoke, Virginia. She received her doctorate from Michigan State University. Her current scholarly work focuses on the theatre of Antonio Buero Vallejo. She has published articles in *Gestos, Neohelicon, Bulletin of Hispanic Studies,* and *Estreno,* and book reviews in a number of journals. Currently, Alison is translating two new works by Marjorie

293

Agosín: a collection of poetry and the sequel to the novel, *I Lived on Butterfly Hill*.

Willa Elizabeth Schmidt is a former academic reference librarian who has lived in Germany and Austria and currently serves as an ESL tutor through the Madison, Wisconsin Literacy Network. Her prose and poetry have been published in journals including *Bellevue Literary Review*, *CALYX*, *Potomac Review*, and *Passages North*. Her fiction was included in the 2014 collection *Best Short Stories from the Saturday Evening Post Great American Fiction Contest*, and a flash memoir is included in the anthology *Two-Countries: U.S. Daughters and Sons of Immigrant Parents* (Red Hen Press). Most recently she was awarded the *Iron Horse Literary Review's* 2017 Trifecta essay prize.

Karen Halvorsen Schreck is the author of *Broken Ground* and *Sing For Me*, along with two novels for young adults and a book for children. Her short stories, interviews, and essays have appeared in *Hypertext Magazine*, *The Rumpus*, *Belt*, and *Literal Latte*. The recipient of a Pushcart Prize and an Illinois State Arts Council Grant, Karen received her doctorate in English and Creative Writing from the University of Illinois at Chicago.

Katey Schultz is the author of *Flashes of War*, an award-winning collection of short stories featuring characters in and around the wars in Iraq and Afghanistan. She has received fellowships in eight states and financial support from local and state arts councils. She mentors writers and also teaches online flash fiction and creativity classes through her business, Maximum Impact. She is currently seeking a home for her novel, *Still Come Home*. www.kateyschultz.com.

Lee Sharkey is the author of *Walking Backwards* (Tupelo, 2016), *Calendars of Fire* (Tupelo, 2013), *A Darker, Sweeter String* (Off the Grid, 2008), and eight earlier full-length poetry collections and chapbooks. A frequent contributor to CONSEQUENCE, her poetry has also appeared in *Crazyhorse*, *FIELD*, *Kenyon Review*, *Massachusetts Review*, and other journals. Her recognitions include the Ballymaloe Poetry Prize, the RHINO Editors' Prize, the Abraham Sutzkever Centennial

Prize, and the Maine Writers and Publishers Alliance's Distinguished Achievement Award.

Theadora Siranian is a graduate of the MFA Program at the University of Massachusetts Boston. She has had poetry appear in *Bryant Literary Review, Amethyst Arsenic,* and *DIAGRAM,* among others. In 2012 she was selected for inclusion in the Best New Poets anthology series, and was shortlisted for both the 2014 *Mississippi Review Prize* and *Southword's* Gregory O'Donoghue International Poetry Prize. She currently lives and teaches in Brooklyn. Italicized phrases in her poems "Ouroboros" and "Götterdämmerung" are borrowed language from letters Lee Miller wrote to her *Vogue* editor, Audrey Withers.

Jamie Zvirzdin teaches in the Master of Arts Science Writing program at Johns Hopkins University. She received her MFA from Bennington College (June 2015), and she has published essays in *The Kenyon Review, Creative Nonfiction Magazine,* and *Issues in Science & Technology.* She currently lives in Managua, Nicaragua, as part of a US Foreign Service family.